Irit Eguavoen, Wolfram Laube (Eds.)

Negotiating Local Governance

ZEF Development Studies

edited by

Solvay Gerke and Hans-Dieter Evers

Volume 14

Center for Development Research (ZEF)
University of Bonn
www.zef.de

LIT

Negotiating Local Governance

Natural Resources Management at the Interface of Communities and the State

edited by

Irit Eguavoen and Wolfram Laube

LIT

Bibliographic information published by the Deutsche Nationalbibliothek
The Deutsche Nationalbibliothek lists this publication in the Deutsche Nationalbibliografie; detailed bibliographic data are available in the Internet at http://dnb.d-nb.de.

ISBN 978-3-643-10673-5

A catalogue record for this book is available from the British Library

Fresnostr. 2 D-48159 Münster
Tel. +49 (0) 2 51-620 320 Fax +49 (0) 2 51-922 60 99
e-Mail: lit@lit-verlag.de http://www.lit-verlag.de

Distribution:

In Germany: LIT Verlag Fresnostr. 2, D-48159 Münster
Tel. +49 (0) 2 51-620 32 22, Fax +49 (0) 2 51-922 60 99, e-Mail: vertrieb@lit-verlag.de

In Austria: Medienlogistik Pichler-ÖBZ, e-mail: mlo@medien-logistik.at

In Switzerland: B + M Buch- und Medienvertrieb, e-mail: order@buch-medien.ch

In the UK: Global Book Marketing, e-mail: mo@centralbooks.com

In North America by:

Transaction Publishers
New Brunswick (U.S.A.) and London (U.K.)

Transaction Publishers
Rutgers University
35 Berrue Circle
Piscataway, NJ 08854

Phone: +1 (732) 445 - 2280
Fax: + 1 (732) 445 - 3138
for orders (U. S. only):
toll free (888) 999 - 6778
e-mail: orders@transactionpub.com

CONTENTS

Chapter 1

Natural Resources Governance – negotiations at the interface of community and state in developing countries

Irit Eguavoen and Wolfram Laube

The focus of this book – administrative decentralisation versus local governance

If one refers to policy papers regarding natural resources management, one gains an understanding of local governance determined mainly by shifting responsibilities from national bureaucracies to lower levels of administration such as the region or the district. Nevertheless, local governance of natural resources refers to at least two different dynamics linked to each other in various ways. The first is created by governments' attempts to decentralise the management of natural resources by drafting new policies, by the reorganisation of administrative roles and duties and by initiating new legal frameworks. The motives for this policy shift are manifold, ranging from a shift in political paradigms, often pushed by donor agencies that acknowledge the potential of the participatory and more localised management of natural resources, to the intention to withdraw from responsibilities and cost. The second dynamic stems from the practices of local actors vis-à-vis natural resources. Resource users, often without the interference of official actors, interact on a day to day basis with natural resources which sustain, support or endanger their livelihoods. In this book, authors from different disciplines, working on different natural resources in different countries, describe and analyse the dynamics generated at the interface of local user communities managing natural resources and the national processes of administrative reorganisation of natural resource management.

Most of the authors who contributed to this book edition worked at the Centre for Development Research in Bonn and conducted long-term field research. Despite the fact that all authors work intensively on the subject of the local governance of natural resources, their theoretical as well as methodological approaches vary due to their different disciplinary affiliation and the particular resources and countries under investigation. The individual approaches range from New Institutional Economics and the legal anthropological analysis of property right regimes through to historical perspectives and approaches informed by cultural and political ecology. Recent anthropological approaches focusing on the politics of belonging and conflicts over status and power are also presented in the book. However, while theoretical perspectives vary, all empirical examples show how the negotiation of natural resource governance is taking place, often with inconclusive results.

The natural resources at stake are manifold; represented are studies on the use and management of forests, wildlife, water and land. Often, two or more resources are directly interlinked in the local management regimes inasmuch that land and water, forest and wildlife, forest and wild coffee or fisheries and water are explored in a multi-resource approach in eight countries as diverse as Ethiopia, Mali, Afghanistan and Malaysia.

Among our case studies, political circumstances and the impact on the conditions of the natural resources vary highly. In Vietnam, for example, a large part of the forest resources and mangroves were irrecoverably destroyed by the American utilisation of herbicides as a military tool during the Vietnam War. Later, in the 1960s, many tropical forests of the country, which had partly recovered from the herbicides, were cut down by the government for their timber resources before political efforts started to target their conservation and sustainable utilisation.

The situation, though, looks very different in Afghanistan. Irrigation schemes and customary rules of water governance have persisted despite the decades of war, affecting infrastructure and social relations within irrigating communities. Whilst before the 1980s the political leaders seemed not to have had an appreciation of the importance of natural resources management, political instability during the war resulted in the absence of a legal framework for water governance. Presently, international donors and the Afghan government intend to provide new regulations, foster participatory management and formalise water rights for irrigation. However, local rules and power arrangements seem to continue to be the main point of reference for irrigation management, as well as land and water allocation.

With regard to the local arena, historical and present examples show that authoritarian claims over the ownership of natural resources by elites or ritual specialists are not necessarily formally codified but enshrined in local belief systems and part of the local professional and social stratification. These management patterns may also be reproduced after the state has officially appropriated control over the management and allocation of resources, if they serve the interest of the administration or when governments fail to implement new regulations locally. In case studies at regional or country level the decentralisation of natural resource management was usually preceded by the failed or successful attempts of central authorities, such as administrative units or the nation state, to appropriate and control natural resources. In most of the African and Asian countries referred to in this book, the first conservation policies were implemented by colonial administration; however, the allocation of natural resources in Ethiopia took place under a feudal agricultural system headed by an imperator. Afghanistan, with its own unique history and specific environmental conditions, is another case in which the typical processes of colonial natural resources governance did not take place.

Despite the differing contexts, all studies portray the processes of negotiation that evolve at the interface of environmental policies and the local governance of resources. The order of the chapters is centred on the types of resources, starting with case studies on forest resources and then shifting to water and land. Despite the diverse context of the case studies, some historically contingent similarities can be identified with regard to administrative and academic thinking, as well as in policy making for natural resources. In the following chapters, a number of historical continuities, relevant discourses, shifts of academic paradigms and changing natural resource management policies will be discussed.

Changing discourses on natural resource management: scientific perspectives and political paradigms

Human interaction with natural resources has been a central theme in social and economic sciences for a considerable amount of time. For early evolutionists and structuralists alike, the way human populations have organised their subsistence and the utilisation of natural resources through technological advancement, as well as through the generation and defence of property rights, has been identified as one of the main drivers of the evolution/development of human societies (Engels 1972; Morgan 1877). At the same time, the destructive pressure of human populations on natural resources has been the theme of critical comments of scientists since Malthus (Malthus 1826) published his essay on the "principles of population" and painted a gloomy picture about growing human populations and the dangers of a degrading natural resource base in 1798. While debates about the need to conserve natural treasures (often in the tropics) from human destruction (Grove 1990) continued throughout the colonial period, it was not until the

1960s that people in Western industrialised countries started to reflect widely on the negative impacts of industrialisation and modernisation on the environment.

The advancement of reflexive modernisation (Beck 1992) may explain the widespread reception that greeted Hardin's (Hardin 1968) article on the "tragedy of the commons" among scientists. He showed that ecological degradation is the logical consequence of actors' rational economic use of resources under an open access regime, and postulated that economically-minded actors can only be expected to use natural resources sustainably under predictable state management or private property right regimes. Hardin sparked a debate about the need to protect common environmental goods and to manage natural resources sustainably. Simultaneously, in many developed countries – where the influence of powerful political or economic interest groups did not prohibit their existence – environmental movements and a new public interest in the protection of natural resources led to new forms of environmental protection and natural resource management. Although private property regimes, along with institutionalised title registry and cadastres, often existed, environmental legislation was passed and governance agencies equipped with sufficient mandates and funds for environmental monitoring and enforcement.

The picture in the developing world differed somewhat. Under colonial rule, pre-colonial natural resource management regimes, which existed almost everywhere at that time, were often altered to fit colonial interest, or natural resources were even declared state property. However, limited monitoring and enforcement capabilities largely limited colonial influence to areas of prime importance to the colonial enterprise (e.g. settlement areas, administrative capitols, plantations, mines, harbours, roads, railway lines). Elsewhere an ambiguous situation of legal pluralism (Griffiths 1986) was created whereby locally developed patterns of resource governance continued to persist and determine patterns of resource use and allocation de facto, while colonial legislation, which sometimes integrated customary law in official legislation if not viewed as "repugnant" or "in inconsistence" with written law (Okoth-Ogendo 1979), was officially promoted and could be referred to by interested actors. After independence, colonial legislation often remained valid. In many other countries, where independence governments subscribed to socialist ideas, natural resources were nationalised and supposed to be governed by the state. However, quite similar to the colonial situation, governments in many countries lacked the funds, power and/or interests to engage in the comprehensive management of natural resources. Even where sufficient resources for environmental management existed, they were often captured and misappropriated by political elites. The official de-legitimisation of local patterns of resource management, accompanied by the failure to institutionalise effective official natural resource governance, has frequently had negative environmental consequences, especially in countries beset with endemic poverty, population growth, migratory shifts, conflicts and an overall economic dependence on the exploitation of natural resources (see Chapter 7).

In the 1980s and early 1990s, the failure or inability of many developing countries' governments to implement natural resource governance and conservation strategies effectively became increasingly obvious. The numbers of animals in national parks, for instance, decreased and deforestation became a widespread phenomenon (see Chapters 2, 4 and 6). In line with these shortcomings, political and scientific paradigms shifted. Neo-liberal economic principles promoted by international donors focused on the reduction of the role of the state in many developing countries. Structural adjustment programmes, on which continued financial and technical assistance of Western donors depended, forced developing countries' governments to cut budgets, privatise state businesses, lay-off government staff and (at least partially) withdraw from the direct management of infrastructure and resources.

In parallel, scientists scrutinised Hardin's hypothesis and found multiple evidence that access to many natural resources, even if not granted through the state or well-defined private property rights, was actually not open and did not necessarily lead to resource degradation. Scholars were able to show that in many (developing) countries, local communities and resource users were able to manage natural resources sustainably (Feeny et al. 1990; Ostrom 1990). Successful examples for Common Pool Resource (CPR) management were analysed, and principles for the successful and sustainable governance of CPRs deduced and developed into scientific blueprints for Community-Based Resource Management (CBNRM) (Bromley 1992; Ostrom 1992). Scientific findings were eagerly adopted by policy makers and implementing agencies, which resulted in CBNRM becoming a dominant development discourse. With regard to ecological conservation and the management of natural parks, the need to involve local communities had been stressed even earlier. Here, the emphasis was less on the local management of resources, as it had been realised that fortress conservation approaches were bound to fail in circumstances in which poor local communities were bereft of the resources on which their livelihoods depended. Thus, in 1980, the World Conservation Strategy of the International Union for Conversation (IUCN), for instance, emphasised the need to enhance conservation through the involvement and economic development of neighbouring communities. In the ensuing years, internationally-sponsored conservation with development (CWD) projects abounded (Stocking and Perkin 1992).

However, incorporative and participatory forms of natural resource management failed to live up to the high expectations placed upon them, so some of their underlying assumptions and discourses have been put under scrutiny. Two strands of criticism will be discussed below, the first of which addresses the neo-Malthusian narratives of natural resource degradation that underlie many natural management policies and projects. Many scholars claim that such resource degradation narratives do not represent what can be classed as 'actual' natural resource dynamics, arguing that they are based on false assumptions and maintained because they legitimise scientific and administrative projects alike. Other critics have emphasised the failure to understand the socially and politically embedded and ambivalent nature of local natural resource governance, which, on the one hand, may lead to naïve perceptions of local communities and their ability to participate effectively in the multi-stakeholder governance of resources. On the other hand, it may lead to an overestimation of the power of governments in the developing world to implement natural resource governance effectively within a context characterised by polycentric governance structures and legal pluralism.

Deconstructing the narratives of conservation and degradation

Discourses of resource degradation can be found in almost all parts of the world. While they are often based on visible and measurable ecological trends, there is also mounting evidence that some of these narratives are social constructions – often dating back to colonialism – that do not necessarily reflect the actual development of the natural resource base, but rather the economic and political interests, as well as ideological convictions, of interested actors.

Colonial claims for control over natural resources manifested not only in the occupation of land, the drawing of administrative borders, the exploitation of mineral, botanical, zoological and other natural resources, but also by the launching of conservation policies and laws. Consequently, respective bureaucracies within the colonial administration were established, while typical ecological interventions included the gazetting of game reserves, the declaration of forest reserves, the enclosure of grazing lands, diverse soil conservation measures, the draining of wetlands and the destruction of local irrigation systems or the creation of new irrigation schemes.

Explorative travels through the colonies in addition to extensive surveys conducted on geology, geo-hydrology, forest, wildlife and agriculture provided colonial administrative bodies with information on the quantity, quality and location of natural resources, which were then recorded in maps and reports to provide a rich database for resource governance. Thus, these inventories served as a precondition for political agendas informed by and implemented with attitudes of legibility (Scott 1998). Nonetheless, the colonial world comprised a high diversity of ecological zones, a wide repertoire of natural resources and various forms of livelihood systems. Additionally, colonial administrations only had a limited reservoir of knowledge on tropical ecology and anthropogenic impacts. Empirical observations made in one part of the colonial world were communicated in the forms of popular ideas and paradigms, by internationally acting scientists and administrators, to other ecological zones under colonial rule. One example for such knowledge transfer is the desiccation theory, which claimed an empirical link between deforestation, change in precipitation and generalised climate change, and was one of main ideational drivers of forest conservation applied to Africa and India after 1840 (Grove 1990).

In some cases, this transfer of knowledge led to the misunderstanding of ecological relationships and misinformed conservation policies (Basset and Crummey 2003). Occasionally, it even resulted in local opposition movements that had clear ecological agendas, often versed in spiritual or cultural discourses, as "*[c]olonial ecological interventions, especially deforestation and subsequently forest conservation, irrigation and soil 'protection', exercised a far more profound influence over most people than the more conspicuous and dramatic aspects of colonial rule that have traditionally preoccupied historians*" (Grove 1990: 17). However, an organic understanding of nature (Escobar 1999) also strengthened opposition movements by providing spiritual dependency narrations, which were able to mobilise local populations against the ruling class (e.g. Sanders 2008).

Paradoxically, whilst colonial enterprises were motivated by the overall exploitation of resources, it was also the paradigm of natural degradation and required conservation that guided colonial administrations in their agricultural, wildlife and forest policies. According to Grove (1990), the motivation of conservation was threefold: first, to promote political control in order to enable resource appropriation by private capital investors and the state; second, contemporary anxieties of resource degradation and climate change, which could have had direct negative effects (droughts endangering the agricultural production) or an indirect negative impact (social unrest and disorder caused by drought and famine); and finally, exoticism and constructed images of wilderness.

Besides the notion of political control, which was always prevalent, the idea of (capitalist) nature, a rather Western concept (Escobar 1999), in need of conservation gained clear policy priority over the requirements of the local populations whose livelihoods were based on the use of natural resources. Consequently, colonial policy was characterised by fencing and fortress approaches, as clearly recognisable in cases of forest and wildlife conservation (see Chapters 4, 5, and 6). "*In every instance, these reserves and parks were directed to the exclusion of local peoples, whose historic patterns of land use had created the landscapes which colonial rulers now deemed worthy of protection, and this exclusion continues to the present*" (Basset and Crummey 2003: 14).

Colonialism did not allow an acknowledgement of the ways in which local residents shaped environments by harvesting, nursing and conserving natural resources; rather, attention was paid to their assumingly devastating impact on nature through practices such as burning soil, cutting trees or hunting bush animals. Missionaries, social anthropologists and colonial officers documented local livelihoods, belief systems and social stratification, but failed woefully to link this data in a systematic way to resource management and the impact on natural resources. Data collection was driven rather by curiosity for the exotic, as well as by the intention to document cultures and societies undergoing rapid social changes. Similarly, natural scientists described landscapes and collected and recorded flora and fauna without showing sufficient interest in the long-term impact of local management practices that shaped these landscapes. While the short- and long-term dynamics at the interface of resource users and the environment remained underexplored, ecological impacts were assumed and empirical evidence from one setting applied to other, dissimilar locations. Some local resource management practices gained particularly special and at times excessive political attention. The shifting cultivation of forest dwellers, for example, developed into a thorn in the flesh and obsession of forest officers from the 1840s onwards (Grove 1990).

The fear of losing the ethnographic and ecologic status quo seems to have been one characteristic of the colonial period. Nevertheless, whilst socially this status quo was obviously endangered by the changes induced by colonialism itself, the degradation of natural environments caused by colonial subjects was generally assumed without providing sufficient empirical evidence. Naturally, the observation of ecological changes would also have required long-term data series, which were still in their infancy at that particular time. Furthermore, not yet familiar with the local environment, officers and scientists were not able to recognise and value the anthropogenic nature of tropical landscapes and the role of local forms of natural resource governance.

Instead of evidence, colonial perceptions of environment in the colonies were shaped by ambiguous images of tropical landscapes as wild paradises, accompanied by narratives of human destruction by ignorant natives (Anderson and Grove 1987). Some of these colonial narratives were passed on and continued to dominate discourses over natural resource management in former colonies, as colonial policies were often maintained or copied after independence. Even though the images of nature in narrations and terminologies have shifted during the past centuries from untouched paradisiacal sceneries to valuable, vulnerable biodiversity hotspots, many local residents and resource users worldwide are still accused of lacking the necessary knowledge and tools, as well as the sufficient care and interest, to sustain the conditions of their environment.

However, some of the underlying Malthusian assumptions, as well as the discursive construction of environmental degradation narratives, are increasingly questioned. Malthus's hypothesis of an inevitably degrading natural resource base under conditions of exponential population growth, which at least implicitly underlay many colonial and conservationist arguments, has long been refuted. Boserup (1965), for instance, has long argued that extreme population growth will not lead to crises, but rather spark innovation and agricultural intensification. Such processes have been documented in the context of many developing countries. Tiffen et al., for instance, have been able to show how in the context of the Kenyan Machakos, a hilly and densely populated agricultural region, strong population growth led to the process of agricultural innovation and intensification that halted and even reversed land degradation (Tiffen et al. 1994).

Similarly, discourses of natural resource degradation, which have often been passed on since colonial times, have been deconstructed and provided contradictory evidence. Using the social construction of the "fuel wood crisis" in the West African Sahel as an example, Fairhead and Leach (Fairhead and Leach 1996) showed how environmental narratives based on insufficient understanding of local practices were perpetuated from colonial times until the 1990s. Similar evidence could be provided for other contexts, which would demonstrate how the "received wisdom" of environmental degradation continues to discredit partially well-adapted local natural resource management strategies. These narratives often help to construct the authority of experts (scientists, consultants, etc.), who then prescribe scientifically "sound" solutions, which governments and donors turn into NRM policies and projects – at times with disastrous results (Hoben 1995; Leach and Mearns 1996).

Proponents of this deconstructivist approach are far from stating that problems of environmental degradation do not exist and that there is no need to review the management of specific natural resources; however, they do argue for careful and open-ended environmental research that pays attention to the long-term process of environmental change and local environmental knowledge. Furthermore, more inclusive and democratic forms of resource governance are argued for.

Questioning paradigms on natural resource governance

In the debate following the publication of Hardin's (1968) article on the 'Tragedy of the Commons', it has become clear that most natural resources, especially in developing countries, where the direct influence of the state and formal institutions may be less effective, are usually governed locally. Local knowledge, belief systems, institutions (norms, rules and concomitant monitoring and sanctioning authorities) and different forms of social organisation have always contributed to local resource governance. The use and allocation of natural resources often followed tacit rules that reflected environmental risks, without being formulated in an explicit way (e.g. settling far from streams to avoid floods and wild animals, differentiation between village and bush and respective behavioural rules). In other cases, environmental risks were addressed by clearly spelled out rules (food taboos, rules concerning totemic animals or harvesting periods and methods), by allocating tasks to particular strata (e.g. young male hunters) or by defining access via property rights or the declaration of sacred territories. Such decisions were often driven by the need to ensure resource sustainability and security, even though this was seldom made explicit, but often veiled in metaphysical parlance. Reference was made, for example, to the will of ancestors or spirits inhabiting nature. Other resources were governed by ritual specialists such as an earth priest or 'Master of the Water' (see Chapter 7), or access limited to particular ethno-professional groups (ibid), who depended largely on the exploitation of particular natural resources. These groups often developed a thorough knowledge of the natural resources and technologies for their sustainable use, while access rights to natural resources were often allocated within the framework of kinship relations. However, the scope of management activities and resource regulation was rather limited to the local arena; often, the over-regional or long-term impacts of local practices were not yet understood or, as a consequence, heeded.

As shown above, during colonial times existing institutions and patterns of resource governance were often not acknowledged out of ignorance or for ideological, economical and/or political reasons. Moreover, colonial governments often perceived authoritarian interventions as the necessary means to effectively exploit or sustainably manage natural resources.

Based on their 19th and early 20th century natural science knowledge, gleaned from diverse areas around the world, colonial administrators introduced policies which linked the management of different resources. Forest reserves, for instance, were declared to restrict access to protected watersheds or to allow game populations to recover. To justify their paternalistic approaches, colonial officers ignored local experience and local capacities to manage natural resources. In areas of prime economic interest (mining areas and plantations, urban and industrial sites, white settlements) or of special ecological value (national parks, reserves), colonial resource governance was implemented forcefully, fully replacing local management regimes and even leading to the outright dispossession of the local population.

However, one has to be careful to not overstate the colonial impact, as it varied widely. In remote areas and in areas without imperial importance, colonial legislation was valid but hardly or only sporadically implemented; the actual impact varied from region to region and resource to resource. In the context of the Gold Coast, Plange (1979), for example, stresses the difference in the colonial treatment of local resources such as grasses, firewood or leather on the one hand and colonial resources such as gold, timber and cocoa on the other. As a result, some resources were targeted by regulations whilst others were neglected in policies. Furthermore, the political power of the colonial state often did not effectively reach to the local level, especially rural areas at the periphery. In certain areas, colonial legislation was ignored completely (or not even known). In other areas, where (as for instance in many British colonies) local governance was left in the hands of local "traditional" authorities, local pre-colonial institutions were transformed into customary laws that were officially acknowledged. However, in the process of codification, local rules and regulations lost their negotiability and flexibility, and were redefined in ways that frequently served the political elites favoured by the colonialists (Chanock 1991). Often, codified law, customary law and local institutional regimes based on traditional norms or religious beliefs existed side by side and afforded individual actors significant room for manoeuvre (Benda-Beckmann 1981).

In many cases, colonial resource governance was followed by the nationalisation of natural resources when independent countries created their own national constitutions and legislative frameworks. The public ownership of all natural resources was introduced for varying reasons, while state ownership was part and parcel of the socialist ideology adopted by many independent governments. Colonial resource governance often favoured social groups (for instance chiefs) that had been opponents in the struggle for independence, although after independence, many new governments wanted to dis-empower them by curtailing their control of natural resources. Furthermore, the control of natural resources was seen as a means to display governmental authority and to set a symbol of emancipation from colonial domination.

Nevertheless, in many countries, aspects of colonial resource governance found their way into new legislative frameworks and organisational set-ups; "received wisdom" and master narratives around environmental degradation were adopted without the necessary reflection (Basset and Crummey 2003). Furthermore, national resource governance did not continue to develop independently. Through the advice of international experts, regulations controlling development projects, loan conditionalities and national laws continued to be influenced by the agendas and discourses of international (donor) organisations (for examples, see Conca 2006; Klug 2002; Laube 2007).

As evidenced in colonial times, the impact of national legislation on actual resource governance was mixed. Governments tried to control strategic resources, but the lack of funds, staff and resources, lack of political will or political opposition often made it difficult to establish control over resources and to implement official regulations, especially in the periphery of the newly independent states. Struggles over the control of valuable resources and raw materials such as oil, gold, timber and diamonds often led to conflicts and had detrimental effects for the economic performance and governance of resource-rich developing countries (Auty 1993; Auty 2001; Le Billon 2001). However, the comprehensive control of widely distributed and less profitable natural resources such as water, land, forests, pasture or fisheries was difficult to achieve, since local populations ignored, opposed and subverted official legislation or adapted it in ways to serve their own interests (Moore 1978; Scott 1985). Official objectives to transform local economies, often through the control and (re-) allocation of natural resources, did not materialise, as profit-oriented production did not correspond with local norms emphasising reciprocity that help to minimise risks in subsistence-oriented production (Hyden 1980). Furthermore, the political economy of many developing states, where elites captured (natural) resources in order to maximise personal profit and thus rendered new patterns of production and resource allocation unprofitable for large parts of the rural population, made it rational for local actors to withdraw from and resist official policies and natural resource governance (Bates 1981; Scott 1976). Conversely, they continued to stick to old patterns of allocation and relied on and invested in social institutions such as kinship, membership in ethnic groups or patronage networks, in order to obtain access to resources (Berry 1989). Thus, governments often failed to establish their hegemony successfully over natural resources, and local resource governance continued to be reigned by legal pluralism and 'polycephalous institutions', developed in a process of historical accumulation that continues to use and to be used by local actors in a strategic manner (Benda-Beckmann 1981; Bierschenk 2002).

Contrary to theories that believe that the establishment of robust and effective institutions maintained or protected either the state or strong local authorities, the often fluid, negotiable and sometimes conflicting nature of local natural resource governance has been the focus of much literature since the late 1990s. Issues of social 'belonging' and access to resources, the hybrid nature of institutions and the creative adaptation or circumvention of official resource regimes, as well as inherent struggles over power and authority in local arenas in developing countries, have been highlighted by a wide range of scholars.

In the context of West Africa, it could be shown, for instance, how the 'politics of belonging' – the social construction of ethnic or kinship identity – are an important factor in the way access to natural resources is claimed and granted inasmuch that both secular and spiritual claims to the control of resources are transformed into political power and vice versa (Kuba and Lentz 2006). As argued above, the control or governance of natural resources is greatly related to issues of decentralisation and the establishment of governmental control over local arenas plagued by legal pluralism and polycentric governance (Ribot et al. 2006; Sikor and Lund 2009). The failure to devolve power and the reliance on top-down approaches masked in discourses of decentralisation and participation often leads to conflicts that preclude the sustainable and equitable management of resources. Conflicts also arise, because an institutional streamlining of resource governance often fails to account for the complex nature of pre-existing property right regimes and existing conflicts over resources. Efforts to privatise and regularise property rights, for instance, often threaten to override rights and interests based on the particular 'moral economy' or patterns of social belonging typical of the socio-cultural context of implementation (Cleaver 2000). At the same time, pending conflicts that often have been inconclusive for long periods of time are likely to re-emerge (Berry 2001; Lund 1998). In the context of developing countries, where the hegemony of governmental authorities is weak, these factors lead to situations in which resource governance is not a straightforward process with clear-cut mandates, powers and rights, but rather consists of – often inconclusive – negotiations in which issues such as access, property, belonging, power and authority are at stake. These configurations are utilised to describe and analyse the different case studies in this book from different angles.

About the case studies

The intention of this volume is to present empirical examples of the negotiations surrounding the governance of natural resources in a wide variety of countries. Presenting empirical evidence, we wish to enhance a dialogue in the study of institutional change, as well as carve out relevant questions for the local governance of natural resources.

Chapter 2 shows how the decentralisation of forest governance in Vietnam not only established a number of contradictory sets of rules, which enhanced local pluralism in land rights, but also encouraged village elites to take advantage of the confusing legal framework. These elites were able to monopolise and channel information systematically to guarantee land use certificates for themselves as well as for their kin and to exclude other villagers from benefits provided under the national forest protection policy for the protection of household plots. In short, land allocation for local households and the issuing of land use certificates became a farce. To Xuang Phuc demonstrates that when the programme ended, no set of rules was provided by the national government and existing administrative units were dissolved, leading to an open access situation and the unregulated (over-)exploitation of forest resources at the local level.

The montane rainforests of South-western and Southern Ethiopia witness high rates of degradation and deforestation, which not only cause the increasing scarcity of essential forest products, land degradation and erosion, each one enhancing rural poverty, but also the irreversible loss of biodiversity and the *Coffea Arabica* 'wild' coffee gene pool. The third chapter, by Till Stellmacher and Ralf Nolten, illustrates the structure and performance of community-initiated forest use rights by providing a case study from the

Bale Mountains. It examines the prospects and limitations for institutional change 'from below' and suggests that action should rather be taken to make already existing community-initiated frameworks work better, rather than designing institutions at government level and implementing them in the local arena. The chapter focuses on the question of how existing local forest use right regimes could be used to institutionally underpin future forest management projects.

Examining the costs and benefits of forest conservation policies, Paul Guthiga and John Mburu compare three different but aligned management approaches in a Kenyan national park. This fourth chapter suggests that even though the fortress policy implemented by one national management authority deprives local communities of access to forest resources, local levels of satisfaction with this forest conservation policy are higher than with less restrictive management regimes. This situation has arisen because, obviously, the fortressed forest has regenerated over the past decades whilst other areas have suffered loss in forest cover and quality. The authors argue that local communities appreciate the idea of conserving the forest for future generations, but also stress that it is mainly the local communities who subsidise the cost of forest conservation by bearing the opportunity costs of its existence without getting the chance to participate in decision-making.

An alternative set of rules and regulations for forest management is provided by the Ekpwe society in Cameroon, a traditional association which originally served as a legislative framework in pre-colonial Nigeria, and is now regulating access to forest resources in local arenas of present Cameroon and Nigeria. This fifth chapter, written by Charles Eyong, illustrates through the use of numerous examples how the old institution of Ekpwe provides an efficient system of rules and sanctions which successfully respond to current challenges such as the smuggling of forest resources across the national border or the abuse of industrially produced poison for fishing. His argument is that the property right approach is not sufficient enough to cover up the local governance of natural resources; alternatively, kinship, local associations, cosmologies and political legitimacy deserve at least equal academic attention. Further, he shows that Ekpwe gains power through its multi-functionality and linkage to almost every aspect of community life and the livelihoods of its inhabitants, and is therefore more efficient in the local management arena than state law and the national system of law enforcement, both of which lack legitimacy.

The contribution of a wildlife management area in Tanzania, described by Devesh Rustagi, hints at the fact that wildlife conservation may entail different benefits not distributed equally among the adherent communities, as well as the cost for local communities in the form of crop, livestock and human losses and higher foregone opportunities. Benefits and costs shape local attitudes in supporting official conservation programs. Even though all communities consider it their moral duty to conserve wildlife and secure bush meat provision, they are not fully integrated in the decision-making processes under the conservation programme, which follows a participatory post-fortress approach while remaining top-down in character.

Chapter 7 results from a comparative research project in African floodplains, and analyses institutional change in the governance of common pool resources (CPRs) from the perspective of New Institutionalism, including a legal pluralism focus. Historical changes in the institutional design of common property regimes for common pool resources such as fisheries, pasture, wildlife and water forests in complex ecosystems are investigated. In line with other contributions to this book, Tobias Haller explains how external factors have led to changes in the relative prices of goods and services, making floodplain CPRs more attractive, yet seriously affecting local-level bargaining power and institutional change. The states create de facto open access situations because they lack the financial means to enforce laws and are unable to monitor or exclude immigrant users, whilst local rules are eroded, weakened or transformed by powerful local people. Further, the chapter argues that the practice of traditional institutions granting rents to powerful people persists (rent hypothesis), while immigrants refer to the ideology of citizenship to gain free access to CPRs, hindering local collective action (paradox of the present absence of the state). Finally, actors make extensive use of the institution forum shopping strategy. The approach of New Institutionalism is opened up towards post-modernist perspectives focusing on power, ideology and discourses/ narratives.

Katja Mielke, Usman Sha and Iskandar Abdulaew show in Chapter 8 how water rights are in the process of being (re-)defined in the current course of state and institution building in Afghanistan. Their chapter is an attempt to understand and describe the technical, social and institutional aspects of water rights undergoing change in five study canals feeding from the Kunduz River. In the context of the Kunduz River Basin Program, institutional inventions such as water user groups, water user associations and canal committees are currently being introduced at the local level, with the objective of formalising water rights in order to enhance irrigation performance and efficiency for higher agricultural yields and the longer-term improvement of rural livelihoods. They argue that as long as current reforms aim exclusively at legal definitions and formal institutional inventions, equity benefits for local user communities are likely to remain an illusion.

In Chapter 9, Welyne Jehom Jeffreys describes the negotiations that evolved around compensations for re-settlers during the construction of the Bakun hydroelectric project in Sarawak, Malaysia. The outcome of the compensation programme was determined by state officials, who were supposed to record the amount of land, fruit trees and other assets lost by the native community due to the project. Flawed recording by public officials, local ignorance regarding compensation procedures and the consequent confusion surrounding ill-defined local land rights led to a situation in which local communities were unable to press for adequate compensation for their assets. Local leaders failed to act as speakers for the community or resolve local land conflicts. Moreover, the local community was unable to verse native claims within the framework of the officially recognised Native Customary Law *(adat)*, which local actors and custodians of the land apparently no longer refer to when dealing with land matters.

References

Anderson, D. and Grove, R. 1987. Introduction: The Scramble for Eden. Past, present and future in African conservation. In: *Conservation in Africa. Peoples, policies and practices.* (D. Anderson and R. Grove, Eds.), Cambridge UP. Cambridge.

Auty, R. M. 1993. Sustaining Development In Mineral Economies. The resource curse thesis. London: Routledge.

Auty, R. M. 2001. Sustaining Development In Mineral Economies. Oxford: Oxford University Press.

Basset, T. and Crummey, D. 2003. *African Savannas. Global Narratives & Local Knowledge of Environmental Change.* Currey. Oxford.

Beck, U. 1992. Risk Society: Towards a New Modernity. New Delhi: Sage.

Benda-Beckmann, K. von et al. 1981. Forum Shopping and Shopping Forums. Dispute Settlement in a Minangkabau Village in West Sumatra. Journal of Legal Pluralism 19:117.

Berry, S. 1989. Social Institutions and Access to Resources. Africa: Journal of the International African Institute 59(1):41-55.

Berry, S. 2001. Chiefs Know Their Boundaries. Essays on Property, Power, and the Past in Asante, 1896-1996. Oxford: James Currey.

Bierschenk, T. and J.-P. Olivier de Sardan 2002. Powers in the Village: Rural Benin Between Democratisation and Decentralisation. Pp. 27. Mainz: Institut für Ethnologie und Afrikastudien.

Boserup, E. 1965. The Conditions of Agricultural Growth. Chicago: Aldne.

Bromley, D.W., ed. 1992. Making the Commons Work: Theory, Practice and Policy. San Francisco, CA: Institute for Contemporary Studies Press.

Chanock, M. 1991. A Peculiar Sharpness: An Essay on Property in the History of Customary Law in Colonial Africa. The Journal of African History 32(1):65-88.

Cleaver, F. 2000. Moral Ecological Rationality, Institutions and the Management of Common Property Resources. Development and Change 31(2):361.

Conca, K. 2006. Governing Water: Contentious Transnational Politics and Global Institution Building. Cambridge: MIT Press.

Engels, F. 1972. The origin of the family, private property and the state (1884). New York: International publishers.

Escobar, A. 1999. After Nature. Steps to an Anti-essentialist Political Ecology. *Current*, 40, 1-30.

Fairhead, J., and M. Leach 1996. Enriching the Landscape: Social History and the Management of Transition Ecology in the Forest. Savanna Mosaic of the Republic of Guinea. Africa: Journal of the International African Institute 66(1):14-36.

Feeny, D. et al. 1990. The tragedy of the commons: twenty-two years later. Human Ecology; New York 18(1):1.

Gausset, Q. Whyte M.A. and Birch-Thomsen, T. (eds.) 2005. *Beyond Territory and Scarcity. Exploring Conflicts over Natural Resources Management.* Nordiska Afrikainstitutet. Stockholm.

Griffiths, J. 1986. What is legal pluralism? Journal of Legal Pluralism and Unofficial Law 24(1):1-56.

Grove, R.H. 1990. Colonial conservation, ecological hegemony and popular resistance. Towards a global synthesis. In: McKenzie, J. (ed.) *Imperialism and the Natural World*, 15-50.

Hardin, G. 1968. The Tragedy of the Commons. Science 162:1243-1248.

Hoben, A. 1995. Paradigms and politics: The cultural construction of environmental policy in Ethiopia. World Development 23(6):1007-1021.

Hyden, G. 1980. Beyond Ujamaa in Tanzania. Underdevelopment and an Uncaptured Peasantry. London: Heinemann.

Klug, H. 2002. Hybrid(ity) Rules: Creating Local Law in a Globalized World. *In* Global Prescriptions. The Production, Exportation, and Importation of a New Legal Orthodoxy. Y. Dezalay and B.G. Garth, eds. Ann Arbor: University of Michigan Press.

Kuba, R. and C. Lentz, eds. 2006. Land and the politics of belonging in West Africa. Leiden: Brill.

Laube, W. 2007. The promise and perils of water reform: perspectives from Northern Ghana. Afrika spectrum 42(3):419.

Le Billon, P. 2001. The political ecology of war: natural resources and armed conflicts. Political Geography 20(5):561-584.

Leach, M., and R. Mearns (eds.) 1996. The Lie of the Land: Challenging Received Wisdom on the African Environment. Oxford: James Currey.

Lund, C. 1998. Law, Power and Politics in Niger. Land Struggles and the Rural Code. Volume 1. Hamburg: LIT Verlag.

Malthus, T. R. 1826. An essay on the principle of population: or, A view of its past and present effects on human happiness with an inquiry into our prospects respecting the future removal or mitigation of the evils which it occasions (6th edition). London: John Murray.

Moore, S. F. 1978. Law as Process. London: Routledge & Kegan Paul.

Morgan, L. H. 1877. Ancient Society. Researches in the Lines of Human Progress from Savagery through Barbarism to Civilization. London: MacMillan and Co.

Okoth-Ogendo, H. W. O. 1979. The Imposition of Property Law in Kenya. *In* The Imposition of Law. S.B. Bruman and B.E. Harrell-Bond (eds.) New York: Academic Press.

Olivier de Sardan, J.-P. 2005. *Anthropology and Development: Understanding Contemporary Social Change.* Zed Books, London/ New York.

Ostrom, E. 1990. Governing the commons: the evolution of institutions for collective action. Cambridge ; New York: Cambridge University Press.

Ostrom, E. 1992. Grafting Institutions for Self-Governing Irrigation Systems. San Francisco: Institute for Contemporary Studies.

Plange, N.K. 1979. Underdevelopment in Northern Ghana. Natural Causes or Colonial Capitalism? *Review of African Political Economy 6*, 4-14.

Ribot, J. C., A. Agrawal, and A. M. Larson 2006. Recentralizing While Decentralizing: How National Governments Reappropriate Forest Resources. World Development 34(11):1864-1886.

Robbins, P. 2004. *Political Ecology. Critical Introductions to Geography.* Blackwell Publishing. Oxford.

Sanders, T. 2008. *Beyond Bodies. Rainmaking and Sense Making in Tanzania.* University of Toronto Press. Toronto.

Scott, J. C. 1976. The Moral Economy of the Peasant. New Heaven: Yale University Press.

Scott, J C. 1985. Weapons of the Weak. Everyday forms of Peasant Resistance. New Haven and London: Yale University Press.

Scott, J. C. 1998. *Seeing it like a State. How Certain Schemes to Improve the Human Condition Have Failed.* Yale UP. New Haven/ London.

Sikor, T., and C. Lund 2009. Access and Property: A Question of Power and Authority. Development and Change 40(1):1-22.

Stocking, M., and S. Perkin 1992. Conservation-with-development: an application of the concept in the Usambara Mountains, Tanzania. Transactions of the Institute of British Geographers 17(3):337.

Tiffen, M., M. Mortimore, and F. Gichuki 1994. More people, less erosion: environmental recovery in Kenya. Chichester: Wiley. Wiber, M., Milley, c. (eds.) 2008. After Recognition. Implementing Special Rights in Natural Resources Management. Lit. Berlin.

Chapter 2

Legal Pluralism in Forest Use and Management in Luoi Hai Mountain Forest, Vietnam

To Xuan Phuc

Introduction

Forest cover in Vietnam has been substantially reduced over the past several decades. To increase forest cover, the Vietnamese government issued a new forest policy in the 1990s. The Land Law, enacted in 1993, mandated the state to allocate land previously managed by provincial and district governments and state forest enterprises to local households. This process is called forest devolution. The law substantially expands the scope of tenure rights and the duration of rights granted to land recipients. The government believes that the increase in tenure security can lead to stability of resources and improvement of local livelihoods. Forest cover has always been a preoccupation of the government. In addition to enacting the new law, the government also spent a good deal on forest development programs aimed at increasing forest cover.

In this paper, I focus on the effects of forest devolution policy and forest development programs on forest use at the local level. Specifically, I demonstrate how different bundles of rights on the same piece of forest are given to various legitimate holders such as individuals and households, and how this situation brings about a variety of contestations among these actors. In doing so, two questions will receive special attention. First, how has the implementation of the devolution policy influenced the way villagers use forest land and forest resources? Second, what factors work to shape the social relationships between these actors and forest outcomes?

Many studies show that the development of new property regimes established by property reform after collectivization in postsocialist countries is a complex process. For instance, in a book on the impacts of property reform on resource uses in postsocialist Romania, Katherine Verdery (1999) argues that local dynamics of resource use is highly complex because various actors hold different ownership right and claims on the same resources. This is a situation of legal pluralism, which arises from a lack of routinized rules and crystallized practices concerning resource use. Under certain conditions, this situation leads to conflicts. In another example, Sturgeon (2004), notes a huge discrepancy in the perceptions of rural landscapes between the Chinese government and the Akha people, a national minority group. While the Chinese state promotes fixed property rights that should facilitate an expansion of the production of a limited number of crops, the Akha stress the spatial complexity and temporal flexibility of rural landscapes. This difference leads to conflicts between the two. In the same vein, Sowerwine (2004), found that land which is officially classified as forestland in upland Vietnam – and would thus be subject to forest production or protection – is in fact used in flexible patterns for multi-purpose land use practices. Different notions of rural landscapes between the Vietnamese state and the Dao people (an ethnic minority) lead to conflicts between the two. Similarily, Sikor (2004) discovered that the government land policy in the Vietnamese uplands, which emphasizes exclusive and territorial property rights, differs greatly from local land relations. The latter is more flexible in terms of time and space, while the former is very rigid, and not able to accommodate overlapping rights of various users. Conflicts over forest resources also arise when different state agencies follow conflicting strategies on forest resources use (Sturgeon, 2004).

While the forest devolution policy of the Vietnamese state clearly determines property rights, forest use at the local level is highly legally pluralistic, combining various systems of rights remaining from socialism and those newly established by the policy. On the one hand, this legally pluralistic context ends up creating opportunities for the local elite, which have access to political power, and capture most of the benefits derived from forestland and forest resources. Whereas villagers, on the other hand, do not have bargaining power to challenge the local elite, for they are neither adequately linked to the state, nor do they have the social and political power possessed by the local elite. The unequal distribution of land and access to the forest is obvious to local people, but they lack the means to effectively change the situation.

I begin my argument with a brief discussion of Vietnam's legal pluralism framework concerning natural resource management. Next, I describe the policy of forest devolution in Vietnam, the study village, and local forest management practices prior to implementation. In the following, I then discuss the implementation of the devolution policy at the village level, and explain how the current pluralistic context stems from a mixed legacy of socialism and neoliberal practices that are embedded in local power relations. The summary and linkage between the findings and the legal pluralism framework concludes the paper.

Legal pluralism in Natural Resources Management (NRM)

From a neoliberal perspective, clearly-defined use rights form the basis for capitalist development. Following this notion, governments around the globe have adopted property right reforms aimed at giving local people more and better defined rights to natural resources. However, the objective of property rights reform is not always achieved. One of the reasons is that reform notions concerning property rights often do not reflect the reality. In practice, there are many different bundles of rights to, and claims over, resources (Meinzen-Dick et al., 2002). The coexistence and interaction of multiple legal orders within a social setting or domain of social life is often referred to as legal pluralism (Ibid., 2001; von Benda-Beckmann, 1981; Wollenberg et al., 2006). In a social setting, law of the state may exist as well as religious law, customary law, project law, organizational law, and various kinds of local norms (Meinzen-Dick et al., 2001). During disputes over resources, disputants seek the legal foundations that best suit their needs, in order to justify their asserted claims in the form of forum shopping (von Benda-Beckmann, 1981).

Studies looking into resources access and control often highlight patron-client relationships. Patron-client contracts tie people of significantly different socioeconomic status or power to one another by allowing these actors to exchange different kinds of goods and services. Patron-client contracts are phrased vertically, and can be thought of as asymmetrical for partners who differ from each other in position and obligations (Foster, 1963 quoted in Ensminger, 1992). According to Ensminger (1992), there are three forms of patron-client relationship. The first form is exploitative patronage. Like a monopolist, a patron takes advantage of a client in an unfair exchange pattern. Thus, the relationship between the patron and client is based on class exploitation. The second form of patron-client relationship emphasizes the benefit that accrues to the client in the relationship. This relationship guarantees subsistence. The third form is individual exchange viewing the relationship between the patron and client as one of market equilibrium in terms of goods and services (Ibid., 1992).

One of the most important characteristics of patron-client relationships is unequal bargaining power between the patron and client. Following Ensminger (1992) bargaining power is one's ability to get what one wants from others, and may come from greater wealth or social position or the ability to manipulate the ideology of others. Bargaining power is consistent with ´voluntary´ exchange, as when one uses wealth to get compliance, or ´involunatory´ exchange, as when one uses force to compel others to act in one's interest. According to Ensminger, this definition subsumes both the common usage of Weber, i.e. the ability to coerce others into doing what they would otherwise not perceive to be in their best interest, as well as of the popular contemporary usage of Foucault, i.e. the ability to control the consciousness of others. I highlight how the implementation of the forest devolution policy facilitates the emergence of patron-client relationship in the village and demonstrate how this relationship changes social relations in the village.

Forest devolution policy in Vietnam

In Vietnam, forest area accounts for two thirds of the total land area of the country. Prior to the country's independence in 1954, the country's forests were, de jure, managed by the French colonial government. During this time, however, virtually all forests in the uplands were de facto managed by local communities. This is because the French were mainly interested in controlling fertile deltas and the uplands where cash crop could be planted (Nguyen Van Thang, in Poffenberger et al., 1998). After defeating its colonial rulers, the Vietnamese government nationalized all forests in 1954. From the 1950s-1980s, forests were managed by a large number of state forest enterprises (SFEs), belonging to either the Ministry of Forestry or local provincial and district authorities.[1] During this period, local people were not allowed to involve in forest management and their access to forest was constrained. The SFEs also had competing functions (Van Dang, 2001), as each had the duty to protect the forest, while at the same time exploiting timber reserves to fulfill logging quotas determined by the central government. In practice, SFEs merely focused on timber exploitation, and disregarded the duty of protecting the forest (Ibid., 2001; Sikor, 1998).

At the end of the 1980s, state forestry underwent a crisis. Many conflicts arose between SFEs and local villagers, as villagers demanded access to land that had been monopolized by the SFEs. In August 1991, in order to respond to the problem, the National Assembly passed the Forest Protection

[1] In 1989, there were 413 SFEs of which 76 were directly under the control of the Ministry of Forestry, 199 under local authorities of provinces, and 138 under the local authority of districts (Van Dang, 2001).

and Development Law. The law classified three types of forest and established different legal regulations for managing each type accordingly. According to the law, the first type, protected forest (*rung phong ho*), accounting for about 30 percent of the total forest area in the country, was managed mainly for the protection of watersheds, soils and the environment in general. Management of protected forest rested with state agencies, either in the form of SFEs or Management Boards (MBs). However, MBs had the right to give protection and planting contracts to the third parties such as organizations or individuals. Special-use forest (*rung dac dung*), the second type, accounts for about 10 percent of the total forest area, was primarily set aside for the protection of ecosystems, flora, fauna and genetic resources, as well as the conservation of important historical and environmental sites. This forest was also managed by MBs, which can also contract the forest to third parties for forest protection purposes. Productive forest (*rung san xuat*), the third type, which accounts for roughly 60 percent of the total forest area, and was principally meant for the production of wood and forest-based products, but managed in a way that ensured the protection of the environment. The use rights of productive forest were granted to organizations and individuals as well. The state also offered barren land to local people to encourage them to plant trees, in order to grow new productive forests, and promised to support and enable people to plant trees and to process and market their products. The law, however, set rigid limits on which rights granted to recipients could be exercised. Land-use recipients were required to follow state regulations when using the land, and required to submit a plan to state authorities at different administrative levels for approval. Also, land-use recipients were required to protect or replant forest in areas where forest resources were exhausted. In general, although the government classified different types of forest and established separate legal regulations for their management, the state still maintained the primary control over economically and ecologically important forests, and granted local households access only to poor-value forests - forest without standing trees or even barren land. Further, the use of such forest land was still subject to various restrictions, and disobedience of state law entailed the retraction of land by the state.

The new land law passed in 1993 strengthened tenure security for local people. Land recepients were granted use of the land for 50 years. During this time, they could exchange or lease their land to others, or offer their land as collateral in order to secure loans from banks. Land recepients could also transfer their land to a third party or bequeath it to their heirs. To concretize the new law with regard to the management and use of forests, the government issued Decree 02/CP in January 1994 for guiding the allocation of productive forest land to individual households. This process is known as forest land allocation, or *giao* in Vietnamese. According to this decree, all rights that the new law granted were extended to productive forest lands. Recipients of production forest land were granted land use certificates by the government, and these certificates served as legitimate claim to land. In January 1995, the government issued Decree 01/CP, guiding the contraction (*khoan*) of land in protective and special-use forests to local households. There is a large difference between *giao* applied to productive forest land, and *khoan* applied to land in special-use forests and protection forests. Under *khoan*, the control over land still rests with state entities, particularly MBs. Furthermore, households did not receive access to land for productive purposes, but rather for forest protection and planting. Both the extent and duration of use rights granted to households were highly restricted depending on the terms specified in the contracts signed between MBs and local households.

As the expansion of forest cover represents an important element of forest devolution policy, the government launched Program 327 in September 1992. This programme aims at reforestation, the protection of the environment, and encouragement of fixed agriculture and sedentarization for swiddeners. Under the program, SFEs were regarded management units and local households were considered production units. SFEs allocated barren land to household for forest planting, or contracted forest land on which forest existed to households for forest protection. In return, households received a planting or a protection fee. The program also served to increase the area of protected and special-use forests, by turning large areas of productive forest into protection and special use forests. When Program 327 ended in 1998, the government launched Program 661. This program was designed to induce the reforestation of five million hectares by the end of 2010.[2] The Vietnamese government expects that the percentage of area covered by forest will increase from approximately 30 per cent in 1999 up to 43 per cent by the year 2010. Unlike in Program 327, local people are now considered a primary force in the expansion and protection of forests, and are also supposed to be the main beneficiaries. Poor households living around the forest were prioritized to receive land in protection and special use forests. Further, unlike under Program 327, where a benefit sharing mechanism was totally absent, local people received use rights within the

---

[2] Of these five million ha, two million are protection and special use forests, one perennial crops and fruit trees, and the other one is softwood forest.

protection forests. They are allowed to harvest firewood and selectively cut some of the trees they have planted. The government also provides support for marketing of forest products such as timber, but it still maintains primary control over high value forests.

The study village – Thanh Cong

Thanh Cong is a small upland village in Van Mieu Commune, Thanh Son District of Phu Tho Province. The village is located at an altitude between 500-600m on Luoi Hai Mountain, which is covered by natural forest (see Figure 1). It is difficult to reach the village during the rainy season for the only access is via a dirt road which is crosscut by streams. In Vietnamese, Thanh Cog literally means success. The name was given to the village by local authorities in 1968 when they successfully persuaded the Dao villagers who practiced slash-and-burn cultivation to take up permanent residence in the present village. When the villagers moved to the present residence, the land for the cultivation of paddy rice was already occupied by a state agricultural enterprise and the forest was managed by a SFE named Tam Cuu. This enterprise belonged to the Department of Forestry of Vinh Phu Province (currently Phu Tho Province). The agricultural enterprise taught the villagers paddy rice cultivation techniques and villagers looked for suitable land to farm their own paddy rice. When the Thanh Cong Agricultural Cooperative was established in May 1970, the cadres of the cooperative encouraged the villagers to contribute their privately owned land to the cooperative, but many households retained a certain amount of their own land.[3] In addition to collective paddy land, the cooperative also worked a large area of swidden land. During the time Tam Cuu Forest Enterprise managed the forest, to have access to land for swidden cultivation, cadres of the cooperative had to ask permission from the enterprise. All households in the village also had their private fields for swidden cultivation outside the collective fields.

At the end of the 1980s, the cooperative was dismantled. The paddy rice farms were distributed to all 28 households in the village according to their labour availability within the families. Each main labourer received 195m^2 of paddy land from the cooperative. Collective land under swidden cultivation

[3] In Vietnam, collectivization existed from the 1950s to 1980s. Initially to form the cooperative, people were encouraged and sometimes forced to contribute their means of productions (e.g. land, buffaloes) to cooperative. These assets then became collective property. Eventually, this collective form of production broke down in the late 1980s.

was abandoned. In principle, all forest land was still managed by Tam Cuu Forest Enterprise.

Figure 1 Sketch map of the village Thang Cong

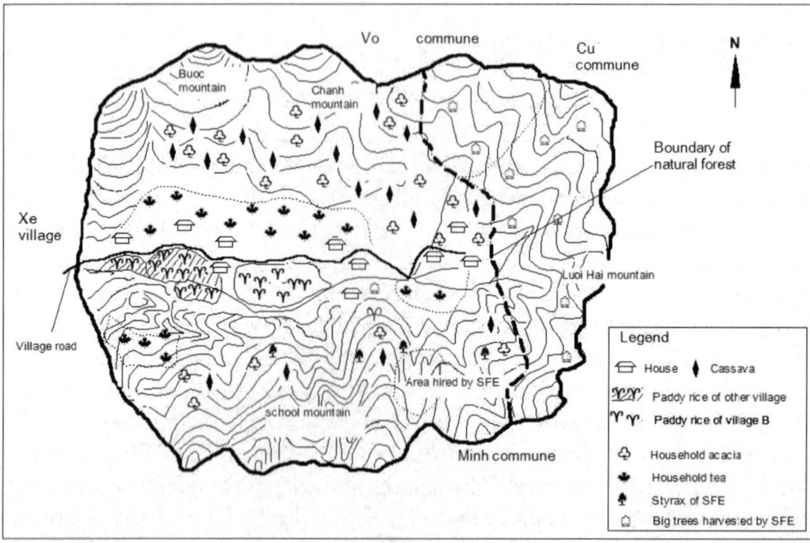

Source: Participatory mapping, 2004

However, owing to loose control over swidden land exercised by the enterprise, households in Thanh Cong were free to practice swidden agriculture in the forest. In 1996 and again in 1998, forest land allocation was implemented in the village. On average, each household received 6.4 ha of forest land. All forest land on the Luoi Hai Mountain was not allocated to households, but was directly managed by local authorities at the commune. Currently, there are 40 households in Thanh Cong, making up a population of 187 Dao people. On average, each household has 941 m^2 of paddy land formerly owned by the cooperative, and 741 m^2 of rice farms established by themselves. The land, however, is not sufficient for household requirements. At present, half of the households in the village lack rice for about one to three months per year. In the village, income from the sale of timber and firewood accounts for the largest proportion of household income (36 percent), followed by the income from cassava (33 percent) and from tea (16 percent). Recently, villagers have become increasingly involved in the market economy. While paddy fields are important for the production of rice for domestic consumption, forest land is the basis for capital accumulation. Since the late 1990s, many households use their forest land to plant cash crops, like cassava, tea and softwood trees. Income derived from crops and trees planted on the forest land is an important source of household income. Before proceeding, and to better account for this shift in household production activities, in the next section I provide an account of the historical background of forest management prior to the implementation of forest devolution policy in the village.

Thanh Cong before forest devolution

After 1968, the Dao people in Thanh Cong abandoned their nomadic life and settled in the current village. Villagers recall that prior to collectivization; households were free to practice swidden agriculture in the forest on individually owned household plots. Timber logging for commercial purposes was totally absent, and trees were only cut for the construction of houses. During the period of collectivisation, control over the forest was exercised by the Xuan Dai Forest Enterprise. Land with a slope of more than 25 degrees was classified as forest that was to be managed by Xuan Dai Forest Enterprise, while land with a slope below 25 degrees was to be managed by the local authorities of the commune and to be used for farms, home gardens and settlement. In practice, the enterprise also managed much of the land below 25 degree of slope, while the local authorities of the commune mainly managed the collective paddy land.

State control over swidden practices exercised by the enterprise was very loose during the collective period. In principle, the enterprise only allowed the cooperative to clear the land on which no trees grew. However, with the consent of the enterprise, the cooperative was free to choose land for swidden practices anywhere in the forest. As the control over swidden land was very loose all households had their own swidden plots in the forest. "*The enterprise never went down to the village to check*", explained my host in the village. Although, the enterprise had to manage the forest, it actually focused solely on timber extraction. In the early 1980s, in order to be able to extract timber from the forest around the village, the enterprise started to construct a logging road in the Luoi Hai Mountain. Logging in the region took place from 1984 to 1991. During this period, the enterprise hired a large number of loggers from the lowland to work at Luoi Hai. The former vice chairman of the Thanh Cong Cooperative pointed his finger to Luoi Hai Forest when we were standing at the bottom of the valley and told me, "*Dozens of trucks laden with ironwood running out of the forest every day.*" When the Xuan Dai Forest Enterprise stopped logging the timber in 1992, virtually all good timber trees had been cut, and after the enterprise had left Luoi Hai, no form of forest management continued. From 1992 to 1996, prior to forest land allocation, the control over timber extraction in Luoi Hai and over transportation of timber was very lax. As a result, villagers in Thanh Cong and other nearby villages began to glean (*mot*) the remaining timber of the forest.[4] Private traders came directly to the village to buy timber from villagers. Villagers repeatedly told me that no officers from local authorities came to the village to protect the timber trees.

In November 1991, the government decided to restructure those state-owned enterprises that were not effectively operating in the market economy.[5] One year later, the Ministry of Forestry decided to restructure a large number of SFEs.[6] All SFEs had to do an inventory of their resources (human, capital, land, machineries, etc.) and were asked to hand over the forests they were not able to manage to local authorities. Under this restructuring, the Tam Cuu Forest Enterprise (currently Xuan Dai Forest Enterprise) had to hand over 73 percent of its forests to 12 communes in Thanh Son district. The Van Mieu Commune, to which Thanh Cong village belongs to, received 966.1 ha. However, the transfer of land from the enterprise to the local authorities was merely made on paper. After the transfer, local authorities in the district started to implement forest land allocation. At the local level, management power of forest land and forest resources was controlled by the People's Committee of the commune, and the Forest Protection Department (*kiem lam*) of the district. The section below reviews the process of policy implementation in the study village.

Implementation of the devolution policy in Thanh Cong

Forest land allocation

Without consultation with Xuan Dai Forest Enterprise, local authorities of the Van Mieu Commune collaborating with the Forest Protection Department began allocating land received from the enterprise to local households in 1996. A total of 31 land recipients belonging to 26 households in Thanh Cong received 225.5 ha of production forest in 1996, and three more land recipients received 29.5 ha of production forest in 1998.[6] However, part of

---

[4] Villagers use the term mot (to glean) to refer to the process through which they extracted left-over timber after the Xuan Dai enterprise left

[5] The Decree 388-HDBT, on the restructuring of state-own enterprises, was issued by the Ministerial Council (currently the government) on 20th November 1991

[6] Most of households in Thanh Cong were allocated the land in 1996 but a few had to wait until 1998. The process of the FLA in the village was very top-down and

the land in Luoi Hai Forest (see Figure 1) was not allocated to households in Thanh Cong, but kept by local authorities of the commune for the purpose that I explain below. In 1997, the local authorities of the district granted land use certificates to the land recipients who received land in 1996. Those who received the land in 1998 received land use certificates a year later.

Difficulties in deriving benefit from productive forest

When I arrived in Thanh Cong in 2004, I was surprised to discover that in order to clear production forest land to plant timber trees and cassava, villagers had to seek the permission of the Forest Protection Department with written consent from the chairman of the village and the chairman of the commune. This was strange, for the law allowed households to use productive forestland to plant trees and food crops without having to ask for permission from local authorities. I visited the head of the Forest Protection Department to ask for clarification. According to its head officer, forcing villagers to obtain consent would better protect the forest in three ways. First, villagers would be less likely to practice swidden cultivation on the land, and that in turn reduced the risk of forest fire.[7] Second, although villagers have been allocated the use right for productive forest land, they are not allowed to clear land that has good forest cover, because this practice would be considered as forest destruction. Third, it is easier for the Forest Protection Department to check the origin of woods which are traded and transported, if they are to control the clearing. If villagers have wood to sell without having written permission from the Forest Protection Department the wood is considered illegally harvested, and the villagers and traders are subject to a fine.

Indeed, some households in Thanh Cong do not ask for permission from the Forest Protection Department for clearing the land to plant trees and cassava, for the forest cover on their land does not provide enough income for them. Where the land has good forest cover, permission for the clearing

---

had shortcomings. It resulted in an unequal distribution of land among households. Description of this implementation process, however, goes beyond the scope of this paper. Further, according to the law, each household is entitled to receive one land use certificate (LUC). In the village, three households received more than one each. The issue of distribution also goes beyond the scope of this paper.

[7] After slashing vegetation on the land, villagers would normally burn residuals in order to clear the land for planting. Some years back, however, there was forest fire in Luoi Hai. The reason is still unknown. After the fire, the *kiem lam* was strongly criticized by the local authorities of the district, and became very cautious about forest fires. They now discourage villagers from burning residuals.

of land is sought. Such permission allows households and traders to market the forest trees without interference, even if the trees are illegally cut.[8] In all cases, villagers must collaborate with both traders and local officials to market the trees. They must obtain permission from the Forest Protection Department by writing letters of request, to which have been affixed the written consent of the chairmen of the village and of the commune. The letters are then given to traders who deal with the Forest Protection Department. For the traders, it is not difficult to get the permission from the Forest Protection Department, because they each understand the process very well.[9] Traders then keep these letters with them as permits for the transportation of wood. To a large extent, then, villagers are dependent on traders for permissions. As a result, traders are in a strong position to negotiate and manipulate the price of wood and to control the market. Having weak bargaining power, villagers tend to accept any price offered by traders.

Under the forest devolution policy, although having granted stronger property rights to land, villagers find it difficult to exercise these rights as various restrictions exist. The evidence from Thanh Cong shows that restrictions do not come from the policy itself, but from legal regulations set up by local authorities particularly the Forest Protection Department to prevent villagers from using forestland and forest resources. Through licensing, the Forest Protection Department are able to control the use of forests, thus creating room for rent-seeking behaviour. In addition, licensing helps to strengthen the bargaining power of outsiders, in this case wood traders. Villagers, on the other hand, even though they have rights to forest trees, have weak bargaining power and are forced to tie to traders in order to derive a benefit from the trees.

Implementation of forest development programs in Thangh Cong

In Thanh Cong the Program 327 of 1992 was implemented by the Tam Cuu Forest Enterprise in 1994. A total of 102 ha of forest on the Luoi Hai Mountain were designated for protection. The protection fee was set up by the government at 40,000 Vietnamese Dong (VND), or around $3.6 US per

---

[8] In this paper, I use the term illegality to refer to local practices that are not allowed in the law. I am aware that many of these illegal practices are legitimate in the local setting. Illegality in this paper does not refer to illegitimacy and vice versa.

[9] During my field research, I stayed in the office of the Forest Protection Department several times and observed wood traders who came to the office to gain wood marketing permits. I assumed that the permission was facilitated through bribes. Villagers in *Thanh Cong* also told me that to get the permission from the Forest Protection Department, traders have to pay quite a lot of money as bribes.

ha per year.[10] However, except for the household of the village chairman, no households in the village knew about the protection program. The village chairman abused his power given by the state to monopolize the protection contract. Backed up by local authorities of the commune, and backed by officials of the enterprise, the chairman signed a protection contract with the enterprise. The contract came into effect in 1994 and would remain in effect for 10 years. When the contract was made public, the chairman told villagers that he was appointed to protect the forest on Luoi Hai, and that villagers were not allowed to extract forest resources from the mountain. By monopolizing the protection contract, the chairman was able to capture all benefits from the forest protection fee.

In 1998, Program 327 ended, shifting to Program 661. In Thanh Cong, though the forest protection contract was still in effect (supposedly up to 2003), it was terminated by local authorities. Management control of the Program 661 no longer rested with the enterprise but the newly-established Project Management Unit based at the district center. Under the new forest protection program, the area designated for protection on the Luoi Hai expanded substantially. The total forest area under protection of the new program went up to 321 ha of which 100 ha was transferred from program 327. In the village, only four households including that of the village chairman received the protection contracts. A forest protection fee was set at 50,000 VND ($ 3.3 US) per ha per year. The Project Management Unit, however, subtracted 15,000 VND, and the local authorities of the commune 4,000 VND per ha from the amount

The village chairman had selected four individuals, including himself, to sign the contracts with the Project Management Unit. Eventually, the vice chairman of the village (the chairman's brother) received a contract of 74.7 ha. The chairman of the veterans union (the chairman's father-in-law) received a contract of 90 ha. A villager with whom the chairman had very close relations received a contract of 56.3 ha. The village chairman himself received a contract of 100 ha. All remaining households in the village were excluded.

In principle, these protection contracts should be signed between the Project Management Unit and the entire village represented by the village chairman, the farmer organization, veteran organization, and women's or-

---

[10] However, the enterprise subtracted 15,000 VND ($1.25 US) per ha for a designing fee, and the commune administration subtracted another 2,000 VND ($0.17 US) for unknown reasons.

ganization represented by the heads of these organizations. Following the terms of reference, the chairman and the heads were entitled to 30 percent of the protection fee. The remaining 70 percent was to be turned over to the village and these organizations to spend on public works such as improvement of the village road and/or school. In practice, the village chairman kept all money under his control. To protect the forest on the Luoi Hai, he established a forest protection team. Each contract signer was allowed to send a member from his household to work for the team. The chairman included a son and three sons-in-law in the team. He also recruited the head of the farmer organization, the head of the youth organization, and one of his relatives. In total, there were eleven members in the protection team including the chairman as the team leader. The team members took turns going to the forest. The chairman recorded the labour days each member contributed to the protection work. The relationship between the chairman and members of the team is based on a patron-client relationship model. All team members, including the chairman's sons, were clients of the chairman.

By controlling the protection contracts and the contractors, the chairman was able to capture a large share of the payments. Although the protection team had to protect all 321 ha, the chairman kept the protection fee paid for his own contract of 100 ha for himself. The remaining fees were divided among the team members based on their labor input. As the team leader, the chairman also claimed a large share from this amount. In the end, most of the protection payment was captured by the chairman. The patron-client relationship between the chairman and the members of the protection team was a form of exploitation. As noted previously, in such a situation, the patron exploited the members by mobilizing their labor, which was contributed to protection of the forest. The clients, the team members, were dependent on the patron in order to derive certain gains from the forest protection program of the state, while all other households in the village were excluded from the program.

The monopolization of the contracts initiated some forms of collective action among the villagers who were excluded from the forest protection program. In response to the chairman's capturing of contracts, villagers tried to fight back. During the village meetings, they requested the village chairman to add more members to the protection team. They also argued that the forest on Luoi Hai belonged to the village, and that all villagers should be entitled to the protection fee. However, the chairman was so powerful that the villagers' request was sidelined. The chairman always argued that the team had enough members. The villagers then wrote to the commune chairman and complained that the village chairman had manipulated the forest protection contracts. However, their attempt proved unsuccessful, as the commune chairman was an ally of the village chairman. The state power of the chairman, coupled with the backing of the local authorities, placed the chairman in a good position to challenge the collective action initiated by the villagers. Eventually, local villagers ended up loosing out. Apparently, the implementation of the forest protection program in the village was entirely embedded in local power relations. In the village, anyone without access to political power, or a close relationship with the village chairman, could not benefit from the forest protection program.

Where does the power of the chairman that provides him the advantage in monopolizing the benefit from the forest protection program come from? Answering this question needs an account on the historical background of the power relations during socialism. The current state power vested in the chairman, who I call Anh Tho, is strongly correlated with the state power given to his father-in-law during the socialism. Specifically speaking, Anh Tho came from another Dao village. He, together with others, migrated to the village during the socialist period. He then married the daughter of the chairman of the agricultural cooperative and remained with the family. Being a member of the family of the cooperative chairman provided him access to political power. His father-in-law put him in contact with local authorities of the commune, taught him management skills, and then got him the position of the vice chairman of the cooperative. After his father-in-law retired, and with the backing of the local authorities, Anh Tho took up his father-in-law's seat and became the chairman of the cooperative. When the cooperative broke down at the end of the 1980s, he simultaneously became the chairman of the village. He has been the chairman of the village ever since. Gradually, the state power given to his father-in-law transferred to him, and this power will likely be transferred to his son. During my time in the village in 2004, Anh Tho was about to retire. He was preparing to transfer his power to his son, who met all the formal requirements (e.g. being a member of the political party, good education background, having experience in managing village organization) of the government to become the chairman. On the ground, the chairman is gaining a lot of benefits derived from the forest by making use of the presence and absence of the state. On one the hand, at the village-level, state power is not really present in the eye of the chairman. Local authorities rarely go to the village to check on forest management practices, but instead merely rely on information provided by the village chairman to know what is happening on the ground. Shortages of checks and balances allow the chairman to manipulate the village in general, and monopolize the forest protection program. On the other hand, the chairman tries to stress the fact that he has been given state power to be in charge of village affairs. By doing this, he is able to exclude villagers from the forest protection program.

Land allocation on Luoi Hai Mountain

According to the law, land is managed by the state that allocates it to local recipients for use and management. The law also says that the management of the land at the local level rests with local authorities, thus, local authorities are managers of the land, whereas land recipients are merely land users. However, local authorities at the district and the commune-levels wanted to keep all the land on Luoi Hai Mountain for themselves for several reasons. First, up to now, the government still refuses land with good forest standing to local households. Second, through the forest protection program, forest provides a source of income for local authorities. As mentioned earlier, local authorities at the commune always subtract a certain amount of money from protection fees supposedly to be paid to contractors. Giving the land to households would mean that local authorities would lose this source of income. Third, local authorities are not clear about whether the forest on Luoi Hai is still productive forest or will be protected forest in the future. Some years back, the Forest Protection Department of the district proposed to their boss at the province to change Luoi Hai Mountain forest from productive to protection status. The proposal had not yet been approved in 2004 when I left the field site. If approved, there would be trouble if the land was already allocated to households for production purposes. Finally, there exists a conflict between the Xuan Dai Forest Enterprise and the commune administration over 102 ha of land on Luoi Hai. As mentioned earlier, the forest protection contract under Program 327 was terminated in Thanh Cong in 1998, without any liquidation measures. Thus, the Xuan Dai Forest Enterprise still considers its claim over 102 ha of land in Luoi Hai valid and requests this land back from the chairman of the commune. To be able to keep the forest on Luoi Hai under its control, local authorities secretly allocated most of the land (255.7 ha) to 16 households in 1999. The allocation, however, was only made on paper. Local authorities did not inform any land recipients about the allocation. Of the 16 land recipients, only five were from Thanh Cong village. The remaining were cadres from the commune. This is illegal, as the land law states that local villagers have priority in any land allocation within their village. Only if the villagers, are not interested in the land, can local authorities allocate the land to people from other villages. When I talked to villagers in Thanh Cong, almost all of them were interested in receiving forest land on Luoi Hai, yet they were never offered the land. None knew about the allocation to people in other villages. Yet in

2000, the district authorities issued 16 land use certificates corresponding to the 16 land recipients. The commune chairman, however, did not give these land use certificates to the households but kept them in his office. When I asked him why he did not give out these land use certificates to the households, he told me that the land on Luoi Hai belongs to the commune, and thus people are not entitled to the land and land use certificates. Although some commune cadres knew that they were given the land (on paper) on Luoi Hai, they did not ask the commune chairman for their land. Knowing that they were entitled to the land, two households in Thanh Cong came to ask the commune chairman. The chairman told them that the land on Luoi Hai was under the control of local authorities.

Allocating the land to 16 households and issuing the land use certificates is a tactic strategy of local authorities to remove the claim over the land of Xuan Dai Forest Enterprise, to stabilize their newly established claims on this forest, and to justify their behaviour to their bosses. Currently, whenever Xuan Dai Forest Enterprise requests land from the commune, the chairman of the commune argues that the land has already been allocated to the households and these households already received their legal titles for the land thus the former claims over the land are no longer valid. In addition, the local authorities of the district and commune are able to tell their bosses that they have successfully completed the land allocation in the area.

Open access to Luoi Hai Mountain Forest

The situation of the forest on Luoi Hai has become much more complicated since the Forest Protection Project ended in April 2004 and the Project Management Unit stopped all the contracts. The Project Management Unit entitled the four households with whom it had previously signed the protection contracts to derive some benefit from the 321 ha of forest as a result of their protection services. This benefit is determined by the government's Decree 178/CP.[11] However, the provincial director of the Forest Protection Department told me that this Decree is "*too difficult to implement.*" According to him, implementing the decree would require an assessment of the existing value of forest resources (timber and non timber products), for which the province does not have funds.

[11] Decree 178/CP was issued by the government on 12th November 2001. The Decree states that when forest products reach their maturity, the households who have protected the forest are entitled to 1.5-2 percent of the total value of these products (e.g. timber) for each year they protected the forest.

After the ending of the protection contracts, protection fees were no longer available. At the village, the forest protection team established by the village chairman was dissolved. With no law enforcement mechanism, the forest on Luoi Hai has become *vo chu* (open access). Many villagers used the term *vo chu* when talking about this forest in 2004. As a result, a timber rush took place, and villagers reported that from April to October 2004, about 25 m^3 of timber had been extracted by residents of Thanh Cong. Villagers also suspected that a much larger amount was extracted by people from surrounding villages.

The local authorities of the commune try to retain benefits from the forest on Luoi Hai, while they avoid the duty to protect it. The commune chairman argues that given the available labour and financial resources, it is impossible for local commune authorities to protect the forest. The Forest Protection Department of the district, on the other hand, argues that the forest protection task at the local level rests with the local commune authorities and that the Forest Protection Department can only give advice. The existing vacuum with regard to the protection of the forest creates the opportunity for villagers and traders to extract timber and firewood. Neither commune administrators nor the Forest Protection Department make any real effort to halt this exploitation, as they benefit from bribes traders offer for them to ignore their illegal activities.

This situation started to change, however, when the ´open access´ of the forest was exposed by two journalists, one published with the provincial newspaper and the other with the "Weekly News" in Hanoi. In response to the articles, authorities in the province demanded an immediate investigation. Various meetings were organized by provincial and district authorities. An investigation team was established. The team comprised of the head of the Forest Protection Department of the district, the chairman of the commune and various commune officials under the leadership of the director of the Forest Protection Department of the province. Although the team members came to investigate in Thanh Cong several times, they never came across any evidence. The Forest Protection Department of the district had always sent messengers to the village before the investigation, who asked the villagers to ´clean up´ evidence of logging. Therefore, the team concluded that the articles were overstated. The team leader told me, "*They* [the journalists] *reported nonsense. You see, the forest here is much better than in other areas.*" He would have drawn a different conclusion if the team had ever visited the forest, where evidence of ongoing logging could easily be found.

After this incident, control over the forest on Luoi Hai has been tightened and timber trading has ceased, with logging in the forest substantially reduced. Before I left the village at the end 2004, the Forest Protection Department of the district had hired my host in the village to protect the forest. This may be ineffective as the area is too large to be protected by one person. Especially, as the Luoi Hai forest borders three communes (see Figure 1), which complicates its control. Villagers in Thanh Cong do not believe that one person can protect Luoi Hai Forest and are unhappy that outsiders without rights enter their forest. In sum, the situation of forest access and control on Luoi Hai is very complicated, highly reflective of a legally pluralistic situation as demonstrated in the table below.

Figure 2 Legal pluralism in Luoi Hai Mountain Forest

Actors at local level	**Rights, duties and de jure benefits**	**Justification of claims (main sources)**	**De facto rights and benefit**
Local authorities of the Van Mieu Commune	• Control over 321 ha of forest land and forest resources • Duties to protect the forest	• Land Law • Law on Forest Protection and Development	• Direct control over the land • Access to benefit from Forest Protection Project
Forest Protection Department at district *(Kiem lam)*	• Control over vegetation (trees, bushes) of 321 ha • Control over transportation and trade of forest products • Duties to protect the vegetation	• Land Law • Law on Forest Protection and Development	• Direct control over transportation and trade • Benefit (bribes) derived from the control
Xuan Dai Forest Enterprise	• Control over 102 ha of forestland under Program 327 • Duties to protect this forest as a land recipient	• The land brought into protection project has not been formally liquidated	• Excluded

11 households (various villages of the commune) holding land use certificates	• Use rights over 168.1 ha of land • Duties to protect the forest on the land	• Land Law • Decree 02/CP	• Excluded
5 households (Thanh Cong) holding land use certificates	• Use rights over 87.6 ha of land • Duties to protect the forest on the land	• Land Law • Decree 02/CP	• Excluded
4 households (Thanh Cong) involved in Forest Protection Project under Program 661 (all belong to the five above-mentioned ones)	• Rights to benefit from forest trees and NTFPs of 321 ha • Duties to protect forest resources due	• Land Law • Decree 178/CP	• Excluded
Villagers in Thanh Cong	• None	• Moral claims over forest resources • Absence of law enforcement mechanisms	• Access to wood and firewood
Villagers in three near by communes	• None	• Moral claims • Absence of law enforcement mechanisms	• Access to wood and firewood

As the table above shows, different actors hold different claims over the same piece of (forest) land and different actors justify their claims as the respective claims with reference to different moral and legal frameworks. Local authorities of the commune seek the Land Law and the Law on Forest Protection and Development as foundation to justify their claims. This is to maintain their direct control over the forest and retain a certain amount of benefit derived from the Forest Protection Project. Their duty of protecting the forest mandated by the law is not taken seriously in their account. Based on the same source of legal framework, the Forest Protection Department of the district tries to avoid its duty to protect the vegetation, but increases its surveillance in controlling the transportation and the trading of wood in order to derive benefits from the forest through bribing. Having maintained legitimate claims on the forest from the socialis socialist era does not guarantee a benefit to Xuan Dai Forest Enterprise. Based on a different legal foundation, the local authorities have found ways to remove the enterprise's claim on the forest and they exclude the enterprise from a benefit stream. Though entitled to the land, 16 households in the commune of which five are from Thanh Cong are generally excluded from benefiting from the forest on Luoi Hai. The eleven households which received land on Luoi Hai in the paper are entirely excluded from the forest, as they don't live close to it. The five households in Thanh Cong benefit from the forest due to the 'open access' situation (just as do allother households in Thang Cong who assert claims based on moral principles). Therefore, it is the local authorities of the commune who use their own argument to justify their monopolization in controlling the forest in Luoi Hai Mountain. Of the five households in Thanh Cong, four are entitled to the benefit from the forest area which they earlier provided protective service under the Forest Protection project. Their legal foundation to justify their claims is legitimate, deriving from different sets of government policy. Households of surrounding villages also make use of the lack of law enforcement mechanisms on the ground, and base their claims on moral issues as a way to gain some access to the forest. This situation of legal pluralism does not guarantee flexibility of forest use and management at the local level; instead, it creates a variety of struggles among various actors.

Conclusion

In this chapter, I have examined the impacts of forest devolution policy on forest use and management at the local level. In particularly, I have looked at legal pluralism in the context of forest access and control in an upland Dao village in northern Vietnam. I have highlighted that despite the abstract set of rules deriving from forest devolution policies, actual forest use and management on the ground is complicated, and often contested among different actors. Legal pluralism arises as a result of the imbalance between rights and duties re-adjusted by local authorities for their own gain, and when various legal frameworks governing the use and management of forest are all working on the ground. In legally pluralistic situations, various actors assert claims based on different legitimate legal foundations to justify their access to the forest. They all try to gain benefit to the forest by ´shopping´ among various legal frameworks and pick up the ones that suite them best. This ´forum shopping´ does not promote more equity as Wollenberg et al. (2005) suggested, nor does it allow more flexibility under certain circumstances; neither does it generate innovation illustrated by flexible ideas. Instead, the existence of 'shopping for a' creates a lot of confusion, overlapping claims, and contestations over the forest among different actors. In addition to that, the legal pluralism brings about forest degradation.

References

Benda-Beckmann, K. von 1981. Forum Shopping and Shopping Forum: Dispute Processing in a Minagkabau Village in West Sumatra. Journal of Legal Pluralism. 19: 117-159.

Ensminger, J. 1992. Making a Market: The Institutional Transformation of an African Society. Cambridge University Press. Cambridge (USA).

Meinzen-Dick, R. and Pradhan, R. 2002. Legal Pluralism and Dynamic of Property Rights. CAPRi Working Paper 22. Washington (USA).

Poffenberger, M. (ed.) 1998. Stewards of Vietnam's Upland Forest. Asia Forest Network. Berkeley, C.A.

Sikor, T. 2004. Conflicting Concepts: Contested Land Relations in North-western Vietnam. Conservation and Society. 2/1: 75-95.

Sikor, T. 1998. Forest Policy Reform: From State to Household Forestry. In: Poffenberger, Mark (ed.): Stewards of Vietnam's Upland Forests. Berkeley, C.A.: Asia Forest Network: 18-38.

Sowerwine, J. 2004. Territorialization and the Politics of Highland Landscapes in Vietnam: Negotiating Property Relations in Policy, Meaning and Practice. Conservation and Society. 2/1: 97-136.

Sturgeon, J. 2004. Post-socialist Property Rights for Akha in China. Conservation and Society. 2/1: 137-161.

Van Dang, N. 2001. Lâm Nghiệp Việt Nam. 1945-2000: Quá trình phát triển và những bài học kinh nghiệm. [Vietnam Forestry 1945-2000: Development Process and Lessons Learnt]. Hanoi Agricultural Publishing House. Hanoi.

Verdery, K. 1999. Fuzzy Property: Rights, Power, and Identity in Transylvania's Decollectivization. In: Burawoy, M. and Verdery, K. (eds.): Uncertain Transition: Ethnographies of Change in the Postsocialist World. Rowmen & Littlefield Publishers. England.

Wollenberg, L., Moeliono, M., Limberg, G., Iwan, R., Rhee, S., Sudana, M. 2006. Between State and Society: Local Governance of Forests in Malinau, Indonesia. Forest Policy and Economics. 8: 421-433.

Government documents

Chairman of the Council Ministers. Quyet Dinh so 327/CT Ve Mot So Chu Truong Chinh Sach Su Dung Dat Trong, Doi Nui Troc, Rung, Bai Boi Ven Bien Va Mat Nuoc (Decision on Directions and Policies on the Use of Barren Land, Denuded Hills, Forest, Coastal Sediments, and Water Surfaces) 15. September 1992.

Prime Minister. Nghi Dinh So 02/CP Ban Hanh Ve Viec Giao Dat Cho Cac To Chuc, Ho Gia Dinh, Ca Nhan Su Dung On Dinh, Lau Dai Vao Muc Dich Lam Nghiep (Decree on Regulating the Allocation of Forestry Land to Organizations, Households, and Individuals for Long Term and Stable Use for Forestry Purpose). 15. January 1994

Prime Minister. Nghi Sinh So 01/CP Ban Hanh Quy Dinh Ve Viec Giao Dat Su Dung Vao Muc Dich San Xuat Nong Nghiep, Lam Nghiep, Nuoi Trong Thuy San Trong Cac Doanh Nghiep Nha Nuoc. (The Decree on Regulation the Allocation of Land for Agriculture, Forestry, and Aquacultural Productions in State Enterprises). 4. January 1995

Prime Minister. Quyet Dinh 661/QD-TTg Ve Muc Tieu, Nhiem Vu, Chinh Sach Va To Chuc Thuc Hien Du An Trong Moi 5 Trieu Ha Rung (The Decision on Purpose, Tasks, Policies and Organization of the Implementation of the Project on 5 Million Hectare Afforestation). 29 July 1998.

Prime Minister. Quyet Dinh so 178/2001/QD-TTg Cua Thu Tuong Chinh Phu Ve Quyen Huong Loi, Nghia Vu Cua Ho Gia Dinh, Ca Nhan Duoc Giao, Duoc Thue, Nhan Khoan Rung Va Dat Lam Nghiep. (Decision on Benefit Sharing Mechanism and Duties of the Households, Individuals Who Are Allocated, Rented, and Contracted forest and Forest Land). 12. November 2001.

Vietnamese National Assembly. Luat Bao Ve vA Phat Trien Rung (Forest Protection and Development Act). 12. August 1991.

Vietnamese National Assembly. Luat Dat Dai (Land Law). 14. July 1993

Chapter 3

Forest Resource Use and Local Decision Making in the Bale Mountains Coffee Forests, Ethiopia.

Till Stellmacher and Ralf Nolten

Introduction

This chapter aims to portray the institutional framework and the interaction between actors that shape local peoples' decision making processes in an afro-montane high forest in south-central Ethiopia. As such, the focus will be on the use and management of forest products, especially on naturally regenerating coffee populations (*Coffea arabica*) that grow under the coverage of the forest canopy.

The contemporary decision making processes of the local forest resource is understandable only in the context of a decades-old history of change and persistence of institutions and actors, and a variety of localised reactions and adaptations. Since the revolution in 1974, and the subsequent land reform, all land in Ethiopia, including forest land, has been nationalized. Successive Ethiopian governments established different organisations and institutional frameworks aimed at the governance of the country's forests. The policies basically emphasized forest ecosystem protection through the exclusion of human interference.

This chapter provides a case study of a village located inside a state-protected coffee forest. It shows that under the 'layer' of state legislation, local institutions determine forest resource use and management by the village inhabitants. Local rules precisely define who of the local peasantry enjoys which use rights to particular forest resources in which forest areas and to what extent. With administrative and juridical backing through neighbourhood working groups, and a council of elders, these institutions outlasted revolutionary changes and persisted over three decades of state-initiated institutional change 'from above'. The case study also illustrates the attempt of the local state administration to enforce exclusionary state policies by relocating the entire case study village out of the forest.

The chapter concludes with the argument that external efforts directed at the sustainable use and conservation of Ethiopian coffee forests can strengthen these local institutions, e.g. by legalising the hereditary use rights for forest coffee and honey. But it is also noted that the system needs adjustment to demographic and socio-economic challenges that add pressure on the forest ecosystem, such as the influx of new settlers into the coffee forests.

Theoretical and methodological background

The degradation of environmental resources in rural Ethiopia is predominantly the result of decisions made at the local level, in this case, by individuals living in a village within a primary montane high forest that harbours naturally regenerating populations of Arabica coffee. In order to understand the underlying decision making processes, one needs to assess both, endogenous and exogenous factors affecting forest resource management. The theoretical base of this study is the Institutional Analysis and Development (IAD) framework, successively developed by Ostrom & Ostrom to analyse structural variables of institutional arrangements (Ostrom et al., 1971; Ostrom et al., 1994; Ostrom, 2004).[1] A set of rather diverse organisational entities and institutions[2] are considered to be relevant, most importantly local institutions initiated and maintained by the communities themselves.[3] Institutions are not always coherent units, and existing institutions can impact, cooperate with or be at cross-purposes with other institutions. Hence, the intra- and inter-institutional levels need to be taken into account as well. The practical documentation and analysis of observed conflicts among locals and the state due to opposing forest governance philosophies support the choice of the theoretical frame.

---

[1]The approach has several advantages for empirical studies in resource management: it is sufficiently broad for interdisciplinary research and different institutional arrangements; it is open for institutional change and for heterogeneity among the target groups. Thereby the action arena – the social space of individual interaction in the institutional setting – can be defined freely, depending on the research perspective. Even while analysing the intermediate level, it is possible to take different actors at the micro-level into account if needed (Ostrom et al., 1994; Ostrom, 2005; Vasenda, 2001).

[2] In this paper, institutions are referred to as the "rules of the game" that "shape human interaction" (North, 1990).

[3] It is, however, not assumed that these institutions necessarily provide for efficient and sustainable systems of resource management (Baland et al., 1996).

The local level case study approach justifies the use of qualitative instruments of empirical social research. Focussed and problem-centred interviews, participatory observations, transect walks, focus group discussions and visual communication techniques like mental mapping were used. Supplementary socio-economic data was obtained by means of a total household census in the case study village Kankicho. Kankicho was chosen for four reasons: a) the area is situated within a coffee forest belt that stretches around the Bale Mountains massif, b) the utilisation of coffee plays a crucial role in the income generation of the local population, c) the village with 35 households is relatively concise in terms of its population size, and d) both, the forest as well as the village area is located within a formally state-protected "Regional Forest Priority Area" (RFPA). The triangulation of methods and sources required a field stay of several months as well as a strong reflection of the authors' own preliminary theoretical considerations.

Background

Before the military coup d'état in 1974, land tenure and property right arrangements in Ethiopia were fragmented in serfdom-, kinship-, private-, communal-, village-, state- and church-dominated land holding systems, a complexity not yet thoroughly studied (EEA/ EEPRI, 2002). In the Bale Mountains, the most prevalent land tenure system was the *gult*[4], in which landlords, the *bala kaarnii* (Oromiffa for "man with the receipt"), held sway over their populace in a way that resembles the exploitative serfdom system of the European Middle Ages. The *bala kaarnii* allocated both agricultural land, and also forest areas - including coffee forests - to local peasants. In return, they received a full range of services, including taxes and tributes in kind and labour (Hoben, 1995). The peasants' tributary relationship with individual landowners as well as the peasants' tenure of specific forest plots was hereditary (Crummey, 2000; Stellmacher, 2007a).

After the socialist revolution in 1974, the new military government, popularly known as the *derg*,[5] proclaimed the abolition of the feudal land tenure system with the slogan 'land to the tiller'. The land reform in 1975 put the proclamation into practice, and a land tenure system based on the socialist model was established. Pausewang (1990) depicted it as "*one of the most radical land reform ever attempted in Africa*". All existing land tenure arrangements in

---

[4] Also referred to the *neftegna - gebber* system (deriving from Amharic for "landlord" and "peasant").

[5] *Derg* (or *dergue*) is Amharic for "committee" and is used as a short form for "Armed Forces Coordinating Committee".

Ethiopia including the *gult* were abolished, landlords were dispossessed, and all land, whether farmland, grazing land or forests, were nationalized and came under direct control of the state. The following land law allocated land use rights for farmland but made no clear statements regarding rights to use forest resources, traditionally of great importance for livelihoods in and around the forest areas (Zewdie, 2003; Popp, 2005; Teklu Tesfaye, 2006; Stellmacher, 2007b).

Concerning the conservation of Ethiopian forests, however, state initiatives resulted in the establishment of different types of protected areas such as national parks, game reserves and "National Forest Priority Areas" (NFPAs). The latter are the most geographically dispersed with a country-wide number of 58 NFPAs covering a total area of 4.8 Mio ha in the early 1990s (EFAP 1994). By statute, settlement inside the NFPAs is prohibited, and the use of their forest resources by the local population restricted (Kubsa et al., 2003).

After the demise of the *derg* in 1991, the new government, lead by the "Ethiopian People's Revolutionary Democratic Front" (EPRDF), did not develop a comprehensive environmental policy, but instead issued proclamations that were meant to serve as the legal basis for the utilisation, management and conservation of natural resources, including forests. The "Proclamation to Provide for the Conservation, Development and Utilisation of Forests", No. 9/1994, assigned forest administration to Ethiopia's regional states, and permitted the involvement of the private sector in forest use and management. As a result, five forest administration categories, namely "National Forests", "National Forest Priority Areas", "Regional Forests", "Regional Forest Priority Areas", and "Private Forests" were established (Mengistu, 2002). In 1997, recognizing the magnitude of ongoing environmental destruction and the need for sustainable use of natural resources, the EPRFD-led government approved a comprehensive environmental policy, which addressed a wide variety of sectoral and cross-sectoral environmental concerns, including the management and conservation of forests.

Kankicho village in the Bale Mountains Coffee Forests

The Bale Mountains massif is located east of the greater rift valley, approximately 300 km south-east of Addis Ababa. It is peaked by the Sanetti Plateau, which reaches 4,300 meters above sea level (asl). South of the plateau, at an altitude between 1,300 and 3,000 meters asl, stretches a mountainous rain forest with an estimated size of 1,000 square kilometers. This area forms one of the largest connected primary rain forests in Ethiopia. The forest is a prime example of an Afromontane *podocapus* forest, and is considered a biodiversity hotspot within the country. Within this larger forest complex, naturally regenerating *Coffea arabica* populations with high physiological variability occur as a dominant under story shrub, basically at an altitude between 1,400 and 1,600 meters asl (Woody Biomass Project, 2001; Senbeta, 2006).

The case study village named Kankicho[6] is located right within this 'coffee belt', with forest and semi-forest coffee within an area of about two hours walking distance to the North and the South of the village respectively.[7]

Figure 1: Kankicho village, located in the "Mena Angetu Regional Forest Priority Area"

[6] In locally spoken Oromiffa language, Kankicho literally stands for "free space".

[7] Kankicho Forest is the major coffee production area in Mena Angetu *woreda.* In 2003, it contained 1,333 ha of coffee land, predominantly semi-forest coffee (MARLNRAWO, 2003).

Administratively, Kankicho is under the auspices of Burkito *kebele*[8], and part of Mena Angetu *woreda*[9] in Bale Zone. Since the mid 1980s, the village area and its surrounding coffee forests lie within the boarders of the "Mena Angetu National Forest Priority Area" (Mena Angetu NFPA), which was changed into a "Regional Forest Priority Area" (RFPA) after the promulgation of Forest Proclamation No. 9/1994.[10] However, similar to most other state-protected forests in Ethiopia, no management plan has ever been put up for Mena Angetu NFPA/ RFPA (Woody Biomass Project, 2001; Teklu Tesfaye, 2006).

The state agencies currently in charge of the management of Mena Angetu are the "Oromiya Rural Land and Natural Resources Administration Authority" located in Addis Ababa and its lower-level branches at the zonal[11], *woreda* and *kebele* level. However, interviews with the officers responsible for the administration of the area indicate that they have no means to govern or guide the decision-making processes regarding the use, management and conservation of the forests concerned. They stated: "*We can't control the forest area, we don't have enough budget.*" (Interview with the head of the "*Woreda* Rural Land and Natural Resources Administration Office") or "*We have not been to the protected forest area since four years.*" (Interview with the head of the "Zonal Rural Land and Natural Resources Administration Desk").

The use and management of forest resources in a state protected forest

The people of Kanchiko earn their living through small-holder agriculture (basically maize, *teff*, wheat), which includes animal husbandry for food purpose, and the utilisation of a variety of forest resources. The generation of cash-income is dominated by coffee selling, produced in forest and semi-forest coffee production systems.[12] A second source for cash-income is honey. Beyond these marketable forest products, the surrounding forest

---

[8] A *kebele* is the smallest administrative unit of the Ethiopian state.

[9] A *woreda* is an administrative sub-unit, equivalent to a district.

[10] With a size of 180,548 ha Mena Angetu RFPA is the fourth largest RFPA in Oromiya Region. In 2001, 91 percent of its land was reported to be covered by forest which is a particularly high rate in comparison to other RFPAs and NFPAs that often do not comprise any forest at all (Woody Biomass Project, 2001).

[11] In the form of the "Zonal Natural Resources and Rural Land Administration Desk" (ZNRRLAD) under the "Zonal Agricultural Development Office".

[12] Garden coffee production only plays a marginal role in Kankicho. For the difference between forest and semi-forest production system see Senbeta (2006).

provides a significant amount of other resources, such as firewood, timber, cattle fodder, and medicinal plants (Stellmacher, 2007b).

The appropriation of forest resources follows definite rules and regulations. The relevant institutions have their roots in the pre-revolutionary *gult* systems, which have been passed down over generations in the local community.[13]

The village community of Kankicho is characterised by the existence of a number of social organisations that impact villagers' decision-making regarding the use, management and conservation of forest resources. Most forest resources are not used and managed individually, but within reciprocal neighbouring working groups, referred to locally as *dschiga.* The forest-related work that these groups engage in is manifold. For example, forest undergrowth is slashed in order to provide the coffee with better growing conditions. Timber is cut for the construction of houses, fences or household and farming equipment (e. g. ploughs), and beehives are made from large tree trunks and hung in the forests' canopy.

The *dschiga* system promotes social coherence, control and knowledge transfer among its members. However, the working groups neither operate spontaneously, nor autonomously. Households call for the assistance of working groups at village meetings. Their formation, membership policy and activities are based on cultural norms promoted and imposed by the *yarsa* (Oromiffa for "old men"), a council of elders of the village. In Kankicho, this group consists of four people, of which one is the wealthiest man in the village in terms of agricultural land and cattle holding, and two are sons of the former *bala kaarnii*, the former landlord in this area. Local decision-making is therefore still widely dominated by a village elite originating from the pre-revolutionary feudal system.

As the highest authority in local forest resource management, the *yarsa* set up rules for how working groups ought to operate in the forest, and define the way in which the forest coffee is harvested by the Kankicho villagers. A peasant stated: "*When coffee is matured, the villagers and elders make a yearly assembly and discuss about this years coffee, for example the right time to pick. After that we can go in the forest and collect. If somebody collects coffee before this assembly the elders will treat him as a thief. They will say to stop*" (Interview with Abduro Borisso from Kankicho).

---

[13] Accordingly, the term community-enforced will be applied here in order to emphasize the place of the institutions' genesis and to avoid using the imprecise and emotion-loaded label "tradition".

The regulations not only define who picks the forest coffee at which time, but also determine the location of coffee collection sites in the forests. The coffee forest surrounding Kankicho village is located in geographically dispersed plots on which households hold use rights. The location of the use right plots and the plot-holding household (indicated by the name of the head of the household) is illustrated in the following sketch, a mental map drawn in a group discussion by local peasants, and confirmed in conjoint transect walks.

Figure 2: Mental map of individual forest resource use rights around Kankicho village

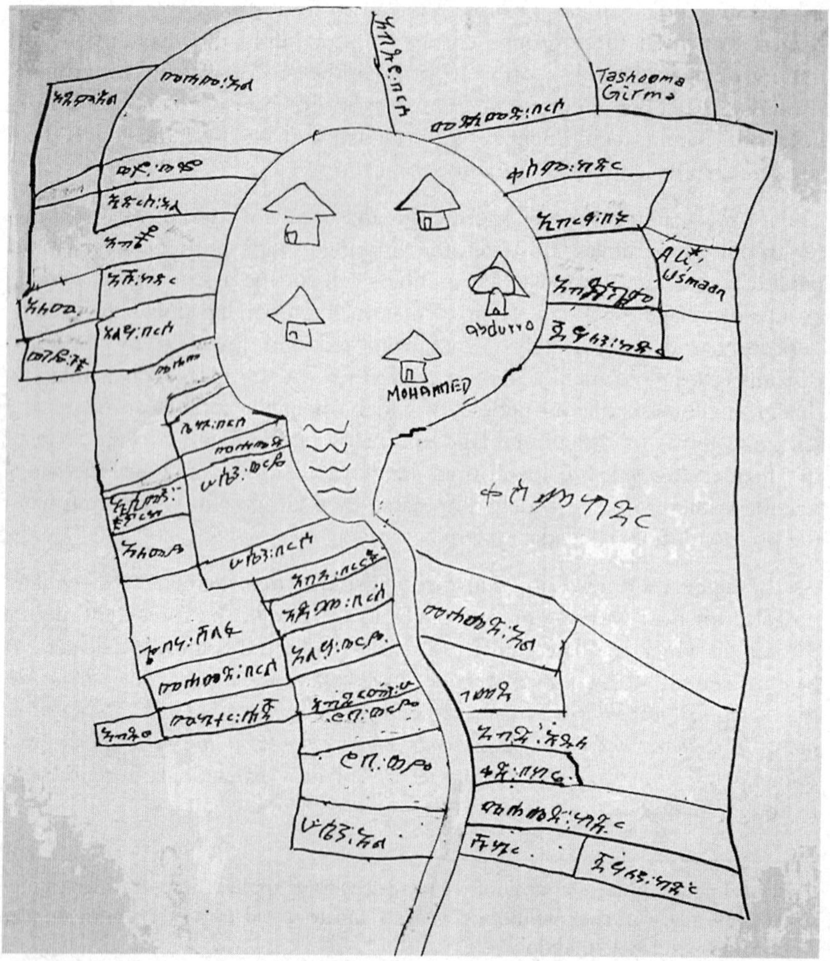

The five house symbols stand for Kankicho village. The lines indicate the forest plot boundaries, and the writing, the names of the forest 'owners'. Plots located close to Kankicho village mostly belong to Kankicho households, more distant plots are more often owned by households from neighbouring villages.
The plot distribution pattern principally reflects the status before the land reform in 1975. The *gebber* continued to exert the forest use rights they received from the *neftegna* and consolidated the system after 1975 through patrilinear inheritance from one generation to another. Today, peasants speak about "*my forest*", "*my neighbours' forest*", or "*the forest of other villages*" and have a strong emotional connection and binding to their plots. The delineation of the forest plots is part of the villagers' local knowledge, particularly of those working together in *dschiga* groups. This information was in no way formally recorded or documented until this research.

Due to today's state laws, however, these forest use rights are considered illegal. First, the distribution of land use rights in Ethiopia is the sole responsibility of the state. Second, the concerned forest is part of the Mena Angetu RFPA, and statutes do not permit the allocation of forest land use rights to individual peasants.

Nevertheless, the forest use rights do not apply for all resources found in a certain forest area. Different use and management rights are defined for different forest resources. Only coffee and honey - the most important cash crops - and wild lemons can be exclusively used by plot-holding households. The appropriation of forest resources - firewood and house construction materials for example - is less regulated. For these forest products, access for subsistence purposes is open. By and large, the scarcer and more valuable a forest resource is, and the more long term management input is needed for its utilisation, the more limited the access to it will be.

The compliance to local access rules is enforced by the elders. One peasant stated: "*When somebody hangs his beehives in my forest I will bring him to the elders.* [...] *When a person cuts standing trees and I catch him, I will bring him to the elders.* [...] *If I catch somebody collecting my lemon, I remove him from my forest and if he continues collecting I bring him to elders.*" (Interview with Abduro Borisso from Kankicho). The council of elders may then use its authority to "*punish the people according to our culture. They say: Why did you do like this? You never do it a second time.*" (Interview ibid.). As illustrated in these statements, elders play a critical administrational and juridical role regarding the use and management of resources from the surrounding forest. Elder's duties, however, reach beyond the borders of the village. They also act as village representatives to the outside, and negotiate and cooperate with local state bodies. The council of elders also supports tax collection, as it determines the annual income tax rates that each household in the village has to pay to the *kebele*. Hence, the elders - and not the state administration - factor-in villagers' income from their *de jure* illegal use of forest coffee and other economically relevant forest resources into the fixing of state taxes.

However, the existence of Kankicho is threatened, and its future uncertain. For several years people from Kankicho and state bodies have fought over the displacement of the whole village from the RFPA. In 1998-99,[14] large forest fires devastated parts of Mena Angetu RFPA. During the fire, all villagers were evacuated to a place roughly six kilometres to the south, close to Burkito, a village outside of the forest. However, the exact justification and course of action of the resettlement is difficult to assess. The account of the events given by villagers and state representatives differed considerably. Villagers emphasise that they were evacuated involuntary and that several people who tried to escape the resettlement were temporarily imprisoned. "*I got prison for one week and again for two weeks because I refused to go. Around twenty people of Kankicho went into prison*" (Interview with Mohammed Kadir Burisso from Kankicho). After the fire, the *woreda* administration forced the villagers to permanently abandon their original village and the surrounding farms and forests and to migrate close to Burkito. This request was legally justified as "*there are no settlements allowed in the state forest priority area*" (Statement of a Forest Officer from Dolo Mena). However, the villagers refused, and returned to their ancestral village about one year later. One interviewee from Kankicho summarised the story as follows: "*The forest burned, we all left the area, we were given a bad place and we turned back*" (Interview with Adam Hussein Mohammed from Kankicho).

At the end of the field research phase in 2004, the resettlement issue was still pending at the *woreda* court in Dolo Mena and Kankicho villagers still feared forceful resettlement. The relationship between the village community and state bodies, particularly the *kebele*, was substantially disrupted and characterized by mistrust.

Conclusions

The use of forest resources in the Bale Mountains is determined by local institutions that define which people are allowed to use and manage which

[14] Interview partners used the Ethiopian calendar to indicate dates. In this article, though, all dates are communicated in the Gregorian calendar.

forest resources to what extent. The forests are divided into use right plots that are individually held by local households and inherited over generations. The plot owners, however, have no exclusive use right over all forest resources on their plots. Exclusive utilisation is limited to the economically most important non-timber resources forest coffee and honey, whereas the access to less valuable resources follows more open access governance. People undertake most use and management activities collectively within neighbouring working groups, administered by the village elders. Elders are the main administrative and juridical local body. They control the adherence to the forest use restrictions and punish in case of non-compliance, e.g. when somebody illegitimately collects coffee from another villagers' forest plot.

This local forest governance system runs counter to contemporary Ethiopian state law at a fundamental level. The country's constitution proclaims all land to be a "common property of the Nations, Nationalities and Peoples of Ethiopia" (FDRE, 1995: Art. 40), in other words to be governed by the state. For more than two decades, the case study village and surrounding forest have been designated a state-protected "forest priority area" in which settlement and most forest use and management activities are prohibited. On the one hand, and as one would expect, this situation causes conflict, culminating in the attempt of local state bodies to resettle the entire village outside the protected forest. On the other hand, the state is a paper tiger whose self-proclaimed responsibility exceeds its practical capability.

In the early years of research on institutions, local 'traditional' institutions were largely ignored or stigmatised as chaotic, weak or even liable for environmental degradation (Hardin, 1968). Later, scholars tended to idealize them as locally well adapted, flexible and suitable for sustainable resource governance (Ostrom, 1990). The research findings supporting our argument identified these institutions as major determinants for the use and management of forest resources. The institutions are tailor-made to regulate long-term human-forest relationship under local conditions. Accordingly, external efforts for the sustainable use and conservation of Ethiopian coffee forests should help strengthening these local institutions, e.g. by pushing forward legalisation concerning hereditary use rights for forest coffee and honey, instead of developing and trying to implement new concepts - as a third 'layer' of forest governance.

However, the Ethiopian coffee forests are subject to internally- and externally-induced change, such as natural population growth and influx of new settlers, constantly increasing pressure on the coffee forest ecosystem. The mere preservation and perpetuation of local institutions, though, will not tackle these challenges and is no panacea for the sustainable conservation of the forests. This is mainly attributed to the local institutions' village-internality, their non-validity for non-villagers, and their lack of formal backing by the state. These are fundamental problems to be solved when integrating local institutions into external forest conservation efforts. Further research, however, is needed to elaborate on the correlation between local institutions, their enforcement and the loss and depletion of Ethiopian coffee forests.

References

Baland, J.-M., Platteau, J.-Ph. 1996. Halting Degradation of Natural Resources. FAO and Oxford University Press. New York.

Crummey, D. 2000. Land and Society in the Christian Kingdom of Ethiopia. From the Thirteenth To the Twentieth Century. University of Illinois Press. Urbana and Chicago.

EEA / EEPRI 2002. Land Tenure and Agricultural Development in Ethiopia. Ethiopian Economic Association / Ethiopian Economic Policy Research Institute. Addis Ababa.

EFAP 1994. Ethiopian Forestry Action Program. Synopsis Report. Addis Ababa, Transitional Government of Ethiopia, Ministry of Natural Resources Development and Environmental Protection.

FDRE 1995. The Constitution of the Federal Democratic Republic of Ethiopia. Addis Ababa.

Hardin, G. 1968. The Tragedy of the Commons. Science. 162: 1243-1248.

Hoben, A. 1995. Paradigms and Politics: The Cultural Construction of Environmental Policy in Ethiopia. World Development. 23: 1007-1021.

Kubsa, A., Mariame, A., Amante, G., Lipp, H.-J., Tadesse, T. 2003. Wajib: An Alternative Forest Conservation Approach for Ethiopia's Forests. Bishoftu/Debre Zeyd (Ethiopia).

MARLNRAWO 2003. Mena Angetu Socio-economic Survey. Dolo Mena, Mena Angetu Rural Land and Natural Resources Administration woreda Office (unpublished).

Mengistu, K. 2002. Tropical Secondary Forest Management in Africa. Reality and Perspectives. Ethiopia Country Paper. Workshop on Tropical Secondary Forest Management in Africa, Nairobi, ICRAF / CIFOR.

North, D. 1990. Institutions, Institutional Change and Economic Performance. Cambridge University Press. Cambridge.

Ostrom, E. 1990. Governing the Commons: The Evolution of Institutions for Collective Action. Cambridge University Press. New York.

Ostrom, E. 2004. Applying the IAD Framework. Workshop in Political Theory and Policy Analysis. Indiana University. Bloomington.

Ostrom, E. 2005. Understanding Institutional Diversity. Workshop in Political Theory and Policy Analysis, Indiana University, Bloomington.

Ostrom, E., Gardener, R., Walker, J. 1994. Rules, Games, and Common-Pool Resources. The University of Michigan Press. Ann Arbor.

Ostrom, V., Ostrom, E. 1971. Public Choice: A Different Approach to the Study of Public Administration. Public Administration Review.13: 203-16.

Patton, M. 1990. Qualitative Evaluation and Research Methods. Sage Publications. Newbury Park, CA.

Pausewang, S. 1990. The Peasant Perspective. In: Pausewang, S., Cheru, F., Brüne, S., Chole, E.: Ethiopia: Rural Development Options. Zed Books Ltd. London and New Jersey: 213-226.

Popp, M.W. 2005. Conflicting Practices of Environment Construction in Bale, Ethiopia. Berliner Beiträge zur Ethnologie: Band 9. Weissensee Verlag. Berlin.

Senbeta, F. 2006. Biodiversity and ecology of Afromontane rainforests with wild Coffea arabica L. populations in Ethiopia. Cuvillier Verlag. Göttingen.

Stellmacher, T. 2007a. The historical development of local forest governance in Ethiopia - from the imperial times to the military regime of the Derg. Afrika Spectrum. 42/3: 519-530

Stellmacher, T. 2007b. Governing the Ethiopian Coffee Forests: A local level Institutional Analysis in Kaffa and Bale Mountains. Shaker Publishing. Aachen.

Teklu Tesfaye, T. 2006. Coffee Forest Conservation: Local-level Institutions Influencing the Conservation and Use of Coffee Forests in Southwest Ethiopia. Margraf Publishers. Weikersheim.

Vasenda, S. 2001. Waking the Russian Bear: Institutional Change in the Russian Forest Sector. International Institute for Applied Systems Analysis. 34. Laxenburg/Austria.

Woody Biomass Project 2003. A Strategic Plan for the Sustainable Development, Conservation, and Management of the Woody Biomass Resources. Issue on Oromiya State. Addis Ababa, unpublished.

Zewdie, Y. 2003. Not by Maize alone: Forest Access and Rural Livelihoods in Southwest Ethiopia. ETFRN News 39/40.

Chapter 4

Local extraction needs and forest conservation outcomes under diverse management regimes in Kakamega forest, Kenya.

Paul Maina Guthiga and John Mburu

Introduction

Among other outcomes, forest management regimes ought to meet the requirements of local residents, ensure equitable benefit sharing, facilitate appropriate conflict resolution and encourage participatory decision-making of the local stakeholders. Forests may be managed under four different regimes. Under centralized management, state agencies assume the lead role whereby under decentralized management, local communities or local governments are involved at varying levels. Forests may also be managed privately where private entities own the resource. Finally, there are co-management regimes, where state, local communities and other actors share management functions, rights and responsibilities (Meinzen-Dick et al., 2002; Mburu et al., 2007). Such management regimes not only differently define and assign property rights to various stakeholders, but they also guide the use of resources, and therefore, consequently determine conservation outcomes (Oakerson, 1992; Meinzen-Dick et al., 2004). The actual operations of forest management regimes and their outcomes depend very much on local conditions concerning the nature of resources, as well as the diversity and interests of actors.

The tropical Kakamega Rainforest Forest located in Western Kenya presents a unique opportunity to compare different management regimes. The forest is currently sub-divided into three parts, each managed by a distinct authority and each using a different management approach. Approximately 44 km^2 of the forest is managed as a national reserve by the state agency Kenya Wildlife Service (KWS) under a protectionist regime. This part of the forest is largely conserved in its pristine form as a national reserve, and is used as a tourist attraction with camping and picnic sites as well as nature trails. Local residents are not allowed to extract any products from this part of the forest to support their livelihood. Strict policing and prosecution of offenders ensures that illegal activities are minimized. Secondly, the major bulk of the forest (about 200 km^2) is managed under an incentive-based approach by the central government through the Forest Department (FD). Under this regime, some forest extraction activities are regulated for the local communities. However, the Forest Department has set apart two small nature reserves, i.e. Isecheno and Yala, from which the local people are not allowed to extract any resources (see Figure 1). Thirdly, since the early 1900s, about 130 ha of the forest have been under incentive-based, quasi-private management by the Quakers Church Mission (QCM), which allows local communities limited and regulated extraction of forest products from this rather small forest fragment. As expected, these three management regimes have different outcomes in terms of the conservation status of the forest, the participation of local people in forest management and the distribution of costs and benefits among different actors.

Historically, state-led attempts to fence off or reserve areas for nature and exclude people from these areas have dominated conservation strategies (Adams et al., 2001). This model, variously known as 'fortress conservation', 'coercive conservation' or 'fences and fines', has long dominated international thinking about conservation. In general, this approach has not succeeded to meet the major conservation challenges by preventing deforestation and the associated loss of forest biodiversity (Geist et al., 2002; Tucker, 1999). As a result, the 'fences and fines' approach is challenged by a new approach that recognizes the potentially vital role of local people for forest conservation.

The incentive-based conservation approach is characterized by two distinct elements. First, incentive-based conservation allows people in the vicinity of a protected area, or other holders of property rights to participate in the conservation process. Further, it links the objectives of conservation with the requirements of local livelihood and economic development (Hutton et al., 2003). This approach recognizes the moral implications of imposing costs (such as income losses) on local peopleas well as the pragmatic problem of hostility that displaced or marginalized local people might pose to conservation organizations practicing fortress preservation (Adams et al., 2001). As an approach, the incentive-based conservation adopts sustainable development concepts and incorporates biocentric as well as anthropocentric arguments into conservation. Under this approach, the state transfers property rights to local communities to enable them to take a more active role in conservation efforts. However, the incentive-based approach in its various forms has not necessarily resulted in positive outcomes (Agrawal et al., 1999). Observations indicate that the success or failure of such decentralization policy depends on a case-specific mixture of institutional and on socio-economic factors (Matose, 2006; Agrawal et al., 1999).

In general, public forests as economic resources are managed to generate timber and non-timber products, as well as to provide various ecosystem services, such as watershed protection, carbon sequestration, soil conservation or biodiversity reservoir. Whatever the form of management, associated costs and benefits arise that are borne by different actors involved in conservation. Economic principles require that resources, such as land, capital and labor, are used in a way that maximizes net benefits (Kao et al., 1991). But apart from economic efficiency, understanding distribution of costs and benefits among different actors in conservation is important for guiding equity considerations (Ferraro, 2002). This is particularly important in the case of tropical forests, where many forest-adjacent communities bear the opportunity costs of conservation, because the distribution of cost and benefits determines the incentive structure of the actors for or against conservation.

Apart from economic and equity concerns, the persistence of the degradation of natural resources, and the failure of simple technical or economic prescriptions has lead researchers to consider the more complex aspects of natural resource management. In this respect, research points out the centrality of local communities in the conservation of natural resource (Wiggins et al., 2004; Trakolis, 2001). It is widely argued that success of natural resource conservation efforts will depend on the support of the local communities living adjacent to the resource (Ferraro, 2002; Trakolis, 2001; Rasmussen et al., 1995). Well-meaning measures of environmental conservation may negatively impact the livelihoods of local inhabitants and this may reduce the effectiveness of the intended policies. As noted by Bruce et al. (2002), public acceptance is of utmost importance to every management decision made by public agencies concerning natural resources.

The local communities owned and managed Kakamega Forest before the central government in started 1933 to manage it on their behalf (Mitchell, 2004). Therefore, the local people can be looked at as the 'clients' of these external management agents. One way of evaluating the external management regimes from the local communities' perspective is through generating their satisfaction levels with the way the forest is managed (Andersson, 2004). Another approach to evaluate forest management regimes is to assess the extent to which local people are given an opportunity to organize and actively participate in the forest management.

The objective of this chapter is to explore the outcomes of the three management regimes in terms of degradation status of the forest, distribution of costs and benefits among stakeholders as well as overall satisfaction of the local people with the different management regimes. The next section gives a description of the methodology. Then, an overview of management of Kakamega Forest is presented which is followed by a discussion of the conservation status of the forest under different management regimes. Local participation under the different regimes is discussed in the next section followed by the presentation of local satisfaction levels. Finally, the conclusions are provided.

Study Methods

Information and data used in this study was generated from a primary data collection survey using questionnaire interviews, as well as secondary sources. Primary data was obtained from a random sample of 378 households using semi-structured questionnaires that were administered to the heads of households by trained enumerators. We randomly interspersed the sampled households in the study area and across the three management regimes. The questionnaires elicited information on household demographic and socio-economic characteristics, farming information, type of products and quantities they extract from the forest, as well as costs incurred by farmers and their satisfaction levels with the functioning of management approaches (both overall and with specific aspects of forest management). Formal interviews with forest managers provided information on how the management regimes carry out their functions. Official records from the forest management authorities provided data on management cost and revenues generated. An array of secondary sources was used in eliciting historical aspects of management of the forest and other related information.

Three management options for Kakamega Forest

Kakamega Forest is the only remaining patch of Kenya's Guineo-Congolean rainforest, which spans from West and Central Africa, and is famous for its diversity of unique and numerous flora and fauna (Kokwaro, 1988).[1] This rich biodiversity makes Kakamega Forest an important global conservation

---

[1] Kakamega Forest is not a single forest block. The main forest block is surrounded by several satellite fragments with distinct names as shown in Figure 1. In this chapter the term Kakamega Forest is applied to both the main forest and its fragments.

area. In 1995, the International Union of Conservation of Nature ranked Kakamega Forest as the third highest priority for conservation among forests in Kenya. The forest is currently facing an ominous threat to survival due to deforestation and associated degradation. The size of the forest has rapidly decreased due to human disturbances, which have gradually contributed to the fragmentation and loss of forest over the past three decades (Lung et al., 2006). Currently, the forest covers an area of approximately 244 km^2, with the area surrounding the forest densely populated and used intensively for farming sugar cane, maize and tea among other crops.

Early records indicate that the first physical boundary around the forest was established around 1908-1910. This boundary was modified in 1912-13, and then again in 1929-1932. The annual colonial government report of 1918 indicates that local communities opposed any sort of control of the forest by the government (Mitchell, 2004). After the establishment of the first boundary, Kakamega Forest was still managed by the local communities through their village elders, who were under the authority of the local Native Council. The term 'local community', as used here, refers to members of different sub-tribes of the larger Luhya tribe which inhabits the area around the forest. The South of the forest and the area around the Kaimosi fragment (Figure 1) is inhabited by the Tiriki sub-tribe, while the North is inhabited by the Kabras sub-tribe. Isiukhus are found in the East and West of the forest. As noted by Opole (1991), these sub-tribes managed different parts of the forest and protected it against invasion by neighboring groups. The forest was under the trusteeship of the local elders who decided, for example, which trees would be cut for construction. In 1931, the Forest Department took over the management of the forest against very strong objection from the local people, who wished to retain control. The local people filed complain with the local authorities but without any avail. It is important to note that at the time of the take over, Kenya was a colony of the British and the local people were not represented in government. There were few if any channels available for them to seek justice or formally express their views. The colonial government had total power over the people and their resources.

But despite the local people's opposition, Kakamega Forest was pronounced as a trust land forest on 13th February 1933, which meant that although the forest would remain the property of the local people, the central government, would manage it on their behalf. From 1933 onwards, concessions for prospecting were established in the forest, and led to the opening of the forest to official and commercial scale logging. Local residents were evicted from the forest, and the forest was managed as a

Figure 1 Kakamega forest

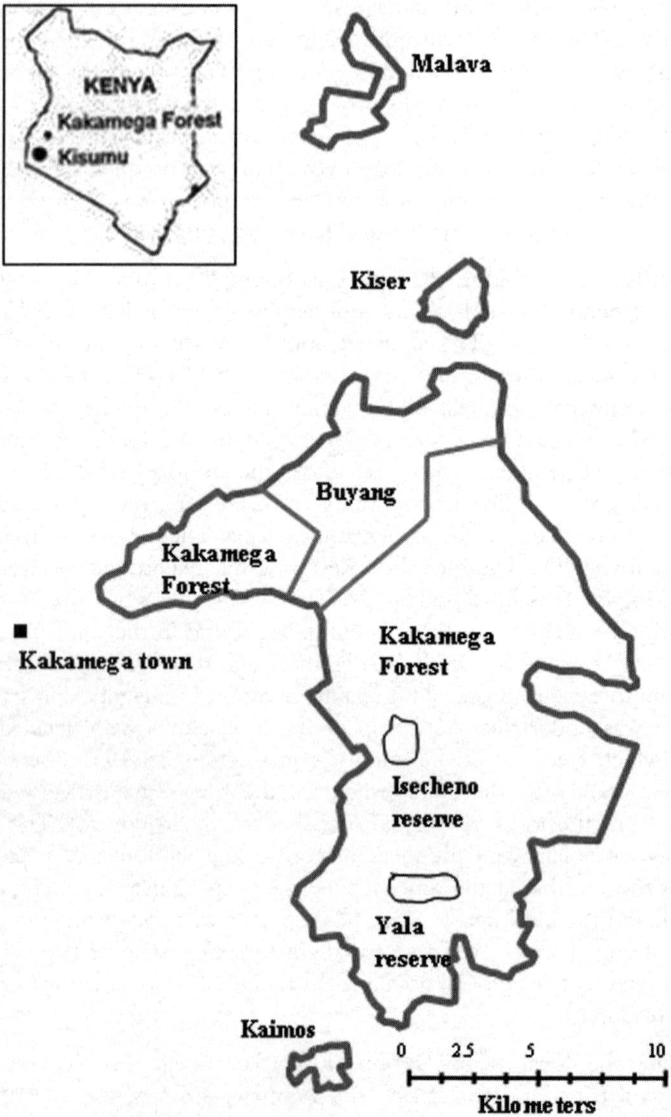

Sources: BIOTA E02; Schaab, 2002

colonial timber enterprise, which led to the establishment of sawmills in the forest (Glenday, 2006). Widespread commercial logging led to clear-felling of some parts of the forest, which were converted to timber plantations of hardwoods (KIFCON, 1994). Thus, resource management and extraction was clearly driven by colonial agendas. But the Forest Department also initiated the non-resident *shamba* cultivation system in the 1940s, in which local farmers were allowed to plant food crops on cleared plots in the forest while tending tree seedlings. This practice was stopped by the Kenyan government in 2003 because of problems associated with encroachment.

In 1964, during the post-colonial period, the forest was declared a central government forest, which technically meant that it now belonged entirely to the state. In 1985, two areas were officially excised from the forest to create the Kakamega National Reserve, encompassing Kisere fragment and the Northwestern part of the main forest block also called Buyangu (see Figure 1). Since then, the two fragments covering approximately 44 km^2 have been managed under the protectionist approach of the KWS on behalf of the central government.

The KWS operates as a semi-autonomous institution under the Ministry of Wildlife and Tourism with authority to raise funds, hire staff and carry out its affairs independent of the parent ministry. It was established under the Wildlife Conservation and Management Act of Kenya in 1976 as an authority to manage and coordinate conservation of wild animals in the country. The KWS is headquartered in Nairobi, but sustains field offices in all regions of the country. The Kakamega office of the KWS consists of a warden, two deputies, five support staff and about 25 armed guards, known as rangers. The KWS provides housing for most of its staff inside the forest at Buyangu, and has two offices which are linked by radio communication (in the forest at Buyangu, and in Kakamega town). During the time of this study, the KWS utilized two operational motor vehicles and one tractor. The gate to the forest at Buyangu is manned at all times by two guards, who collect gate fees and issue receipts to tourists entering the forest. Daily patrols are carried out by armed forest guards. The main challenge for the KWS officers is the lack of sufficient vehicles to cover the whole forest. Therefore, cases of illegal extraction continue, although not as rampantly as in the section of forest managed by the Forest Department.

The Southern part of the main forest block and the Malava fragment are managed by the Forest Department under an incentive-based approach. Here, local communities are allowed to extract forest resources, such as fodder for grazing, dead timber for fuel, mushrooms, fruits and medicinal plants. In 1991, a memorandum of understanding was drawn between the Forest Department and the KWS to closely cooperate in the management of the forest. However, many of the agreed rules are not strictly enforced by the Forest Department while, in contrast, KWS strictly prohibits local use of the forest in the national reserve. However, it is important to note that FD and KWS have somewhat different rules in the forest management. As noted earlier, FD allows some regulated extraction but there are strict conditions for example people are not allowed to go to the forest with harvesting implements such as machetes. The agreement between FD and KWS is based on shared goal of conserving the forest through sharing resources for enforcing rules of extraction, sharing information and such others. The Forest Department operates under the Ministry of Environment and Natural Resources of the Kenyan government. As noted in the introduction of this study, in accordance with a newly enacted law i.e the Forest Act of 2005 there was a process to transform the Forest Department into a semi-autonomous authority under the new name of 'Kenya Forestry Service' which was done in 2006. There is a clear prescription of reporting duties from local to national level. The Kakamega District Forest Officer is based at Lurambi on the outskirts of Kakamega town and is in charge of the management of Kakamega Forest and Bunyala Forests. The officer reports to the forest officer at provincial level (in this case Western province), who is in turn responsible to the Chief conservator of forests based in Nairobi.

The forest station is located about 17 km from Kakamega town in the Southern part of the forest called Isecheno. The station has twelve staff houses, offices, a guest house and a tree nursery. The Forest Department has about 35 forest guards and several technical staff. During the field research, the Forest Department owned three operational vehicles. Informal interviews with the District Forest Officer indicated that illegal activities were going on at high rates and rule enforcement was limited by inadequate budgets, manpower and number of vehicles for patrol.

Since early 1900s, the Southern fragment, also known as the Kaimosi, covering about 130 ha, has been under the incentive-based quasi-private management of the Quaker's Church Mission (QCM). Under the church's management, local communities may pursue a limited and regulated extraction of forest products. The QCM management is headed by a Secretary General who is also responsible for the day-to-day management of the affairs of the mission. The forest is managed as the private property of the church. Therefore, management of the forest falls directly under his jurisdiction. The Secretary General delegates the supervisory functions of the forest to a caretaker, who also acts as a patrolman because the church does not have regular armed guards. Local people extract different types of products from the forest such as wood for fuel and thatch grass, as well as they let their livestock graze inside the forest. The office of the Secretary General occasionally brokers the sale of trees in the forest for logging to individuals from the local community. The church also organizes tree-planting days in collaboration with local schools and the community. Even though the church occasionally organizes public meetings to educate people on the importance of forest conservation, community participation is rather limited.

Degradation status of Kakamega Forest

As noted previously, over the years, Kakamega Forest has been subjected to disturbances of various kinds. In the pre-colonial era, local people actively converted the forest into farmland, but this practice was checked by natural calamities, such as diseases and wars (Mitchell, 2004). During the colonial period, massive disturbances occurred, namely gold mining, logging, and timber extraction by saw millers, fuel wood collection as well as charcoal burning. In the past century, the overall size of the forest shrunk rapidly about roughly 20% (Lung et al., 2006) due to high human population growth and increased resource extraction. The non-resident cultivation practice, known locally as *shamba* system, is also cited as contributing to forest degradation. Official excisions by the government, especially for purposes of resettling people and other public uses further set land apart.

The extent of forest degradation differs under the three management regimes. Recent studies based on GIS and transect analysis show that there is a clear gradient of disturbance across the three parts of the forest, with the KWS-managed part being the least degraded and the QCM fragment being the most degraded (Bleher et al., 2006; Lung et al., 2006). These differences are attributable only to the diverse management styles (Bleher et al., 2006). It is worth noting that since taking over of management 20 years ago, the protectionist regime of KWS has transformed a rather degraded forest into a regenerated forest. The study by Bleher et al (2006) collected data on forest degradation as measured by the presence of tree stumps and forest regeneration. The success of the protectionist regime in conserving the forest can be attributed to its mandate *"to sustainably manage wildlife to meet conservation goals"* (Wildlife Conservation Act of 1985). In order to meet this goal, the protectionist regime applies a rigorous patrolling of the forest using armed guards and prosecutes any offenders caught extracting any products from the forest or even trespassing. Offenders are usually taken to the courts and prosecuted for their offenses with punishments varying from low fines of ksh 500 for trespassing to ksh 3000 for illegal charcoal burning. In contrast, the incentive-based regimes of the Forest Department and QCM attempt to balance the twin goals of conservation and meeting extraction needs of the local people. However, non of the group is very effective in enforcing their rules for extraction, and cases of illegal extraction are more rampant in their areas than those of the KWS. The combination of providing lee-way for some 'allowed' extraction coupled with weak policing power and corruption of the armed guards, works to compromise the ability of the Forest Department to effectively balance the livelihood requirements of the people with its conservation objectives. Many incidences of illegal extraction go unpunished. But it is not only the local communities that break the rules. As expressed by one of the villagers interviewed about the Forest Department managed Malava fragment "*…this forest is almost completely deforested. There are actually trucks which come into the forest to carry logged trees. It is not done by the local people but by people from outside.*" Similarly, the QCM lacks sanctioning ability because it does neither employs armed guards, nor maintains vehicles to police and enforce extraction rules. The QCM mostly depends on local people to volunteer and give information about illegal extraction activities. Based on our observations, we argue that achieving both conservation targets and livelihood objectives simultaneously is a great challenge, especially when sanction capacity is weak. This experience is documented also for other forest conservation projects (see study by Rustagi in this volume).

Local participation in forest management

In the literature on forest conservation, it is widely acknowledged that communities living within the vicinity of protected areas are critical to the success of conservation efforts (Agrawal et al., 1999; Ferraro, 2002; Ostrom, 1999). Local communities are thought to have the knowledge, information and incentive required to manage and conserve the resources which they depend upon (Johnson, 2001; White et al., 2002). However, despite widespread efforts to transfer management of forests to local communities, about 80 % of forests in developing countries are still owned and centrally administered by national governments (White et al., 2002).

As noted earlier, Kakamega Forest is managed under three management regimes. From a historical point of view, the local people living nearby the forest had full property rights to the forest, but these rights were taken away by the state. Over time, there have been attempts by the state to transfer some of these rights back to the people. One way of assessing local participation in conservation is by looking at how the three management regimes grant or share some property rights with members of these communities. To this end, we followed the hierarchical definition of property right as outlined by Schlager and Ostrom (1992).

The basic right is 'access' defined as the right to enter a defined physical area and enjoy non-subtractive benefits. This is followed by the ' right to withdraw' defined as the right to obtain resource units or products of a resource system. 'Management rights' allow the holder to regulate internal use patterns and transform the resource by making improvements. 'Exclusion rights' to determine who will have an access right, and how that right may be transferred and lastly the 'right of alienation' confers the holder with the right to sell or lease exclusion, management or withdrawal rights. The idea is that obtaining at least some rights to the continued use of resources may encourage local users to perceive long term interests in a natural resource. In contrast, it is assumed that limited property rights do not establish strong incentives to manage resources in a sustainable manner (Agrawal et al., 1999). On the one hand, empirical evidence shows that proprietors have sufficient rights and thus incentives to make long term investment in a resource (Ostrom, 2003). On the other hand, there are arguments that people also invest to obtain rights over resources, such as land (Sjaastad et al., 1997). However, in Kakamega Forest, the territorial boundaries of the forest are established and protected by law, and thus property rights are clearly and formally defined.

The property right regimes under the three management approaches are summarized in Figure 2. Under the protectionist management regime of the KWS, nearly all property rights are vested in the central government. The local communities are denied all rights, and may only obtain a temporary right of entry into the forest after paying entry fees into the reserve. The state spends a lot of resources to enforce its overall claim. Illegal activities such as trespassing and extraction have continued and therefore, enforcement costs continue to rise. Management and enforcement costs invariably exceed the direct earnings from tourism. For example, in 2005, official records show that the total management costs for the forest were approximately US $ 62,019, compared to revenue of US $ 43,262 earned from tourism.

Acting jointly with the Forest Department, the KWS has allowed some level of community organization through formation of a community-based organization (CBO) known as Kakamega Environmental Education Program (KEEP). The CBO has two branches: one operating in the KWS managed part, and another in the Forest Department part, with approximately 40

Figure 2 Property rights in Kakamega Forest

Property right type	Management regime		
	KWS	FD	QCM
Withdrawal	Public (Vested exclusively in the state)	Public (Vested in the state but local communities are assigned limited withdrawal right after paying access fees)	Private, communal (Vested in the church but it assigns limited rights to the local communities)
Management	Public Vested exclusively in the state but there is a limited devolution to a CBO-KEEP	Public Vested in the state but there is a limited devolution to a CBO-KEEP	Private, communal Vested in the church but it has devolved limited management right to community elders to a small part of the forest for traditional circumcision ritual
Exclusion	Public Vested exclusively in the state via the forest guards and courts	Public Vested exclusively in the state via the forest guard & the courts	Private, regulated by customary law Vested in the church but the community taboo do not permit unauthorized people to enter the ritual forest
Alienation	Public Vested exclusively in the state	Public Vested exclusively in the state	Private Vested exclusively in the church

members of staff engaged in its day-to-day activities. KEEP is involved in several income generating activities, as well as in environmental education initiatives in schools and other public fora. KEEP runs a tree nursery, butterfly farm, tour guide services, as well as lodging services in traditional huts for tourists all established within the forest grounds. KEEP not only offers employment opportunity for local people, but also increases conservation awareness of the locals and provides them with opportunities to earn income through promotion of butterfly farming and the marketing of butterfly pupae. The formation of KEEP is an example of community empowerment by allowing them some collective choices. This has potential to increase positive incentives to conserve the forest through direct economic benefits, as well as through the opportunity to organize and establish rules of action among its members. However, KEEP represents a rather limited level of devolution of forest management responsibility by the state agencies. It can therefore be argued that the current level of community participation is rather limited under the Forest Department and the KWS.

Under the management of the Forest Department, most property rights are public, but some level of devolution is observable. The local communities have access and limited withdrawal rights, but they do not hold exclusion, management and alienation rights. FD allows people to collect dead wood, thatch grass and use forest resources for grazing but for the latter a fee is required. Prior to 2004, the Forest Department had allowed the *shamba* system. Farmers provided labor for tending tree seedlings while they grew their crops in the forest. However, this practice was stopped by the government in 2004 because of its associated problem of forest encroachment and subsequent degradation. The *shamba* system gave local people limited management rights to the forest, but its discontinuation has been an issue of great discontent among locals.

Under the QCM, all property rights are vested in a private entity, i.e. the local Quaker church, and the church has granted limited access and withdrawal rights to the local communities. As shown in Figure 2, the forest under QCM generates sizeable benefits to the local communities. It has also set apart a small part of its forest for the practice of traditional circumcision of the local Tiriki sub-tribe (QCM Secretary, 2006, personal communication). Local communities have primary rights over this small forest patch. This is an important aspect for the local acceptance of the management regime, because the circumcision rituals which are performed once every five years are integral to community life. The management of this forest patch falls under the council of elders guided by a set of traditional norms and taboos. For example, no one can enter into this forest patch, or extract any product unless first authorized by the elders. Despite being the full owners of the forest, the QCM faces the huge challenge of excluding unauthorized people from extracting from the forest because it uses few unarmed people to guard the forest.

In summary, under Forest Department and KWS forest management, most property rights are vested in the central government. It can therefore be argued that local communities do not have sufficient incentives to conserve the forest. The current system of management places the burden of enforcement with the national government, and also to the Quakers church. However, it is important to note that the current level of withdrawal rights allowed by both the Forest Department and the QCM contribute in a significant way to the livelihoods of the local communities through the products that they extract from the forest. But as noted, this extraction is largely at the expense of forest conservation. At the time of the study there was little conflict arising from external forest users due to ban on logging by the central government through the FD.

Distribution of costs and benefits among the stakeholders

Overall, the financial values of direct non-timber forest products extracted from the Kakamega Forest in 2004-05 are summarized in Figure 3 below. For ease of comparison, extraction values are presented on a hectare of forest basis (US $/ ha) by dividing the total monetary value of products extracted by the area of the forest. As expected, there are differences in the values of direct-extracted products across the three management approaches. In absolute terms the protectionist approach of the KWS offered the least benefits in terms of direct-extracted products, while the incentive-based management of the Forest Department generated the largest amount of benefits for the local people. However, it is important to note that in relative terms, the quasi-private incentive-based approach of the QCM generated the highest extractive benefits per unit area, due to the small size of the forest in comparison to the number of people extracting from it.

Figure 3 Financial values of extracted forest products by local people in 2005

Forest product	KWS		FD		QCM		Total	
	Overall (US $)	US $/ha	Overall (US $)	US $/ha	Overall (US $)	US $/ha	Overall (US $)	US $/ha
Fodder/ Grazing	-	-	769,837	38.49	16,720	128.62	786, 558	32.77
Firewood	5649	1.28	656,818	32.84	39,113	300.87	701,579	28.75
Charcoal	-	-	25,424	21.19	-	-	25,424	21.19
Thatch grass	-	-	147, 312	7.37	-	-	147, 312	7.37

Source: Guthiga (2007)

In general, the average total value of non-timber products harvested from Kakamega Forest averaged about US $ 69.20 per hectare per year. This figure closely coincides with figures generated by other studies in tropical forests areas, for example, Pearce (2001) report values between US $ 0-100/ha per year.

Different categories of costs are incurred in the process of conserving and utilizing the forest (see Figure 4 below). Opportunity costs are the largest category of cost and are mainly incurred at the local level. Other local costs consist mainly of extraction labor costs, participation costs (arising out of involvement in conservation activities), access fees and transaction costs that arise from information search in buying and selling of forest products. At the national level, the bulk of costs include management costs incurred in financing the operations of the Forest Department and the KWS.

Figure 4 Annual financial conservation costs

Category of cost	US $/ha		
	FD	KWS	QCM
Opportunity costs	150	150	150
Extraction labor	32	0.1	29
Transaction costs	0.2	0.1	2
Conservation participation costs	0.1	0.3	0.4
Access fees	0.2	0	0
Crop Loss due to wildlife damage	0.1	0.1	0.2
Management costs	13.5	16	0.01

Source: Guthiga (2007)

The main cost at the local level is the opportunity cost of forest conservation, i.e. the forgone earnings from using the forest land for smallholder agriculture. Opportunity costs represented the highest percentage of costs incurred by the local people in the conservation of the forest. Participation costs included costs of participating in forest conservation activities both in form of time, as well as cash. Transaction costs arose mainly from negotiations and searching for information on trade in forest products. These costs are higher than user fees, value of crop loss due to wildlife damage or conservation activities. Another important component of cost incurred by local communities is the cost of crop damage and livestock injury due to wildlife attacks. Kakamega Forest is host to a variety of wild animals, some of which attack crops and domestic animals such as chicken, causing damage and injuries. The findings of the survey revealed that baboons were the most frequently cited culprits. Other animals cited include wild pigs, monkeys, baboons, squirrels, and mongoose. The value of crop loss was obtained by multiplying the quantities of crop harvest lost through wildlife attacks by their market prices. Management costs include remuneration costs for staff, office stationery, vehicle operation costs and other equipment costs. From 2003 to 2005, annual management costs incurred by the Forest Department and the KWS averaged US $ 269,907 and US $ 62,019 respectively. On a per hectare basis, this translates to US $ 13.5 and US $ 16 for the Forest Department and the KWS. The comparison of costs and benefits show that despite the differences between management regimes, in general the local communities subsidize the cost of conservation of Kakamega Forest by bearing the opportunity costs of its existence.

Community satisfaction levels with forest management regimes

Overall levels of satisfaction with forest management approaches were elicited by asking the respondents to score their overall satisfaction with the way the forest nearest to their residence is managed, by assigning a satisfaction rank from among five different levels:1= very satisfied, 2=satisfied, 3=neutral, 4=dissatisfied and 5=very dissatisfied. The results of means and frequencies of satisfaction levels are summarized in Figure 5.

Figure 5 Frequency and mean satisfaction level with forest management

Management approach			% Frequency				
	Mean	SD	V. satisfied	Satisfied	Neutral	Dissatisfied	V. dissatisfied
FD (n=220)	2.64	0.86	-	47.9	37.5	13.9	0.7
QCM (n=83)	2.72	1.06	3.6	54.2	16.9	16.9	8.4
KWS (n=61)	2.23	0.64	8.2	11.5	62.3	16.4	1.6

Source: Guthiga (2007)

Generally, the satisfaction ranking results showed that respondents were relatively more satisfied with the performance of the protectionist approach of the KWS (mean 2.23) than with the incentive-based approaches (2.64 and 2.72 for FD and QCM, respectively). For the Forest Department and the QCM management approaches, satisfaction levels were more or less neutral. The study also tested whether the three mean levels of satisfaction were significantly different from each other. It was found that the satisfaction level associated with the approach used by the KWS was significantly higher than that of the Forest Department and the QCM, but the latter was not significantly different from each other. The higher ranking of the protectionist approach may be attributed to the desire of local communities to have the forest conserved for future generations. It could be argued that local communities are interested in conservation despite the pressing need to extract from the forest. As noted earlier, the KWS has done relatively well in conserving forest biodiversity compared to the Forest Department and the QCM. It should, however, be noted that although the local communities ranked the Forest Department and the QCM approaches lower than that of the KWS, they did not express strong dissatisfaction with their performance. This implies that the communities are willing to live with these management approaches most likely due to the benefits they derive from extraction of non-timber forest products.

Informal interviews conducted among key informants in the community mirror largely these findings. The KWS is viewed by the local communities as committed to conserving the forest by implementing its rules firmly and transparently. On the other hand, the Forest Department and the QCM are viewed as falling short of communities' expectations in implementing conservation rules, despite allowing some level of regulated extraction from the forest. Many of the people interviewed expressed some disappointment with the way both FD and QCM implemented their rules. Therefore, the results of satisfaction ranking can also be interpreted to express the communities' verdict on how the existing management approaches apply and enforce their rules. Although not common, it is not surprising to find instances where people prefer protection-oriented state-led conservation to community conservation.

Conclusions

This study set out to investigate the links between forest extraction and conservation outcome under three different management regimes for a Kenyan tropical rainforest. The study shed light on how the three management regimes assign property rights between different actors, how these property rights are enforced and how it influences conservation outcomes. Distribution of costs and benefits indicate that the Kakamega Forest generates an array of benefits to the local people, but opportunity costs overshadow these benefits except for in the QCM managed section, which in resource terms is the most disturbed section of the forest. This observation raises the question on how to meet the urgent livelihood needs of the forest-adjacent communities, without jeopardizing conservation goals. The results of the overall mean satisfaction survey results indicated that the protectionist management approach was ranked most favorably for its management of the forest. From this result, it cannot be conclusively concluded that local communities in the study area favor the protectionist management approach over incentive-based approaches. However, this finding clearly indicates that in the study area, the local communities have an interest in conservation despite the need to extract from the forest. The challenge that all the three management approaches face is to find a suitable way to achieve their conservation goals while taking into account the needs and aspirations of the local communities.

References

Achard, F., Eva, H. D., Stibig, H. J., Mayaux, P., Gallego J., Richards, T., Malingreau J. P. 2002. Determination of deforestation rates of the World's humid tropical forests. Science 297: 999-1002

Adams, W. and Hulme, D. 2001. Conservation and Community. In: Hulme, D., Murphree, M. (eds): African Wildlife and Livelihoods. James Currey Limited. Oxford.

Agrawal, A., Gibson, C. C., 1999. Enchantment and Disenchantment: The Role of Community in Natural Resource Conservation. World Development. 27: 629-649.

Andersson, K. P., 2004. Who talks with whom? The role of repeated interactions in decentralized forest governance. World Development. 32/2: 233-249.

Argawal, A., Ostrom, E. 1999. Collective action, property rights, and devolution of forest and protected area management. Collective Action, Property Rights and Devolution of Natural Resource Management: Exchange of Knowledge and Implications for Policy Proceedings of the International Conference in Puerto Azul (the Philippines): 21-25 June, 1999.

Bleher, B., Uster, D., Bergsdorf, T. 2006. Assessment of threat status and management effectiveness in Kakamega Forest, Kenya. Biodiversity and Conservation. 15: 1159-1177.

Bruce, S. A., Mark, B., George, S. H. 2002. Social acceptability of forest conditions and management practices: A problem analysis. General Technical Report (PNW-GTR-537). U.S. Department of Agriculture, Forest Service.

Ferraro, P. J. 2002. The local costs of establishing protected areas in low-income nations: Ranomafana national park, Madagascar. Ecological Economics. 43: 261-275

Geist, H. J., Lambin, E. F. 2002. Proximate Causes and Underlying Driving Forces of Tropical Deforestation. BioScience. 52: 143-150.

Glenday, J., 2006. Carbon storage and emissions offset potential in an East African tropical rainforest. Forest Ecology and Management. 235: 72-83.

Guthiga, P. M. 2007. Economic Assessment of Different Management Approaches of a Kenyan Rainforest: Cost-benefit and Community Satisfaction Analysis. VDM Verlag. Germany. 188pp.

Hutton, J. M., Leader-Williams, N. 2003. Sustainable Use and Incentive-Driven Conservation: Realigning Human and Conservation Interests. Oryx. 37: 215-225.

Johnson, C. 2001. Community formation and fisheries conservation in Southern Thailand. Development and Change. 32: 951-974.

Kao, C., Yang, Y. C. 1991. Measuring the efficiency of forest management. Forest Science. 37: 1239-1252.

KIFCON (Kenya Indigenous Forest Project) 1994. A National Profile of Kenya's Indigenous Forests. Forest Department. Nairobi.

Kokwaro, J. O. 1988. Conservation status of the Kakamega Forest in Kenya: the Easternmost relic of the equatorial rainforests of Africa. Monographs Systematic Botany. Missouri Botanical garden. 25: 471-489.

Lung, T., Schaab, G. 2006. Assessing fragmentation and disturbance of west Kenyan rainforests by means of remotely sensed time series data and landscape metrics. African Journal of Ecology. 44: 491-506.

Matose, F. 2006. Co-management options for reserved forests in Zimbabwe and beyond: Policy implications of forest management strategies. Forest Policy and Economics. 8: 363-374.

Mburu, J., Birner, M. 2007. Emergence, Adoption and Implementation of Collaborative Wildlife Management or Wildlife partnerships in Kenya: A look at Conditions for Success. Society and Natural Resources. 20: 379-395.

Meinzen-Dick, R., Di Gregorio, M. 2004. Collective Action and Property Rights for Sustainable Development: Overview. IFPRI Brief 1/16.

Meinzen-Dick, R., Raju, K.V., Gulati, A. 2002. What affects organization and collective action for managing resources? Evidence from canal irrigation systems in India. World Development 30/4: 649-666.

Mitchell, N. 2004. The exploitation and disturbance history of Kakamega Forest, Western Kenya. In: Bleher, B., Dalitz, H. (eds.): BIOTA East Report No. 1. Bielefelder Ökologische Beiträge. 20: 1-77.

Oakerson, R.J. 1992. Analyzing the Commons: A Framework. In: Bromely, D.W. (ed.): Making Commons Work: Theory, Practice and Policy. ICS Press, San Francisco. 41-59.

Opole, M. 1991. User trends and attitudes to management of the Kakamega Forest reserve. Kenya. Indigenous Forest Conservation Programme, Nairobi.

Ostrom, E. 1999. Self governance and forest resources. CIFOR discussion paper 20.

Ostrom, E., 2003. How types of goods and property rights jointly affect collective action. Journal of Theoretical Politics 15/3: 239-270.

Patel, A., Rapport, D. J., Vanderlinden, L., Eyles, J. 1999. Forests and societal values and public perception of forest health. The Environmentalist. 19: 239-249.

Pearce, D. W., 2001. The economic value of forest ecosystems. Ecosystem health. 7: 284-296.

Rasmussen, L. N., Meizen-Dick, R.. 1995. Local Organizations for Natural Resource Management: Lessons from Theoretical and Empirical Literature. EPTD Discussion Paper 11. IFPRI.

Schlager, E., Ostrom E. 1992. Property right regimes and natural resources: A conceptual analysis. Land Economics. 68: 249-262

Sjaastad, E., Bromley, D. 1997. Indigenous land rights in Sub-Saharan Africa: Appropriation, security and investment. American Journal of Agricultural Economics. 81/2: 467-478.

Trakolis, D. 2001. Perceptions, Preferences and Reactions of Local Inhabitants in Vikos-Aoos National Park, Greece. Environmental Management. 28/5: 665-676.

Tucker, C. M., 1999. Private Versus Common Property Forests: Forest Conditions and Tenure in a Honduran Community. Human Ecology. 27: 201-230

White, A. M., Martin, A. 2002. Who owns world's forests? Forest tenure and public forests in transition. Forests Trends and Center for International Environmental Law. Washington D.C.

Wiggins, S., Marfo, K. and Anchirinah, V. 2004. Protecting the Forest or the People? Environmental Policies and Livelihoods in the Forest margins of Southern Ghana. World Development. 32: 1939-1955.

Chapter 5

Why ignore Ekpwe rules? The regulation of forest use by a secret society in Korup National Park, Cameroon

Charles Takoyoh Eyong

Introduction

Officially, the history of forests protection in Cameroon dates back to the colonial era (1884-1961), when forests were put under public ownership and some accorded a strict protection status.[1] The post-colonial state maintained control over protected forests although it was not well equipped to effectively carry out this function. Today, with forest conservation rooting deep into international relations, the capacity of states to coerce their citizens into unpopular conservation and development programs is still limited (Agrawal and Gibson, 1999). On the other hand *"communities down the millennium have developed elaborate rituals and practices to limit off take levels, restrict access to critical resources, and distribute harvests"* (Western et al., 1994: 1). This study is one of the academic voices calling for community-based NRM through an institutional analysis, although, Elinor Ostrom had downplayed the contributions of cultural traits like magic, sacredness, and kinship (Ostrom, 1990). Recently, Ostrom argues that many key problems of common-pool resources can be successfully and flexibly solved by local collective action without requiring external intervention by third parties (Ostrom, 2005). These claims as well as my observations of constrained forest use in the Korup National Park serve as the major inspiration for this chapter. It is so because of the complexity of the property rights regimes that exist for just a single forest. This forest is a common-pool resource for the indigenous population and a public property, according to state law. Whose rules effectively constrain the behaviour of forest users is what is most edifying as shall be seen in subsequent sections. In line with Roberts Chambers (1995), this chapter contends that park managers have not adequately appreciated the richness and validity

---

[1] The French policy of *tèrres vacants et sans maître* and the German *herrenlos* land policies did not recognize and preserve the native rights of communities like British policy did. This marked the idea of state stewardship of forests in the country.

of indigenous knowledge and institutions that constrain free riding by limiting individual access, use and destructive extraction.

National parks fall under the category II of the International Union for the Conservation of Nature (IUCN) classification. They are a natural area of land and/or sea, designated to (i) protect the ecological integrity of one or more ecosystems for present and future generations, (ii) exclude exploitation or occupation inimical to the purposes of designation of the area and (iii) provide a foundation for spiritual, scientific, educational, recreational and visitor opportunities, all of which must be environmentally and culturally compatible (FAO, 2006). National parks are often under the protection of state agents which suggests that they are government property at least on paper but those that inhabit people like Korup National Park, have a different, if not complex reality altogether. They represent avenues where resource use rights are prohibited by state agencies. Korup National Park requires effective macro- or micro-levels institutions for its sustainability. But, micro level institutions [otherwise regarded here as indigenous institutions] have been ignored because academic and Parks protection agencies have for long, downplayed their role in protecting biodiversity (Ostrom, 1999). Unfortunately, these institutions are fast eroding due to colonialism, commercialization, globalization and modernization, lack of efficient codification, breakdown of traditional family structures and functions (the institution that helps in the socialization of tacit knowledge), developmentally induced human displacements, the decline in the practitioner base and many other reasons (Eyong, 2007). This erosion amidst widespread failure of macro-level institutions to provide adequate biodiversity protection, raises concerns over what works best. Continuous empowerment of macro level institutions as most demographers and conservation biologists claim, or should we turn over to micro-level institutions as the Boserupians[2] and some anti-displacements academics[3] argue? Both camps have excellent arguments based on property rights and it is worth reflecting them in the discussion of a detailed survey of the current situation in the Korup National Park. This chapter moves forward from the too limiting and mal-debated property rights approach to a rather responsibility, authority and obligation approach.

The aim of this chapter is twofolds: on the one hand, it aims to provide an understanding of the role of indigenous knowledge and institutions in con-

---

[2] Agrawal, 1995; Binswanger et al., 1988; Boserup, 1965, 1981; Davis, 1991; Simon, 1983, 1990; Tiffen, et al., 1994

[3] Geisler, 2003; Cernea, 1991-2003; Cernea and Schmidt-Soltau, 2003, 2006; Lamb, 1997.

straining resources use in Korup National Park, Cameroon so as to explain how the "green" forestry legislations on conservation and sustainable rural development could recognize indigenous realities that constrain and define interactions in forest communities. International donors withdrew in July 2003 and the Cameroon government is unable to provide protection to the Park. So, the top-down approach that relies on guard patrols and penalties and has imposed hardship on locals failes to provide species protection. The weaknesses of the state-centric approach revives prospects of community-based conservation as a promising option based on common action (Agrawal et al., 1999: 632). This collective action is said to be possible in the so-called 'mythic community'; small, integrated groups using locally evolved norms to manage resources sustainably (*Ibid*: 640). Such characteristics may exist in the Korup forest communities. On the other hand, this chapter is a case study to enlighten the debate that indigenous institutions manage forest sustainably and should be revitalized so that forest peoples could accept as responsibility and obligation authority to use their institutions for an effective multi-level management of Parks. This claim might be valid for Parks that are created with resident communities within its boundaries. It may not be valid for fenced/uninhabited parks.

Materials and Methods

Even though this work is chiefly a product of critical literature review, it is spiced with empirical data based on fieldwork carried out between 1999, 2003 and in 2006. Data were collected using the participatory appraisal methods. Open-ended interviews in Pidgin English (a lingua franca) were conducted with tourists, administrative officers, the Korup Park Service and indigenous NGO workers in Mundemba in South West Cameroon as well as with park villagers using an interview guide with cautious flexibility. Group interviews were held with chiefs and village elders of Ikondo Kondo I and Esukutan, using a special interview guide. The focus of interviews was on the use and conservation of indigenous resources, as well as on the institutions involved. The observation guide covered daily interactions of villagers, ritual sites, and leadership. Content analysis was used to contextualize primary data through secondary sources. To avoid a tunnel-like vision that characterizes most works on national parks, interdisciplinary knowledge from anthropology, sociology, environmental economics and conservation studies has been employed in these analyses so as to provide a holistic view of the issues investigated.

The research setting

The Korup National Park[4]

The biome called Korup National Park, located in South West Cameroon, was not officially recognized until 1937 when it became known as the Korup Native Administration Forest Reserve. The forest is drained by the Korup/Akwayefe and the Mana Rivers in the south and by the Bake/Munnaya and their tributaries in the north-eastern sector. The Ndian River in the center flows towards the southern sector. The western and south-western sectors are drained by the Akpasang and Korup Rivers. It comprises forest areas from both Bakoko and Korup ethnic groups that inhabit it. By 1971, researchers continuously appealed to the government of Cameroon to transform this Korup Forest Reserve into a National Park (Oates, 1999). The increasing awareness and willingness of international donors to support conservation of rainforests in Cameroon also facilitated the creation of the Korup National Park, gazetted by Presidential Decree No. 86/1283 of October 30th 1986. Today, the park embodies three forest reserves of various sizes: the Rumpi Hills (45,843 ha), Nta-ali (35000 ha) and Ejagham (74,851 ha) with a primary forest cover of 125,900 hectares and a 300,000 hectares support zone. For more than 30 years thereafter, no official activities took place in the forest reserve but studies carried out by Struhsaker in 1970, Agland in 1981 and by Gatland in 1984, enabled the Earthlife Foundation to carry out the first conservation activities in the late 1970s and early 1980s (Korup Project, 1999; Schmidt-Soltau, 2004). These studies have exposed the fact that in terms of its biodiversity, Korup forest is Africa's richest rainforest for which comparable data exist. Korup forest is the oldest remaining rainforest in Africa today and has survived the ice age or Pleistocene glaciations, over about 600 million years ago and the single richest lowland site in Africa for herpetofauna, butterflies and birds with high endemism (Korup Management Plan, 2002: 40). Korup is critically important for primate conservation supporting large populations of chimpanzee, drill, red-capped mangabey, red-eared monkey, Preuss's red colobus monkey and Preuss's monkey (Oates, 1996). It is a conservation hot-spot and a first class national park, according to state classification.

---

[4] See figure 1 on details about how it was partitioned into sectors. It is worth noting that during the field visit, locals did not understand the meanings of the partitions, neither did they recognize it beyond their traditional boundaries.

Figure 1: Map of Korup National Park and its Support Zones

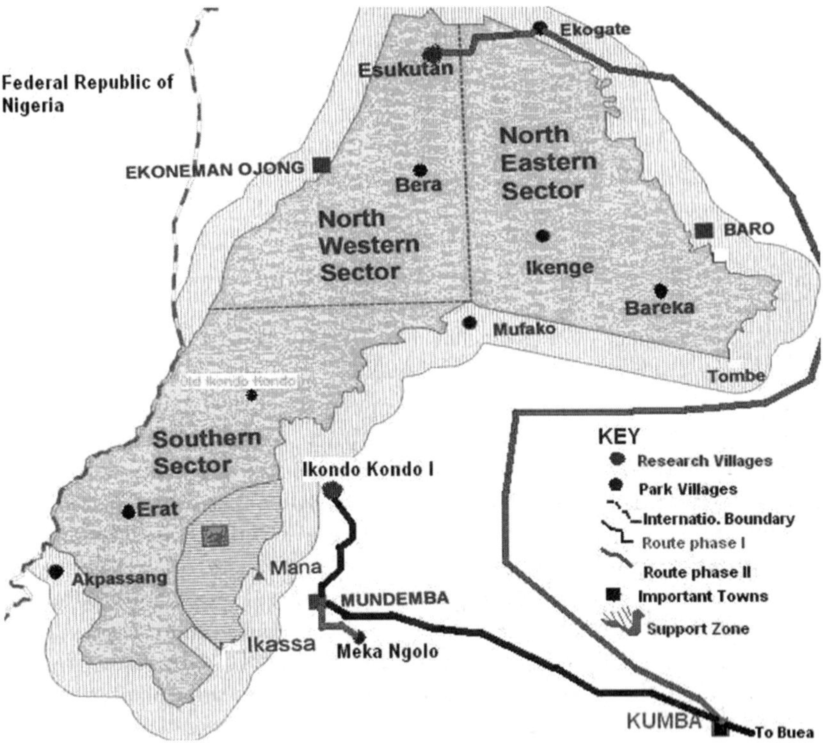

Adapted from Korup Management Plan, 2002

Characteristics of the study villages

Two[5] of the six Park villages are objects of this chapter. Esukutan is a village form the Oroko or Bakoko ethnic group while Ikondo Kondo I is a breakaway from the Ororup ethnic group. Both ethnic groups inhabited the Korup National Park; in need of effective conservation prior to the year 2000

[5] Esukutan and Ikondo Kondo I were selected for this study based on; the need to reflect the ethnic diversity in the park (Ororup and Bakoko, respectively). Both villages extract from a cross section of the park representing the north eastern and south western sectors. Although, Ikondo Kondo I was relocated, the people still extract from the park. These two villages were perceived to be more easily accessible than the others. Lastly, they speak Pidgin English that was used for interviewing with little need for interpreters' errors.

when the latter was displaced as the pilot relocation scheme. Generally, 90% of the village members have acquired basic education and the highest educational level attained so far in the communities is secondary. Their activities are greatly regulated by the dry and rainy seasons. The major livelihood activities are subsistence food and cash crops farming, small-scale fishing, hunting and gathering of None-Timber Forest Products (NTFPs), fetching water, visiting with each other, porting for researchers, produce buyers and other visitors, and making some of their material possessions. They all fall under the national 'poverty line' of US$ 0.86 a day, but life is pretty easy in the sense that they can earn a living with about three hours of work per day. Their protein comes from a variety of natural sources and all of them seek healthcare from indigenous healers as well as drug hawkers from nearby towns.

Indigenous culture is dominated by food taboos, sacred forests, rites, totems and other animistic beliefs and practices. They display a richness in traditional technologies, traditional healing methods, traditional NRM, celebrations, and patterns of social interaction that contribute to group welfare and identity (DMFA, 2002; World Bank, 2003). Social life is organized along kinship ties, descent, patterns of marital exchanges, and the transient charisma of chiefs. Their political organization is headed by a chief who works in collaboration with a village council (with a rotating chair), regent chiefs and lineage heads. This picture was distorted when the Cameroon government through the Korup Project named "government-appointed village chiefs" and employed them as project workers. The government chief represents the village in all official matters with forest protection agencies and the Cameroon Government and is paid a salary. This created a bipolar power structure at village level. People with higher levels of formal education identify rather with the government chief and tend to disobey the indigenous chief. While all government chiefs reside outside and do not own[6] a house or a farm in their respective villages, visitors are formally obliged to contact them for access rights to the park and information about their village. This breeds the danger of misinformation as these chiefs tend to speak for their village even without knowing what is going on there. The indigenous chief resides permanently in the village and takes care of cultural matters but without any economic compensation, except for social recognition, prestige and power endowments. We investigated how the two chiefs exercise power and how this affects the solidarity of the village. In the course of

[6] A complete enumeration of the two villages under investigation in 2006 confirmed this assertion.

the fieldwork, it became very obvious that government chiefs have power over official and stately matters and were most hated in the villages for supporting the draconian conservation policies of the state. Indigenous chief did not conceal their hatred for the government appointed counterparts. It was the indigenous chief who in all instances controls and enjoys the support of most village members as we could observe.

The communities[7] studied are patriarchal and nearly all household heads are men. The culture of widow inheritance and polygamy were not obtrusive. In general, life expectancy is about 49 years, the population has a young age structure and females are slightly more than males in Ikondo Kondo I and vice versa in Esukutan. Storytelling, song and dances are still common and important cultural practices that encourage social cohesion. The stage for such stories is around a fireside after an evening meal or outside in the moonlight. Household members and neighbors could join in storytelling events. Sometimes songs are sung which convey a message that encourages group behaviors and discourages individualism. The most famous myth that is often told young people concerning non-compliance with indigenous rules in regard to forest use is "The moonlight woman".

It tells how during the time of their ancestors, a woman went to the forest on an indigenous holiday (a day set aside for rest so that ancestors could move about the forest unnoticed) to fetch fuel wood carrying her baby on her back. The ancestors on their forest walks, saw her, got angry and then took her to an unknown destination in the moon. So every time that there is moonlight, she is seen carrying her baby and splitting firewood. To the villagers, the image of the woman in the moon reminds every group member of similar consequences, should they repeat her crime. And this fear keeps village members away from disobeying indigenous holidays.

Men and women in Esukutan would readily respond in the affirmative that it works and that ancestors do keep in touch. Another myth is related to

---

[7] Community is approached here as both a descriptive category and as a set of variables because in practice, the two are entwined and often difficult to separate (Frazer, 1999: 76; Smith, 2001). It is treated as the interlocking social networks of neighbourhood, kinship and friendship networks; community life (Frazer, 1999: 73). Communities are distinguished from others by boundaries (both similarity and difference) in the way that people within and outside experience them. Community values include; tolerance, reciprocity and trust or "weak ties" in the form of respect and confidence that individuals will support each other at all times (Putnam, 2000: 274). Inherent in these ties are short- and long-run altruism of the respective social actors. This support for each other has made "community" gain fame in the resource management discourse (Agrawal et al., 1999: 630).

death ceremonies. There is a belief that when someone dies in the villages, villagers could go to the forest during the first four days in order to stock their homes with enough food. On the fifth day it is a taboo to go to the forest because it is the people's beliefs that the dead starts wandering in the forest from this day and so could harm anyone who does not want to let it move freely in the forest. However, not going into the forest for some days in a way greatly reduces forest disturbance, which is good for conservation.

Related to myths are beliefs associated with certain wild trees. Such trees are not felled due to existing beliefs that they possess spirits and powers that could harm the individual. The fear to make expensive and heavy sacrifices before felling such trees deters many from attempting to cut them down. For instance, Ikondo Kondo I elders disclosed that *"We have the red stick (camwood or Baphia nitida) which harbours spirits (gods or ancestors)"*. A more optimistic response was gathered from Ikondo Kondo I elders whose parents told them that ill-omen befell those who went to the forest on a traditional Sunday. The innocent had nothing to worry about while they were in the forest. Hunters were often confronted by gorillas and chimpanzees (believed to be transformed human beings) that ended up killing them, if the hunters tried to shoot them down. Discussions with men and women above 18 years in Esukutan reveal that this belief still exists and ancestors constantly keep in touch to remind them to respect such beliefs. This connection with the spirit realm also helps to reduce pressure on some forest resources, although there is no 100% guarantee that people will always stick to such beliefs. This leads to the conclusion that indigenous beliefs, myths and fears command respect and regulate forest disturbance in the communities, which is what macro-level conservation craves for. There is also a diversity of delicious dishes that symbolize sharing, reciprocity and obligation going along these story telling events.

The villages have a long history of displacements from one to another site for different reasons. Some of the reasons include internal quarrels, attacks by neighboring villages, shortage of fertile land and drinking water, illnesses, plagues by insects or wild animals. Chiefs sent their sons with their families to strategically important sites to enlarge their sphere of influence and to secure them from attacks. Today villagers are forced to leave the Korup National Park because they hunt and collect NTFPs that animals would have fed on. These villages are not isolates but are embedded in a wider economic, ecological, political and legal context. There is much research going on in the national park and supporting research activities has become one source of livelihood for indigenous people who port, help and guide for prospectional, bio-monitoring and socio-economic surveys. Researchers come from both national and international research bodies.[8] Article 78 of the 1994 Forestry Law in Cameroon clearly stipulates that no forms of livelihood should exist in a park consequently, no extension of current farms, hunting or collection of NTFPs is allowed. Attempts have led to arrests, seizures and imprisonments. Notorious poachers were arrested in August 2001 and July 2005 and their guns, cartridges and machetes confiscated. They were jailed. In total, 4 poachers have been arrested from the relocated Ikondo Kondo I village between 2000 and 2005.

Korup indigenes possess experience-based knowledge that has helped them monitor, interpret, and respond to dynamic changes in the forest resources. This knowledge was found to be age, gender and species sensitive. More important for daily management of the park are good local mental maps of the park's features, concepts and ideas This knowledge and its conservation potentials are in line with the Boserupian argument that communities develop rural strategies to counter the effect of population pressures on resources. This knowledge has value not only for the information it contains, but for the cultural framework of respect, reciprocity and responsibility in which it is embedded (Kimmerer, 2002: 432). Current efforts to ignore traditional ecological knowledge have not provided adequate species protection (Sharpe, 1998: 26). There is evidence of how resource users are using indigenous ecological knowledge to enable them to reverse the loss of certain wild plants, also known as local soft management practices (Moegenburg et al., 2002: 320). These Boserupian so called rural [conservation] strategies are an important aspect of ecosystem restoration (Burke et al., 2007). Indigenous ecological knowledge of medicinal plants is vital in modern scientific discoveries. In a way, relocating communities out of the national park is in a way denying the potential contributions indigenous ecological knowledge has made so far to both scientific discoveries and conservation efforts. In total, 36 of the 90 medicinal plants discovered in the park are new to science and the medicinal vine, *Ancistrocladus korupensis* shown (in vitro) to be active against the HIV/AIDS virus was found thanks to the knowledge and cooperation of indigenous healers. This suggests a link between indigenous and modern medicine in the area. Also, seasoned hunters are helping many wild-

---

[8] For instance, Korup Project had links with the Universities of Buea and of Yaounde, in Cameroon. Internationally, the Royal Botanical Garden Kew (UK), Missouri Botanical Garden (USA) and Agricultural University Wageningen (Netherlands) do research in the park. The National Cancer Institute in 1993 researched on the botany and domestication of the medicinal vine, *Ancistrocladus korupensis* found in the park. The EU sponsored Sterling University (1986) and the Smithsonian sponsored Biodiversity Conservation Programme (1996), worked with the Project.

life researchers by taking them to areas in the forest where they can find any type of animal they want. Once pictures of such animals were shown to hunters, they immediately said where and when the species can be found. This can be seen to be a rapid assessment and participatory approach to bio-monitoring, but more in-depth research is needed in this field.

The typical rural economic or rural livelihood activities (Ellis, 2000: 10) are characterized by manufactured goods mostly from Nigeria that are sold in Korup Park villages, while forest products are traded in Nigerian towns. They are increasingly engaging in food and cash crops farming. Cash crop farming involves oil palms and cocoa in small-scale plantations. Food crops cultivated include plantains, bananas, coco yams, beans, maize, caso, essaka, masua and pepper and smaller quantities of yams, mbu, sugar cane, cassava and okra (some are dialect names). They also grow fruits like coco nuts, mangoes, plums, pears, pawpaw, guava, lemon and oranges on their farms. Hunting takes place throughout the year but declines in intensity during December to March, the peak farming season. Hunting in the national park takes two forms: with guns, practised by 14 or 30% of the 47 households in Ikondo Kondo I village and 24 or 51% of households in Esukutan village. About 36% of the households use traps to kill animals. Hunting with guns is carried out at night and in the day time. Expert hunters (mostly from villages within the support zone of Korup National Park) use automatic rifles, double-barrel shotguns and factory-made shotguns. These experts kill mostly large mammals like elephants, buffalos, war tugs, chimpanzees etc. Locals commonly use riffles and the Dane gun. Most of the shotguns are manufactured by local blacksmiths. Bullets and firearms are smuggled from Nigeria. Night hunters use carbide headlamps and torch lights to hunt species like duikers (*Cephalophus spp.),* genets (*Genetta spp.)* and the two-spotted palm civet (*Nandinia binotata*). Fishing is purely for home consumption and villagers formerly used *Strychnos aculeata* a forest plant and fish poison with minimal environmental damage. They collect non-timber forest products (NTFPs) like njangsanga, bush mangoes, njabe, palm nuts, plums, eru, kola nuts, shea nuts, bitter kola, and wild onions as are locally known. Domestication of fowls, goats, dogs, pigs and sheep is for home consumption.

Although they farm, hunt, and collect NTFPs for subsistence, some minimal social surplus generates cash income. The relative contribution of farming, hunting and collection of NTFPs for Esukutan in 2006 was 43%, 30% and 27% respectively (Figure 2). While cocoa fetches much money for men (about 75 euros per 100kg), NTFPs like Njansanga and Bush mango provide over 70% of women's as well as over 30% of household income. These commodities are transported as head loads, and about 30 km is trekked for about 10 hours to the nearest marketing point by family members. Whether sold in the village or transported to a nearby market, the income remains the same when the overhead cost is deducted. Hence, the marketing point does not affect real incomes.

Figure 2: Composition of household incomes

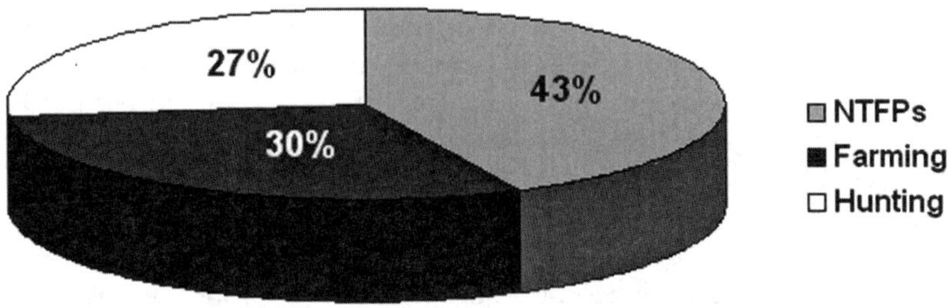

One could also deduce from Figure 2 that NTFP extraction is the highest income earning activity. Since this activity is mostly done by women, there is the temptation to conclude that women are the highest income earners in the communities. However, hunting and gathering activities put together provide 70% of household incomes. The reality is quite different if one considers individual households as units of analysis as some engage more into some activities and less in others. Hence, there is a diversity of portfolios. Hunting contributes more than 44% of some households' incomes, high enough for hunters to engage in it full time. Since, hunting is a sensitive issue in the area, even full time hunter households prefer to declare low incomes from this activity.

Hunting at night as well as hunting with traps is bad because both large and small animals are killed and hunters can not easily determine the sex of the animal. The game sometimes rots because a complete trapping rotation takes 3 days and an individual may own as much as 1000 wire snares. Cash crop farming contributes more than 55% of some households' income. It involves the slash and burn and shifting cultivation methods. Lately, the use of gammalin 40 to poison fish for an easy catch is undesirable because it completely obliterates aquatic animal and plant life in the vicinity and also causes severe health hazards to people who eat poisoned fish. This intensive gathering of leafs, barks, fruits, etc. is considered as an unwanted competition over animal food by the conservator of Korup Park. These people are aware that the forests are able to naturally regenerate as the outtake by them is largely for subsistence and demographically, the population density is low;

about 1 inhabitant per km^2. However, their livelihood activities are based on the knowledge they hold about their environment. There is social differentiation and specialization especially with hunting that is exclusively carried out by young men.

The Government of Cameroon and Korup Eco Guards

The Government supports the idea of the existence of a national park and provides personnel and security for the entire Korup staff. It also provides funding to the Korup Park Service, covering the salaries of the staff. It remains the overall power to make park laws, though it fails to ensure that they are enforced at all costs. Its NRM strategy often disregards the interests of resident indigenous populations. Cameroon's national parks law prohibits human activities other than research, tourism and recreation in national parks and people are legally forbidden to live, collect or harvest natural resources in parks. Even if Korup indigenes were to protest against harsh conservation strategies in the area, their voices will not be heard and the political cost will be low. This is because, the conservation and or exploitation of natural resources of uncertain value in a remote area of the country is "generally very different from openly combative issues such as tax policy, central government spending, or wage policy" (Ascher, 2000). Notably, natural resource sites in Cameroon are remote and economically marginal where property rights are either poorly defined or have passed to state control. Thus protests against resource abuses are stymied by the legal weakness of such claims in addition to the political marginality of the protesters (Ascher, 2000). Also, donors backed out in July 2003 without effectively building the necessary capacity and capability of Cameroon government to sustain the strict management approach adopted for Korup National Park since 1986. Neighbouring communities now take advantage of this macro-level weakness to free-ride on the forest resources whilst resident communities stand out as main losers. Yet conservation in the park is obligatory.

Game or Eco Guards are para-militaries trained to guard the Korup National Park performing a policing function for the Park's surveillance and enforcement unit. Since 1988, 26 have been employed, 1 resigned, 3 died and so there are 22 remaining to guard the 126,900 hectares of closed canopy forest. Few of them are from villages within the park area. Due to irregular salaries and no status, eco guards extensively poach, threatening a park they have to protect. Yet indigenes are blamed for hunting too much meanwhile the reality is that large animals are hunted by professional hunters not from within park villages. Eco guards, who are charged with enforcing national park laws, face stiff and sometimes lethal resistance from resident communities.

The International Donor Community

International actors included: the World Wild Life Fund for Nature (WWF) that assisted the government of Cameroon in creating and managing the Korup National Park in 1986. Until 1996, it remained the major donor and the Korup was its largest conservation project in the world. The German Technical Corporation (GTZ) invited into the project in 1991, financed the forestry and agro-forestry activities in the Support Zone (forest reserves). The Overseas Development Assistance (ODA – DFID) 1986-1997 and the World Conservation Society (WCS) 1989-1993, carried out biological research. The German government through Kreditanstalt für Wiederaufbau (KfW) since 1994 ear-marked Korup for special grants to support rural access tracks, water and sanitation. The US Department of Defense (US DoD) since 1993 committed to financed communal structures at the relocation sites in collaboration with the Cameroon military. The European Commission (EC) funding was effectively provided in 1994. It was the major donor of the Korup project, sponsoring anti-poaching campaigns and ordered the recruitment of 12 more game guards - all of which came from villages within a three-kilometer periphery of the Park - as well as financed access roads. These bodies can be considered as Public Service Contractors which finance and support research activities in the park, elaborate management plans and provide top managers for the Korup Project. Until 2003 the EC and GTZ were major donors, despite the lack of donor coordination, accountability and institutional collaboration (Obase et al., 1997: 6).

The Korup Project

The Korup Project was one of the first Integrated Conservation and Development Projects (ICDPs) established in the tropical rainforest zone since 1988, with the Cameroon Government and international donors as partners. This multi-donor and multi billion Euro bureaucracy, phased out in July 2003 with a 5 percent positive impact amongst the inhabitants of the project area due to its very unpopular relocation programme that started and ended with the pilot village Ikondo Kondo I. The Korup Project aimed to conserve untouched or undisturbed ecosystems in the Korup area through the sustainable management and development of these protected areas and their associated support zone. Indicators at the project purpose level included among others (Korup Management Plan, 2002):

- The time required to obtain bush meat from the forest does not increase;
- The distance traveled to collect NTFP does not increase;
- No elephants shot illegally in forest reserves after September 1999;
- 50% decline in the exploitation of Eru, Njangsanga, Bush-mango and chewing-sticks in the park by villagers from the support zone by 2000.

As an ICDP, Korup Project used a multiplicity of instruments which have faced fierce criticism. First its reliance on the IUCN for directives to transplant a global protection approach to a more complex indigenous situation. Its poor application of the carrot (rural development to villages in the support zone) and the stick (park surveillance) approach, which is very contradictory as it was not sensibly handled (Eyong et al., 2007). Also, the natural resources management component was segregated from the rural development component allowing staff to concentrate on single roles, thus confusing to both staff and clients; there were separate extension channels; as well as separate institutional development activities. Also, the GTZ component functioned independently, parallel and insulated from the Korup Project as a whole (Obase et al., 1997:7). This chaotic instrumental application makes it hard to say if Korup Project achieved its goals because at least three elephants and one buffalo were shot in Ikenge in 2004 and 2005 by a notorious hunter from Manyemen. Eru, Njangsanga and Bush-mango are the main income sources for women in and outside the Park, while chewing stick (Massularia acuminata) has been over- exploited and sold. However, a detailed bio-monitoring survey is necessary to support this argument.

Since 1988, Korup Project with the assistance of the Cameroon Government and international donors, made giant strides if one goes by official records. It facilitated the creation of more than 31 Forest Management Committees and more than 40 infrastructure development projects (including water supply, bridges, culverts, rural access roads, rural community halls and schools), more than 70 Income Generating and Credit Activities (including cassava grinding mills, palm oil presses, improved cocoa driers and sprayers, natural resource plantations, coffee rejuvenation, cattle, goat and pig rearing projects). Ikondo Kondo village was relocated in the Support Zone in 2000. Park boundary cut-line was maintained. A complex headquarter and sub-headquarters, tourist information centers, 115km of trail, five tourist camps, three game guard posts and main equipment were developed and upgraded for tourism and security purposes. Environmental awareness was carried out through the establishment and distribution of environmental magazines, newsletters, pamphlets, posters and calendars of Korup (Obase,

1995) to selected households and curriculum development for primary schools in the villages of the park area, but it proved insufficient as people needed food and not only lectures. A number of bursaries were granted to selected children from the Park villages to acquire technical education and tools costing to about 1000 euros were handed to graduates. However, two years of technical education did not qualify anyone of these beneficiaries to be efficient carpenters, motor mechanics etc as envisaged. A host of them are now wasting in Esukutan with no real skills to fully utilise the donated tools. Environmental awareness, also translated to mean travel abroad made 14 indigenous sponsored abroad for training, meanwhile about 57 nursery, primary and secondary schools were supported with tuition material (books and tools), supplemented wages of teachers employed by parents of school children, school buildings, infrastructure and furniture. Also, the Park surveillance and enforcement unit seized tens of thousands of wire snares, searchlights, tons of guns, GPS instruments and destroyed five hunters' huts. Notorious poachers were arrested in August 2001 and July 2005 and their guns, cartridges and machetes confiscated and were jailed. Despite these, there are many challenges Korup faces.

Challenges, contests and conflicts

Challenges

Korup Project faced a myriad of challenges and phased out in 2003 leaving behind a number of problems and some are now backfiring on the Park's condition. First, the failure to target the issue of poverty and permit some level of forest use through innovative policy actions and sustainable economic alternatives now poses as a hindrance. Korup Project's strategies failed to pay special attention to poverty alleviation that is compatible with conservation, though poverty alleviation was not one of its goal and or long term objective.

Second, the strict and insular management strategy of Korup Project was just a short-term strategy launched by biologists, whose understanding of Parks through the ecological paradigm depicts them as ecological islands as well as an end in themselves. The strict enforcement, insular, hierarchical, output oriented and protective of turf approach adopted for park management perceives indigenous communities as being in the way rather than as partners in conservation. This approach that pays less attention to the social values of a Park fuels degradation of Korup National Park. One may ask why? Whilst one cannot boast of any ready-made answers to this question, it is one that leaves many indifferent. A convincing answer lies in the disassociation and disintegration of the otherwise interwoven values of parks due to a disciplinary (narrow focused) management strategy that seeks to enhance ecological values deceptively ignoring the complementing direct economic and social values. The resultant is transformation of the direct economic and social values of Korup National Park to opportunity costs as they become the opportunities forgone. Like other ICDPs, Korup failed due to lack of a holistic park management strategy to integrate bedfellows like conservation and development.

Third, the growing Nigerian rather than indigenous population increases the demand for forest products. Nigeria is a net importer of NTFPs and over 93% of buyers found in Korup Park villages in 2006 were of Nigerian nationality. They illegally hunt and smuggle firearms through the Park to Nigeria with little benefits as income to Cameroonians and the absence of cross-border cooperation between the Oban Hills project and Korup makes matters worse (Obase et al., 1997: 9). Although Park enclaves are illegal since 1986, they are officially recognized unless relocated and so have to be treated with discretion. However, non-park indigenes use this opportunity to hunt and smuggle goods from neighbouring Nigeria through the Park, making anti-poaching activities a daunting task as it is very difficult to identify each park resident and distinguish him/her from outsiders. Consequently, Cameroon officials claim the Park will be best protected if there are no inhabitants in it. Currently, the indigenes are being sacrificed and deprived since no development is permitted in the Korup National Park.

Fourth, short project cycles of 4 to 8 years are not enough to carry out conservation and development, especially without the right tools and capacity. Donors made short term commitments and withdrew them not because their goals had been attained but due to poor performance, reduced assistance from funding source, better interest elsewhere or bad political climate. When WWF-UK and ODA withdrew in 1998 after a critical mid-term review, rural development activities in the Support Zone were reduced drastically affecting other donors whose activities were complementary and dependent. Short term financial commitments are deleterious because the desired attitudes and behavior change with respect to natural resources use by forest dependent peoples is nothing to occur within 8 years. Also, development is not something to be delivered only through bags of rice, medical tablets, calendars and culverts but also through long term alternatives that create awareness like revitalizing indigenous institutions and forcing the host government to recognize and empower them. For 15 years, Korup Project spent useful energies and resources trying to recover lost grounds but kept losing more grounds.

Fifth, throughout its lifespan, the Korup Project suffered an acute shortage of qualified staff in the government services. Today there is only one conservator who lacks the necessary interdisciplinary skills as well as 3 employed and 23 contracted eco guards to enforce the law prohibiting hunting, fishing and farming in the Park. One resigned, three died and three have been withdrawn to do secretarial duties, leaving 19 to patrol the over 248 km Park boundary. This means a guard is responsible for about 6679 hectares of forest, an amount more than double the 3000 hectares per guard standard that is recommended by the International Union for the Conservation of Nature (IUCN) for a closed canopy forest like Korup. Making matters worse, many of them have little knowledge of the park's boundaries and do not even come from within the Park villages. Also, salaries of eco guards have not been paid a salary for more than two years pushing them to make a living through unorthodox means. In July 2006 the Divisional Officer for Ndian division in Cameroon, said, game guards have turned out to pose a serious threat to the park than indigenous communities. They poach and destroy the wildlife in the park that they are employed to protect and sometimes, they sell whatever is confiscated from poachers.

Sixth, the carrot and stick management strategy was a major disincentive for indigenous survival and livelihood. The Korup Project held the carrot (rural development in the support zone) in one hand and the stick (park surveillance) on the other which is very contradictory if not sensibly handled. This focus on flora and fauna excludes people, their knowledge and institutions that have been the most effective conservation instruments.

Seventh, the relocation scam advocated by the conservator of Korup National Park, ignores and erodes the park's direct economic and social values. To him, human settlements should be separated from park boundaries as if the park is an ecological island. This approach is very expensive as between 1988 and 2000, Korup Project spent about 20 million euros or 1, 3 million euros a year, which is the highest conservation budget per km^2 of forest in West and Central Africa (Cernea et al., 2006). Though expensive, it treats indigenous cultures as barriers to conservation instead of integrating them in conservation agendas as is the case with Kibale National Park, Uganda among others (Borrini-Feyerabend et al., 2004). Indigenous institutions and knowledge of natural resources have been proven to be positive contributions to natural resources management in rural Brazil and that has helped reduced the incessant conflicts over natural resources exploitation and use

(Begossi, 1998). Korup officials still talk of relocating all Park villages, though no official plan is on the table due to lack of funds.

Eighth, lack of funding hindered financing of the heavy-handed policing approach though Korup Project was the most ambitious and heavily funded WWF conservation project in the world which also became a wasteful spender. For instance the entire forced relocation process costed 642,037 Euros exceeding the planned budget by such an extent that insufficient funds remained for the resettlement of the remaining five villages. External funding ceased in July 2003 and today with just fees levied to the discerning numbers of different categories of visitors to the park to run its activities, Africa's richest rainforest risks becoming Africa's poorest rainforest. The government of Cameroon is not able to provide one-tenth of the required 2002-2007 budget of 1,806,368 Euros. Running for almost two years with no salary, the need for survival becomes prior to eco-guards who are now the worst threats to the park. They no longer go on patrol but illusively spend their days in front of the Korup Park Service office in Mundemba hoping for when they shall be paid. Poachers are now enjoying the boon while it lasted and stop at nothing to unsustainably exploit, threatening tourists and researchers who pay to visit the park.

Conservation strategies and the local response: contests and conflicts

As observed in the Himalayas, the restricted access to livelihood resources accelerated the destruction of forest as local people sought to obtain all they could before they are deprived of their traditional rights and ownership (Ives et al., 1989: 61). So, relocation as a conservation strategy provokes a local response that results in a dilemma. Relocation is an idea that is strongly supported by demographers and ecologists but rejected by Boserupians and anti-displacements scholars. Relocation policies are in most cases known to be based on speculative representations that alter locals' attitudes and undermine their role in natural resources governance. In the light, state officials exclude forest dwellers from conservation programmes also generated conflicts between human and wildlife population as well as between park managers and resident communities. Such outright protection of biodiversity by taking control of NRM away from forest residents ignited contests and conflicts for over 25 years with governmental agencies, marked by increased illegal hunting, river poisoning and harvesting of NTFPs as well as sometimes lethal confrontations between eco guards and villagers.

The prohibition strategy is decried by locals as the reason why large mammals such as Elephants, Buffalos, Tigers and Chimpanzees have been destroying food crops on farms in both the forest and in the nearby settlements causing severe hunger, poverty and suffering. Their elders insist that preventing them from their livelihood activities in their surroundings has granted animals more rights to survive than them who are the traditional owners of the forest. Villagers complain that the situation is such that "no amount of hard farm work can counter the destructive effects of these animals" and so the "way out is to face them out rightly". This struggle to eliminate destructive but protected animals has resulted in people-wildlife conflict. As reported, villagers would contribute money to employ experienced hunters from further villages away to kill the destructive and large mammals. Although hunting is illegal according to state law, indigenous beliefs prevent the killing of large mammals that are believed to be the doubles of some elders who have mystical powers in the community. Also, local hunters too do not have good weapons like automatic rifles to kill large mammals.

Another point of contestation is related to the claim of indigenous rights over the forest. In 1986 when the forest was gazetted as a national park, these traditional rights were removed and settlements were declared illegal. The villagers interpret conservation as denying them their rights to harvest, hunt and fish in their immediate vicinity by the state that has nationalized all forests. Such 'legal dualism' in the ownership of forests has since the colonial times, kept causing insecurity and conflicts, resulting in serious encroachments and illegal poaching. Somehow, it leads to extinction of species. As a way out state laws have been enacted to forbid human activities inside parks because such activities may destroy habitats as well as reduce food for wild animals. As was observed during the fieldwork, state control has not deterred over-exploitation of some forest resources. An example is chewing stick (*Massularia acuminata*) that has become rare in the area. The harvesting method was unsustainable as the tree trunks, roots and young trees are harvested and boat loads go to Nigeria on a daily basis. Buyers from Nigeria acknowledge that they no longer come to the area because almost all the chewing sticks have been harvested. The worrying thing is that indigenous children don't attend school at such times because they have to harvest chewing stick to sell. Prohibiting the exploitation of park resources by setting up boundaries marked by 22 pillars, 98 km of planted fast growing conspicuous trees such as *Gmelina arborea* and *Dracaena spp.* and numerous sign posts could have worked if the park did not originally inhabit communities. These barriers to deter human survival and livelihood create suspicion since any attempt to collect resources in their backyard is considered 'poaching', a punishable offence. Since 1988, many villagers have been arrested, detained and released (after a bribe) including four hunters from Ikondo Kondo I village for hunting in their neighborhood - the park. Despite this, excessive degradation of resources is not observable in Korup. This begs that question; who and how have the resources in the park been protected. This brings us to the idea of rule enforcement and effectiveness.

Whose rules matter in the Korup area?

Understanding whose rules matter in the Korup rainforest area requires an actor-oriented approach that identifies and characterizes differing actor strategies and rationales, and their effectiveness for solving conservation problems and the structural outcomes (Long, 2002). Till date, the state enacted laws to govern the park. In the 1990s it created and promoted a number of village NRM committees. 10 years after their creation, a survey found that less than a third of them is functional though ineffective (Schmidt-Soltau et al, 2004). Eco guards who are charged with enforcing the law are constrained by many factors including a lack of understanding of the laws they have to enforce. In effect, all the state enforcement bodies are located far away from the park. They seldom visit the villages whose activities affect the park. Esukutan and Ikondo Kondo villagers lamented that Korup Project workers never really visited their villages. They either were passing-by or briefly held secret meetings with favored village members (Korup Project, 1999). The Project was visible only in the Southern sector with plans to develop the other sectors between 2002 and 2007 (Park Management Plan, 2002), even without a running budget to repair transport vehicles. Also, Esukutan villagers could only remember an instance in 2005 when youths fought with and drove eco-guards in the area. If the protected resources are not being destroyed by free-riders then it raises questions as to whose rules matter in the Korup Park area. An underlying reality, long contested by the conservator of Korup National Park which this study uncovered is what that has constrained resource abuse from pre-colonial to present times. This includes the locally respected indigenous institutions for social control that agents of modernization (Western donors through macro-level institutions overseeing forest protection efforts in Cameroon) have worked hard to silence with little success. What does institution mean in this context?

There has been an upsurge of definitions of institutions both formal and informal as there are publications and scholarly works. Only three are discussed because the intention is not to repeat the literature and all definitions revolve around those presented here. The most classical definition holds that *"Institutions consist of informal constraints, formal rules, and the enforcement characteristics of both"* (North, 1989: 239). Another definition argues that institutions are *"prescriptions humans use to organize repetitive and organized interactions"*

(Ostrom, 2003; 2005). This definition omitted the idea of *"the incentive structures institutions represent and the physical and social environment in which human beings live"* (Ascher, 2000; Chakraborty, 2001: 343). Institutions also refer to the guiding norms, rules, procedures, processes and community organizations that fashion the way group members interact with each other as well as the natural and spiritual environments. They do not necessarily have to be bounded units with physically defined characteristics in time or space (Poteete et al, 2004). For this chapter, indigenous institutions include village associations, cultural sites and processes as well as the control mechanisms put in place by groups with a strong identity and leadership. Such groups draw their existence from forest resources through patterned behaviours that directly or indirectly control and regulate forest use. These control mechanisms are transmitted from generation to generations usually orally and at different levels of socialization. Indigenous institutions set the rules of the game of social interaction that fashion how individual behaviours lead to group expectations of forest use and conditions. Since culture is not a mono-logic entity, deviation is to be expected and this could give rise to unexpected social and ecological change. This change can be positive or negative for nature conservation. If such institutions, as they usually do, evolve as unwritten norms or rules in use, they are difficult for outsiders to observe or get recognized (Poteete et al., 2004: 6).

Since their origin, indigenous people have evolved a set of laws (rules) guiding behavior with respect to community life, including ways in which forest resources are exploited. Today, these rules have become a way of life (culture) for the villagers. These norms define deviance that is punishable by the heavy hand of indigenous legal frameworks with Ekpwe at its helm. For instance, the rule that no one should poison streams and rivers in order to catch fish with inorganic poisons like Gammalin 40 or Gammalin 80 intended for spraying cocoa plants, existed not long ago although the use of biodegradable natural toxins from macerated fruits of *Strychnos aculeata, Blya supida* and *Massularia acuminata,* have always been the norm in all the villages in the Korup National Park. Their non-usage today, has been due to a serious ban village on all forms of poisons used for killing large amounts of fish. In-comers who gained access through the hospitality of the first settlers were involved in all reported cases of deviance in 2006, which re-enforces Elinor Ostrom's idea that unwritten norms are not usually respected by newcomers or non-members until an example is set.

However, rules and norms at individual and peer group level exist. At the personal level, someone could make it a rule not to kill small animals. Such specialized hunters are said to acquire their skills from mystical sources that warned them to hunt only large mammals like elephants, gorillas and chimpanzees. So far, two specialized hunters have been hired by Park villagers to kill elephants that destroy crops. As peers, it is a rule that hunters select their game and normally not kill female, young and pregnant animals. But this is possible only for hunting during the day, as hunters could clearly identify the type, sex and reproductive state of the animals. It is impossible at night because, if eco guards ever patrol the area, they stop working in the evenings, and so hunting in the night is rampant with little or no regard for sex, size and reproductive state of animals. There is widespread disillusionment in the villages and any night hunter is under voluntary surveillance. If a defaulter is reported to the Village Council, a heavy fine involving several bottles of illicit gin (locally called afofo), is charged. No case was reported and the elders in both villages argue that it is a sign of an effective rule. This might be true but it could also be that people fear reporting their friends to avoid such harsh payments.

Whatever the case, rules are enforced by community-based organizations and social institutions for decision-making. These structures which control the use of natural resources in the Korup area include village councils, village chief, traditional chief and village development associations (Malleson, 2000). Government-appointed administrative chiefs are said to head villages (Park Management Plan, 2002: 58). Despite this hierarchy, the indigenous secret or 'juju' society; Ekpwe, remains the most important social institution and governing body in all villages of Korup National Park and Peripheral Zone (Malleson, 2000; Park Management Plan, 2002). Knowledge plays a great role in this power hierarchy. Women confirmed this assertion by stating that "youths know just a little, it is obvious that our parents know better, and the chief knows best about the forest than the rest of our parents" hence, "more knowledge implies more powers, that is why we report cases at levels". We verified these claims from the literature which also failed to detail how these institutions control forest use in the area.[9] Crucial indigenous institutions for NRM in the enclaves were the family, peer and social groups, sacred forests and rivers, indigenous chief, the village council and the Ekpwe society. These bodies operate within a set of norms and rules usually endorsed under the auspices of Ekpwe.

The family is the main unit of primary socialization in the villages. Villagers refer to lineages when talk about of the [nuclear family]. Every village has a

[9] This study will not discuss village development associations and government appointed Chiefs because they have very political undertones and were not visible in the villages studied.

number of lineages with an heir each, whom the rest of the kith and kin are answerable to. In all cases, it is a male who acts as divergence manager, exercising leadership and power over the lineage. He represents the lineage in the Village Council and takes responsibility for the mishaps of his fellow members. *Table 2* is a list of names of the main lineages in Esukutan and Ikondo Kondo I, respectively:

Table 2: Names of lineages in Ikondo Kondo I and Esukutan villages (2006)

No	Esukutan	Ikondo Kondo I
1	Bakumba	Bachouk
2	Biki	Barome
3	Bonakanda	Batanga
4	Bonambere	Besiwan
5	Bonangiri	Bokom
6	Bongwanamba	Borona
7	Bonokongo	Buyen
8	Bosango	Ntui
9	Bosito	-

The functioning of lineage heads to control behavior is interesting. They remain the conflict manger at a level higher than the household. In Esukutan, the heads of the Bositos and Bonangiri acknowledged that they were openly reprimanded in a Village Council meeting in 2005 when members of their lineages poisoned streams to catch fish. At their level, they forced the culprits to pay a fine that was taken to the Village Council. Additionally, every lineage member reports mal behaviors to them for immediate action before consulting higher authorities.

Self-help groups of youth as well as other social groups that work on members' farms on a rotating basis also ensure social control in the villages. Their powers end where those of lineage representatives, Ekpwe, Chief and Village Council begin. When a case is more than them, reports are made to higher authorities. For instance, a former head of the Korup Youth Task Force, commented in 2006 that "actually, when a case arises, we inform the chief, and then able-bodied youths will be sent to arrest the intruders and to equally seize their tools like; guns, bullets, cutlasses and so on". However, youths get remuneration through a share in the fines that culprits pay.

Another form of behavior control with respect to resource use is sacred groves. Korup forest people have for centuries demarcated and protected sections of rivers or streams (called *Itika Bekundi* and *Nkanda* in Esukutan) and forest. For rivers, the idea is to prevent fishing at such points so as to enable the village have fish to feed strangers. For forest, exploitation is prohibited in patches of up to two hectares called *Ekpwe forest.* All these form part of what is called *Spiritual Natural Sites* that have been seen to contribute enormously to biodiversity conservation. These indigenous protected hot-spots were found in Esukutan but not in the relocated Ikondo Kondo I. Thus, rules endorsed by Ekpwe apply in these hot-spots.

Forest use is also controlled by a Village Council that is made up of representatives of the main families in the village. The chair rotates and the laws are endorsed by Ekpwe. Oaths are sworn invoking Ekpwe powers. Forest use and abuse are discussed during meetings. In effect, it is the most democratic body of any village. Through it, laws are repealed or strengthened. This body is very effective in Esukutan which forced Nigerians to pay a token fee before exploiting the village forest. In the early 1980s, Esukutan youths found that when exploiters pay to exploit an authorized quantity of a resource, they take the advantage that the village is not monitoring them and extract more. A Nigerian, who paid about 4 Euros for permission to hunt in the Oroko forest ended up killing many animals, smoked them and after two weeks he came to the village with just a handful of the game to signal his return. He complained that his expedition was not successful. Just when the village council was feasting over a game he offered them, news came from one village hunter that a pile of smoked meat has been found close to the footpath to Nigeria. The Nigerian exploiter was detained, and his pile of hunted game that was seized and youths were sent to see him off to Nigeria. From thence, a law was passed banning the granting of permission to any foreigner to personally hunt or extract resources in the forest and this law was endorsed by Ekpwe.

The indigenous chief exercises control on a level that is somehow higher than that of the village council. Although he is usually a member of Ekpwe and the village council, he does not necessarily head them. Conflicts are reported to him first and he resolves most. His decisions are binding because of his charisma.

Ekpwe is an indigenous association of low intensity segregation that assembles a large number of male adult villagers. Each village has an Ekpwe hall situated at its centre. The Ekpwe society essentially governs the public sphere of the village. Ekpwe laws and powers are supreme and everyone in the village including the Chief must abide by them. Membership in Ekpwe is open to all and is sought individually. It is a graded organization starting with young men. Climbing the social ladder (prestige & power) in the village coincides with climbing the internal grades of the organization. The lowest level of Ekpwe is that of ordinary membership which grants participation rights in the public area. The next level is a federation of inner core representatives of collective political units. This sphere could feature older members in terms of longevity. The associative and status conferring level is the space of inclusion by incorporation and low intensity segregation. Esukutan elders revealed that this level consists of reputed healers and five eldest persons. Segregation is reflected in diurnal, nocturnal or serious religious, ritual, juridical, political and entertainment activities. While hardcore judicial, political and ritual ceremonies are conducted by the constituted core of elders and specialist shamans, hearings are open to all members of the association. Nocturnal activities are access-free to only Ekpwe members and diurnal activities are also shielded from women and non-members. For instance, if jujus are performing in the village, all the women, children and men who are non-members are fiercely sent into hiding. This is done at the sound of the Ekpwe drum to alert everyone of restricted freedom of movement. The parading jujus chase and arrest whoever ignores these orders. Jujus have whipping sticks that are believed to have magical spells that could harm generations yet unborn. The fear of a bad future makes non-members to go into hiding when Ekpwe is displaying.

Although there is some secret knowledge, there are general aspects of Ekpwe that are open to all community members. This secret knowledge is the inner functioning of the Ekpwe that is known only to members. The open access knowledge is what to do when Ekpwe is displaying, the consequences of not complying with an Ekpwe rule or how Ekpwe sanctions its rules. In general, Ekpwe is the arena in which the people as a group construct their public sphere and articulate their collective interests (governance role). By settling disputes, it also plays a judicial role. First, everything from investigation and disproving is open and involves mediums. The most reputed spiritualists are asked to perform magic during investigations. Ekpwe uses coercive investigation procedures and gives tough sanctions. Its diagnostics have hardly been faulty and in all the reported cases the accused pleaded guilty. Some young men are still keen to be Ekpwe members for prestige, enjoyment and to have a say in the village government (Malleson, 2000: 75). This forms part of the general social knowledge and the hierarchies of access to knowledge go with status within Ekpwe since it is an organised knowledge space and each step in its hierarchy from non-membership to the Ekpwe Chief is a gateway to heavily guarded knowledge. Everything from investigation and disproving is open and involves mystic. The most reputed soothsayers perform magic to identify defaulters. As reported in Esukutan village, all the accused pleaded guilty, implying the diagnostics so far have not been wrong. In 2000, a Nigerian called Okoro, got married to an Esukutan woman, poisoned a river with Calisulfan 350 EC and caught large quantities of fish. The Village Council convoked him for detailed explanations. After a painful investigation process through Ekpwe, he acknowledged he intentionally poisoned the river with Calisulfan. He was found guilty, fined 12 bottles of Afofo and about 35 Euro and later banished from the village. Whipping is also another way of punishment for Ekpwe and the idea of open punishment is to send a strong warning signal to everyone that such as act is inexcusable. This punishment levied on Okoro was harsh for two reasons: it took place after a 1998 incident involving Moki Benard, an indigene who also used Gammalin 80 to poison fish. School children who went to fetch water for their classroom saw floating fish and started picking. The catch was so huge that it raised an alarm. Benard hid the catch in his forest hut. At first the only primary school teacher in the village was accused. He declined. Others were accused and they declined. The village council invoked Ekpwe powers and a reputed resident soothsayer performed magic and pointed at Moki Benard who was hiding in the forest. Youths were sent to arrest him and he pleaded guilty. He was seriously warned, thrashed and fined four limps of bush meat, 8 bottles of Afofo and about 15 Euro. His case was an example to others.

Indigenous institutions are closer to the resource, there is a common understanding of their purpose and functioning amongst the villagers and their enforcements are harsh but effective. It is obvious from the examples above that they constitute what kept away foreign and illegal poachers from the area on a continuous basis. These institutions have controlled three quarters of the Korup National Park for 25 years now, with enormous success though greatly resisted by state agencies. One cannot dispute the influence of the indigenous Chief and Ekpwe society during the pre-colonial times. Although they are still effective, they are changing due to external pressures. Current conservation approaches are alienating these institutions through government appointed chiefs and development associations that are practically absent in the villages (see box 1). A case in present times was the Chief of a Peripheral Zone Village who was arrested by state forces for trying to punish illegal poachers in the forest around his village on grounds that he acted unlawfully by taking the law in his hands.

Indigenous property rights and regimes

Officially, the national park forest is a public property and state agencies take decisions for its management. On the ground, it is a communal property for which use rights are restricted to village members (Hanna et al., 1995). For theoretical and practical reasons, definitional clarity is needed for concepts like [private and public] goods, rights, and owners of goods. This is because almost all environmental resources fall within common-pool goods; a foundation to detect the circumstances in which common-property arrangements are appropriate, desirable, and even in some situations utterly essential to sound resource management in general (McKean, 1998). Goods are a natural given, rights are an institutional invention, and owners of rights are entities that make different representational claims to common pool goods like forest (McKean, 1998). Many studies are united on the fact that resource management failures rest pivotally on poorly defined and transferred rights (Ostrom, 2003; Tucker, 1999). The misconception that communities grant open access that leads to reducibility provoked scholarly recommendations for external authorities to impose a different set of institutions. Works from Demsetz (1967), Posner (1977), Simmons et al. (1996) saw private property as the most efficient form of ownership, another by Ophuls (1973) thought government ownership and control is better (Cited in Ostrom, 1999: 2). However, the inability of states to effectively conserve forests, coupled with empirical cases of successful forest management by communities challenge this conventional theory of common-pool resources (Agrawal et al., 2000; Ostrom, 1999) stressing that what is needed is well defined and transferred rights (devolution).

It is important to note that the Korup forest is formally a state property but empirically, customary land use rights and indigenous ownership claims are popular in all enclaves. The same is true for villages within the Peripheral Zone claiming customary use rights that extend well inside Korup National Park. Without being able to refer to any official or legal basis, indigenous people use streams, trees, crops and other physical attributes to demarcate boundaries with adjacent communities. These traditional territories are recognized by indigenous communities whose members normally live, farm, gather and hunt within their own territory. The territory is ordered according to certain criteria and not at all chaotic. The village forest is distributed among households or even families (See figure 3 for the Esukutan example). In these patches, members of the unit carry out livelihood activities and jealously keep away unauthorized members even from the same village. Therefore, we have to acknowledge private ownership and use rights within the overall communal property regime. These private patches are found within 10km around the village. The area of forest beyond the 10km limit is where large scale hunting and collection of NTFPs takes place. It is open to all members of the community in question. This open access does not guarantee exhaustibility because Ekpwe laws are binding for extraction in the entire village forest. However, people from other communities were previously allowed by indigenes to hunt in such an open access territory but not without formal permission to conduct a casual hunting or gathering expedition. This act breeds the conception amongst state officials that indigenes have been hitherto accomplices to poachers mostly from neighboring Nigeria, as they provide these poachers shelter, cover and direction in the Park (Korup Project, 1999). Hence, for the sake of wildlife, the Park would best be protected if there were no people living in it (Obase, 1997).

Figure 3: Map of Korup National Park

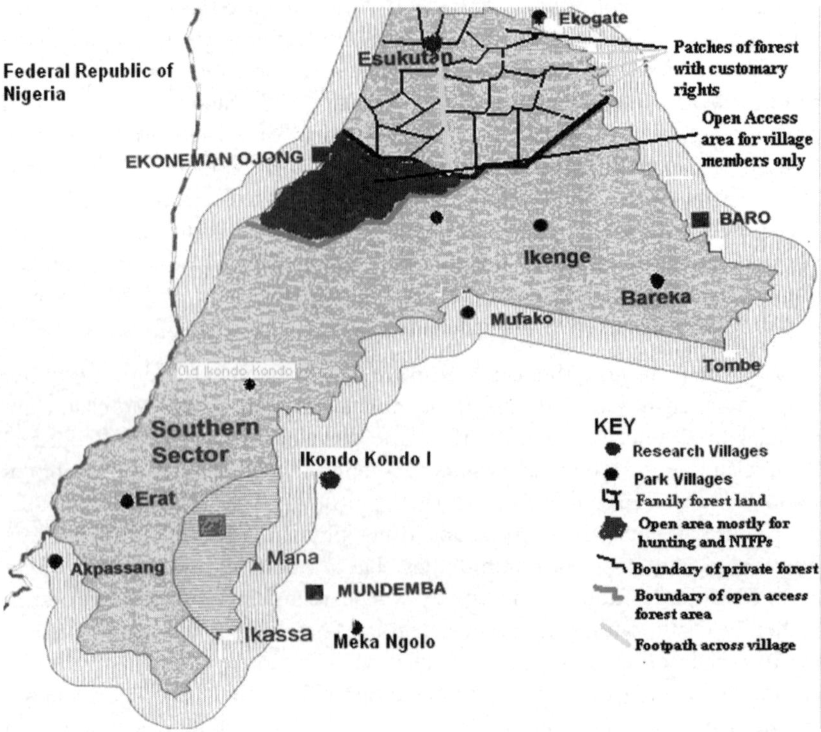

However, Esukutan villagers no longer allow access to foreigners but ask villagers to do the extraction and sell to buyers who must identify themselves at the level of the indigenous chief and the village council. They do so because the forest belongs to them and if people extract everything from their forest their survival will be threatened. At the household level, every family member has an obligation to protect the family forest which also has clear boundaries and well-known neighbours. Unauthorized exploitation is sanctioned by the owners, but if not successful a referral is made to higher authorities. Usually, the lineage head is contacted first, the indigenous chief could be contacted directly who may on his perception of the matter transfer it to the village council for public hearing. If trespass was detected in the "open access but limited to village members forest", then the issue becomes an inter-village affair. The culprit will be arrested and or reported to his or her village of origin. A date will be fixed for hearing; usually in a third party village. The sanctions are usually heavy for such crimes since all three villages are concerned. The defaulter's village is responsible to make sure the fine is paid and to slam harsher sanctions against the culprit for the disgrace and shame brought to it. The harshness of sanctions is partly accountable for the relative compliance in the area as no cases were recorded in the past 15 years.

An indigenous indicator for measuring success and effectiveness of their protection activities is the observation that illegal exploiters no longer encroach. This in no way means misbehavior is effectively constrained by indigenous institutions. Tolerated but bad economic practices by village members in Esukutan and Ikondo Kondo I put bush meat under siege and cause scarcity of NTFPs. These economic activities are fueled by Nigerian buyers whose bid to come closer to the source to reduce cost, have created footpaths in the Park through which valuable forest resources are smuggled to Nigeria and gun powder, bullets and riffles are smuggled in and sold to hunters. These have increased hunting pressures especially from 1981, when indigenes were prohibited from making new investments in the park. Villagers revealed that once they knew that ownership of their source of livelihood had changed hands people felt *"no need to protect what belongs to the government"* since *"government property is no man's property"*. Currently, hunting, fishing and farming goes on during formerly prohibited days of the weeks with impunity in the relocated Ikondo Kondo I. This reveal that relocation weakens indigenous management structures. Strong leadership facilitates effectiveness of institutions for forest use control and this is what obtained when government appointed chiefs were not empowered. Under this condition the presence of dwellers in the park is vital if illegal poachers are to be effectively prevented. So far, eco guards have not been able to control or regulate poachers. Inter-Ekpwe collaboration remains the best option since Ekpwe is also an important institution in villages in Nigeria, with same principles, rules and authority.

Disempowering indigenous institutions has been premised on only the narrow minded conservation theory that upholds only the ecological values in parks. It neglects the fact that most biodiversity hot-spots including Korup are also political and social hot-beds. The park accommodated human populations who are still bent on preserving its richness. Their property or use right that exist on family forest lands, free access to members to the open access forest and constraining foreigners to obtain permission, works well. Although competitive pressures tend to be reduced in this arrangement, more action is necessary in Esukutan village, where newcomers are the notorious hunters spending several months in the forest killing animals on the endangered species list. This action could be successful given their small, stable and highly homogenous populations. There are clearly defined boundaries, villagers get benefits if foreigners extract from their forest, there is effective monitoring, sanctions, and conflict resolution mechanisms (Ostrom, 2005). Relocation, a practice of the past has exhausted its credibility as a way of managing natural resources for poverty alleviation (Cernea et al., 2006). An innovative adaptive strategy to conserve the Korup National Park should reflect on why indigenous institutions have been ignored. Sharing benefits of parks is desirable but the absence of established institutions to safeguard the interest of indigenous communities and vest them the authority and responsibility to protect their source of livelihood based on centuries of innovative knowledge of forest resources causes resentment when anyone talks about relocation.

Conclusion

Theorizing national parks management strategies and bickering over their effectiveness as useful as they can be in the academia, only deliver as much as the words in which they are elaborated. Romanticizing and prescribing the strict enforcement of national park laws in the literature as the *cure-it-all* for the conservation problems only deter what actually constrains forest resources use and abuse in the Korup area. The Ekpwe provides an efficient system of rules and sanctions that have effectively responded to conservation challenges in the Korup National Park. This paper argues that the property right approach is not sufficient to ensure effective governance of natural resources. Kinship, indigenous associations, cosmologies and strong political legitimacy deserve at least equal attention. The Ekpwe association gains its power by its multi-functionality and linkage to almost every aspect of community life and livelihood and is therefore more efficient in the local management arena than state law and the national system of law enforcement. So far the job of keeping away illegal poachers has rested on the Ekpwe mechanism, which raises the question, if Ekpwe rules are effective on the ground, why are indigenous conservation institutions being ignored.

Korup forest peoples have lost confidence and would not support conservation efforts in the Korup National Park, as long as they are being alienated. As demonstrated, they have what it takes to properly secure the resources inside the national park. Moving away from the current resentments requires behavioural change not only through properly defined property rights as just a pure property right approach is insufficient. Responsibility and authority are critical success factors imbedded in the norms, rules and institutions of the Ekpwe. They are well understood by Korup park villagers and this works better than the largely unknown government national park laws.

References

Agrawal, A. 1995. Population Pressure = Forest Degradation: An Oversimplistic Equation? Silviculture. Unasylva 46/2: 50-58.

Agrawal, A. 2001. Common Property Institutions and Sustainable Governance of Resources. World Development. 29/10: 1649-1672.

Agrawal, A., Gibson, C. 1999. Enchantment and disenchantment: The role of community in natural resource conservation. World Development. 27/4: 629-649.

Ascher, W. 2000: Understanding Why Governments in Developing Countries Waste Natural Resources in Environment. Environment: 8-18

Becker, C. D., Gibson, C. C. 1998. The Lack of Institutional Supply: Why a Strong Indigenous Community in Western Ecuador Fails to Protect its Forest, Forest resources and institutions. Forestry Working Papers: pp 223.

Berkes, F., David, F., Bonnie, J. M., James, M. A. 1989. The Benefits of the Commons. Nature. 340/6229: 91-93.

Begossi, A. 1988. Knowledge on the use of natural resources: contributions to local management. In: Hens, L., Borden, R., Suzuki, S., Caravello, G. (eds.): Research in Human Ecology. An interdisciplinary Overview. VUB press. Belgium: 39-51.

Binswanger, H. P., Pingali, P. 1988. Technological priorities for farming in Sub-Saharan Africa. The World Bank Research Observer. 3/1: 81-98

Borrini-Feyerabend, G., Kothari, A., Oviedo, G., 2004. Indigenous and Local Communities and Protected Areas. Towards Equity and Enhanced Conservation. Guidance on policy and practice for Co-managed Protected Areas and Community Conserved Areas. IUCN Guideline Series 1: pp 139.

Boserup, E. 1965. The Conditions of Agricultural Growth: The Economics of Agrarian Change under Population Pressure. G. Allen and Unwin, London. Aldine, Chicago: 124 pp.

Boserup, E. 1981. Population and Technological Change: A Study of Long Term Trends, University of Chicago Press. Chicago.

Burke, S. M., Mitchell, N. 2007. People as Ecological Participants in Ecological Restoration. Restoration Ecology. 15/2: 348-350

Cernea, M. M. (ed.) 1991. Putting People First; Sociological Variables in Rural Development. 2nd edition. World Bank Publication. Oxford University Press. London: pp 600.

Cernea, M. M. 2003. For a new economics of resettlement: a sociological critique of the compensation principle. International Social Science Journal 55/175: 37- 45

Cernea, M. M., Schmidt-Soltau, K. 2003. The end of forcible displacements? Making conservation and impoverishment incompatible. Policy Matters 12: 42-51.

Cernea, M. M., Schmidt-Soltau, K. 2006. Poverty Risks and National Parks: Policy Issues in Conservation and Resettlement. World Development. 34/10: 1808-1830.

Chakraborty, R. N., 2001. Stability and outcomes of common property institutions in forestry: evidence from the Terai region of Nepal, Analysis. Ecological Economics. 36: 341-353.

Chambers, R. 1995. Rural Development: Putting the last first. Prentice Hall, UK.

Danish Ministry of Foreign Affairs (DMFA), 2002: Culture and Development Strategy and Guideline. Danish Ministry of Foreign Affairs Information Office. Denmark. pp 26.

Davis, K. 1991. Population and resources: fact and interpretation. In: Davis, K., Bernstam, M. (eds.): Resources, environment, and population: present knowledge, future options, Population and Development Review. The Population Council. Oxford University Press. New York.

Demsetz, H. 1967. Toward a theory of property rights. American Economic. Review. 57/2: 347-359.

Edwards, J. C., Johnson, E. K., Molidor, J. B. 1990. The interview in the admission process. Academic Medicine. 65/3: 167-77

Ehrlich, P. R., Ehrlich, A. H., 1991. Healing the Planet: Strategies for Resolving the Environmental Crisis. Addison Wesley Publishing Company. Reading, MA: pp366.

Ellis, F. 2000. Rural Livelihoods and Diversity in Developing Countries. Oxford University Press. Oxford.

Eyong, C. T. 2007. Indigenous Knowledge and Sustainable Development in Africa: Case Study on Central Africa. In: Boon, E. K., Hens, L. (eds.): Indigenous Knowledge Systems and Sustainable Development: Relevance for Africa. Tribes and Tribals. Special Volume No. 1: 121-140.

Eyong, C. T., Gerke, S., 2007: Management of National/Natural Parks and Biodiversity Conservation in Africa: An Experience in South West Cameroon. Presented in Parks Conference, Accra (Ghana): 2-6 April, 2007. pp25.

Food and Agricultural Organisation (FAO) 2006. Global Forest Resources Assessment 2005, Chapter 8: Progress towards sustainable forest management: 133-135.

Frazer, E. 1999. The Problem of Communitarian Politics: Unity and conflict. Oxford University Press: Oxford.

Geisler, C. 2003. A new kind of trouble: evictions in Eden. International Social Science Journal. 55/175: 69-78

Gibson, C. C. 1999. Politicians and Poachers: The Political Economy of Wildlife Policy in Africa. Political Economy of Institutions and Decisions. Cambridge University Press. Cambridge. pp 262

Hanna, S., Munasinghe, M. 1995. Property rights and the environment: social and ecological issues. Beijer International Institute of Ecological Economics and the World Bank: ppVII-141

Ives, J. D., Messerli, B. 1989. The Himalayan Dilemma: Reconciling Development and Conservation. Routledge. New York.

Kimmerer, R. W. 2002. Weaving traditional ecological knowledge into biological education: a call to action. BioScience. 52/5: 432-438.

Korup Park Management Plan 2002. A management plan for Korup National Park and its peripheral zones - 2003-2007. Ministry of Environment and Forest, Yaounde: xvii-170.

Korup Project. 1999. The Socio-Economic Impact of the Relocation in the context national park management: The case of Ikondo Kondo I Pilot Project. Korup Project Report: I – 56

Long, N. 2002. An actor-oriented approach to development intervention. Background paper prepared for APO Meeting in Tokyo (Japan): 22-26 April, 2002.

Malleson, R. 2000. Forest livelihoods in southwest province, Cameroon: an evaluation of the Korup experience. Department of Anthropology, University College London.

McKean, M. A. 1998. Common Property: What Is It, What Is It Good For, and What Makes It Work? In: Gibson, C., McKean, M. A., Ostrom, E. (eds.): Forest resources and institutions: Forests, Trees and People Programme. Forestry Department Working Paper 3.

McShane, T. O., Wells, M. P. (eds.) 2004. Getting Biodiversity Projects to Work: Towards More Effective Conservation and Development. Biology and Resource Management Series. Columbia University Press: pp464

Moegenburg, S. M., Levey, D. J. 2002. Prospects for conserving biodiversity in Amazonian extractive reserves. Ecology Letters. 5/3: 320-324.

North, D. C. 1989. Institutional change and economic history. Journal of Institutional and Theoretical Economics. 145: 238–245

Oates, J. F. 1996. African Primates: Status Survey and Conservation Action Plan. Revised Edition, IUCN, Gland (Switzerland).

Oates, J. F. 1999. Myth and Reality in the Rain Forest – How Conservation Strategies are failing in West Africa. University of California Press. Berkley, USA. Pp 340.

Obase, T. M. 1995. Korup Project Management: Achievements and Problems. Ministry of Environment and Forestry. Cameroon. Pp18.

Obase, T. M., Victor, B. S. 1997. Donor collaboration and institutional linkage management in multi-donor projects: Korup National Park Project, Korup Archives. Pp15.

Ophuls, W. 1973. Leviathan or oblivion. In: Daly, H. E. (ed.): Toward a steady state economy. Freeman, Oakland, CA: 215-230.

Ostrom, E. 1990. Governing the Commons: The Evolution of Institutions for Collective Action, Political Economy of Institutions and Decisions, Cambridge University Press. Cambridge.

Ostrom, E. 1999. Institutional Rational Choice: an assessment of the Institutional Analysis and Development Framework. In: Sabatier, P. A. (ed.): Theories of the Policy Process. Westview Press. Boulder. CO: 35-71.

Ostrom, E. 2003. How types of goods and property rights jointly affect collective action. Journal of Theoretical Politics 15/3: 239-270.

Ostrom, E. 2005. Understanding Institutional Diversity. Princeton University Press.

Posner, R. 1977. Economic analysis of law. Little, Brown & Co, Boston, MA.

Putnam, R. D. 2000. Bowling Alone: the collapse and revival of American Community. Simon and Schuster. New York.

Poteete, A. R., Ostrom, E. 2004. Heterogeneity, Group Size and Collective Action: The Role of Institutions in Forest Management, Development and Change. 35/3: 435-461.

Simmons, R. T., Smith, F. L. (Jr.), Georgia, P. 1996. The tragedy of the commons revisited: politics versus private property. Center for Private Conservation. Washington.

Sharpe, B. 1998. First the Forest: Conservation, Community and Participation in South-West Cameroon. Journal of the international African Institute. 68/1: 25-45.

Smith, M. K. 2001. 'Community' in the encyclopedia of informal education. Internet source: http://www.infed.org/community/community.htm.

Schmidt-Soltau, K. 2004. The Costs of Rainforests Conservation: Local responses owards Integrated Conservation and Development Projects in Cameroon. Journal of Contemporary African Studies. 22/1: 93-117.

Schmidt-Soltau, K., Nkwatoh, A., Meboka, M., Saga, P. 2004. Evaluation of the technical, finacial and organizational sustainability of village natural resource management committees in the support zone of Korup National Park. GTZ Report: pp 65.

Tiffen, M., Mortimore, M., Gichuki, F. 1994. More People, Less Erosion. Environmental Recovery in Kenya. John Wiley. New York.

Tucker, C. M. 1999. Private versus Common Property Forests: Forest Conditions and Tenure in a Honduran Community. Human Ecology. 27/2: 201-230

Warren, A. R., Cara, E. W., Marney, T., Michael, N., Jennifer, M. K., Susan, M. L., Julie, A. S. 1999. Assessing the Effectiveness of a Training Program for Interviewing Child Witnesses. Applied Developmental Science. 3/2: 128-135.

Western, D., Wright, R. M. (eds) 1994. Natural Connections: Perspectives in Community-based Conservation. Island Press: Pp 600.

World Bank Group 2003. Culture and Poverty: Learning and Research at the World Bank. Washington DC.

World Health Organization (WHO) 2006. Global Forest Resources Assessment (2005), Progress towards sustainable forest management Chapter 8 Progress towards sustainable forest management, Pp. 134.

Chapter 6

New Wildlife Policy, Local Attitudes, and Wildlife Distribution in JUKUMU Wildlife Management Area, Selous Game Reserve, Tanzania

Devesh Rustagi

Introduction

Over the past few decades, the idea of integrating conservation and development has received increasing attention by both conservation organisations and international development agencies. In fact, attempts to integrate conservation and development were made as early as the 1970s through UNESCO's Man and Biosphere Program and subsequently through the Integrated Conservation Development Program. The Convention on Biodiversity, which was unanimously adopted at the 1992 Earth Summit, also aimed at integrating conservation and development. The Summit emphasised that the effectiveness of protected area as a conservation strategy depends not on its existence as an ecological island but on its integration and management in a broader land use context, with adequate participation by stakeholders, including local communities living on the fringe of protected areas (CBD, 1992).[1] In 2003, in its message to the CBD, the fifth World Park Congress at Durban also endorsed this approach (IUCN, 2003).

In adherence to this trend and after years of pursuing a strict conservation policy, the Tanzanian government passed the Wildlife Policy of Tanzania in 1998. The cornerstone of this policy is the creation of Wildlife Management Areas (WMAs), which are wildlife reserves established on village lands and managed by inter-village associations, with guidance and support from the state Wildlife Division. WMAs are expected to bring wildlife habitats on village lands that fall outside the purview of protected areas, such as dispersal sites, migration corridors, and breeding sites, under legal protection. This habitat expansion is considered especially important for wide-ranging species, such as elephant, buffalo, and wildebeest. In return, the local communi-

---

[1] See www.biodiv.org

ties from the participating villages are entitled to benefits from wildlife found in WMAs, such as wildlife utilization quotas, employment benefits, and revenue from trophy hunting and photographic tourism. In this way, WMAs are expected to encourage the local communities to manage wildlife so that they can continue to benefit from wildlife in the long run.

Though the new policy is definitely a step forward, it has also engendered much debate and discussion on the concept of benefit sharing and devolution of power. For instance, Goldman (2003) argues that even though local communities are now included in the new policy, they are still not allowed to participate actively and to define the ways in which wildlife is managed. For instance, the Wildlife Division solely decides the quota for trophy and meat hunting in WMAs without consulting the local communities. In case the communities disagree, they may file a petition, but the decision is finally made by the Division. There are many such cases in which the Division still holds overall decision-making rights over wildlife and is unwilling to transfer them to the local communities. Seen from this perspective, some argue that the new policy has become a new tool to dispossess the local communities of their customary land from which they could generate several local livelihood benefits (Neumann, 1997; Shauri, 1999; Songorwa, 1999; Sosovele et al., 1999). Others suspect that such programs and policies are not designed for genuine benefit sharing, but instead for reducing the community opposition to protected areas (Songorwa, 1999; Wells et al., 1992). Consequently, the new policy is still seen by some as a top-down approach, with little difference from fortress methods it seeks to replace. Not surprisingly, critics suggest that without community partnership, wildlife does not have much of a future.

This ongoing interest in the new policy in Tanzania, as well as elsewhere, has led to a debate on how and under what conditions the new policy can improve and strengthen relationships between the local communities and wildlife. Since the new policy is based on participation and benefit sharing, one of the key ingredients of such a debate is examining the attitudes of the local communities towards wildlife. Many such studies (Allendorf et al., 2006; Baral et al., 2007; Boer et al., 1998; Gillingham et al., 1999; Lewis et al., 1990; Mehta et al, 1998; Walpole et al., 2001; Weladji et al., 2003) have generally found that genuine benefit sharing builds up positive attitudes, providing extended support for wildlife conservation, whereas higher wildlife induced costs build up negative attitudes, leading to hostile people-wildlife interface. Therefore, an examination of local costs, benefits, and attitudes towards wildlife are important in guiding wildlife policy and management decisions, as well as in generating a baseline for assessing the success and failure of policies in future (Gillingham et al, 1999; Allendorf et al., 2006; Weladji et al., 2003).

Equally significant ingredient of this debate is the impact that such policies have on wildlife and the ecosystems it inhabits. For instance, Lewis and Alpert (1997) reported that due to a lack of systematic census of wildlife, there was no direct evidence that the management of trophy hunting benefited wildlife conservation in Zambia. Consequently, a reliable wildlife census is an important component of benefit-sharing mechanisms. It can provide a valuable feedback not only on whether the new policy is conserving wildlife, but also how to adjust the new policy to improve wildlife conservation (Novaro et al., 2000).

This paper examines how the allocation of wildlife related benefits has influenced the attitudes of the local communities' as well as the distribution of wildlife in JUKUMU[2] WMA, which lies to the north of the Selous Game Reserve - a world heritage site. The study is based on the fieldwork that I conducted from February to March 2005 as a part of my Master's thesis. Here, I present an overview of the attitudes of the local communities towards wildlife in relation to qualitative measures of wildlife related costs and benefits. Further, I also present an overview of the effect of the new policy on key wildlife species and their dispersal patterns in Gonabis, which is the main hunting block of JUKUMU. I find that the new wildlife policy has led to mixed attitudes towards wildlife conservation. While most respondents support wildlife conservation, oppose the construction of a dam on river Ruvu, which will lead to the submergence of Gonabis, and consider Gonabis as an important sector for government spending, few support outright conversion of Gonabis into agricultural land. In general, the attitudes vary with wildlife related costs and benefits. Similarly, the effect of the new policy on wildlife is also mixed. The population of key herbivores in Gonabis, such as wildebeest, zebra, buffalo, impala, and elephant has remained fairly stable in the post new policy period. Despite stable numbers, poaching is still seen as the biggest threat to wildlife in Gonabis. The population of key carnivore species, such as lions, has declined in Gonabis; excessive trophy hunting by tourists was reported as the reason behind this decline. No disturbance was reported in the pattern of wildlife migration between Gonabis and Selous. The paper is organized as follows: it begins with a background of the study area, followed by a description of criteria used in the study,

---

[2] JUKUMU is an abbreviation for Jumiya Ya Kuhifadhi Na Matumizi Bora Ya Maliasili Ukutu, which is the Swahili name of the community based organisation responsible for the management of the WMA.

wildlife related benefits, costs, attitudes, and wildlife distribution. The last section summarizes key findings from this study.

The study area

Selous Game Reserve

Selous Game Reserve is the second largest protected area in the world and the largest in Africa. It covers 48,000 km^2 or roughly 5 % of Tanzania's land area. The Reserve is one of the oldest protected areas in Africa and home to some of the largest and most important populations of elephant, buffalo, Nyasa wildebeest, lion, wild dog, crocodile, and hippo in Africa (Baldus et al., 2003; Baldus, 2006; WCMC, 2003).

The history of the reserve dates back to over a hundred years, when the German colonial administration (1891-1919) established four reserves in the region. Subsequently, over the course of a decade (1936-1947), the boundaries of the reserve were enlarged several times to include wildlife migration routes and dispersal areas. This expansion, together with 'villagization' (Ujama) and a sleeping sickness prevention program, led to a relocation of the local villages to areas adjacent to the reserve. In 1974, the reserve was legally established as Selous Game Reserve. The effect of this relocation and legal establishment on the local villages was the loss of access to bushmeat, which formed an important part of the local people's diet (WCMC, 2003). In the 1980s, Selous witnessed a major wildlife depletion: its elephant population declined from an estimated 110,000 in the 1970s to 55,000 in 1986, and further to 30,000 in 1989. Likewise, its rhino population declined from 3,000 to 300 during the same period (Siege, 2000). This immense decline had its roots in a strict and restrictive wildlife policy, villages bordering Selous, a poor financial base of the poor governance (Baldus et al., 2003). Even though wildlife depletion came to a halt with the launch of Operation Uhai in 1989, it was recognized that the immediate and long-term threat to wildlife came from poaching for meat and trophies, and that local antagonism will only lessen if wildlife is seen to benefit local people (Baldus, 2006).

Alarmed by such a drastic decline in the population of key mammal species, the Tanzanian government launched the 'Selous Conservation Programme' in 1987, with assistance from Germany. One of the three fundamental components of the program was community-based management through sustainable use of wildlife. This was achieved through: a) identifying future WMAs, b) establishing inter-village associations, such as JUKUMU, for managing wildlife in WMAs, and c) recruiting village game scouts to monitor and protect wildlife in these areas. Under the program, five areas bordering Selous were identified as potential WMA sites: Songea District, Tunduru District, Liwale, Rufiji, and JUKUMU. The study was conducted in the JUKUMU Pilot WMA (JWMA), which is also known as the Mgeta River Buffer Zone (MRBZ). JWMA was selected, because it is the oldest pilot WMA in Tanzania. The involvement of the local communities in the area is almost two decades old, and until the late 1980s, was preceded by fortress conservation methods. JWMA also serves as a seasonal wildlife dispersal area for wildlife in the northern sector of Selous.

JUKUMU Wildlife Management Area

JWMA is a narrow strip of land, which extends from Mkulazi Forest Reserve in the east to Mikumi National Park in the west. It is bordered on the north and west by 22 villages, which are members of JWMA. The villages comprise nearly 8,000 households and have a population of over 45,000 (GTZ, 2003). The wildlife rich region and the main hunting block of JWMA is called Gonabis. An inter-village association called JUKUMU society manages JWMA. It is run by elected members and a council comprising three members from each village. The society is responsible for conserving wildlife in Gonabis as well as for securing wildlife related benefits for the villages. For instance, the society executes hunting on behalf of the villages, manages negotiations with tourist and hunting companies, and employs village game scouts, who are responsible for monitoring wildlife in Gonabis and assisting local people in managing wildlife related problems.

Under the JWMA scheme, the following main benefits are available to the local villages: a) annual fee from Sable Mountain Lodge, which is located on the WMA land, b) annual fee from Intercon hunting company for issuing hunting permits within Gonabis, c) local employment opportunities, and d) wildlife utilization quota of three buffaloes and 13 wildebeest per village per year. Bushmeat from Gonabis is sold by JWMA to individual households at a subsidized price of nearly Tsh. 300 per kg. Currently, this is the main benefit available to the local people at an individual level. Other benefits, such as revenues from hunting and tourist companies, are used for community level projects.

The Village Zone

Of the 22 villages forming JWMA, only eight have a direct border with Gonabis. It is these eight villages together with Gonabis that form the main focus of this study. The villages are listed in Table 1 and are hereafter collectively called the 'village zone'. It covers an area of almost 530 km^2, of which only 116 km^2 is revenue land. There are 2,143 households residing in this zone with a total population of 13,097 (GTZ, 2003). Because the data on Kibulumo village was not available, the paper focuses on seven villages from the zone.

Table 1 Demographic profile of villages bordering Gonabis

No.	Village Name	Ward Name	Area (ha)	Population	Households
1	Bonye	Bwakira	9985	3509	585
2	Mbwade	Bwakira	6665	2685	384
3	Kongwa	Mvuha	8816	1153	231
4	Tulo	Mvuha	5373	1023	205
5	Magogoni	Selembala	14958	865	148
6	Bwira Chini	Selembala	3272	2961	370
7	Bwira Juu	Selembala	3849	881	220
8	Kibulumo	Selembala	Data not available		
	Total		**52918**	**13097**	**2143**

Source: GTZ, 2003.

Most villages display a low level of socio-economic development. While Bonye, Mbwade, and Magogoni have access to hand pump water, the remaining villages rely on river water. A primary health care facility is available in four villages and the remaining three villages (Kongwa, Bwila Chini and Bwila Juu), which are relatively remote and inaccessible during the wet season, do not have ready access to primary health care. Concerning transport accessibility, only Bonye and Mbwade are accessible throughout the year, Bwila Juu and Bwila Chini are accessible only during the dry season, while Tulo, Kongwa and Magogoni are located at a distance of 5 to 10 km from the nearest bus stop. In addition, none of the villages have electricity and communication facilities. All the villages, however, do have access to a primary school.

Most households in the village zone rely on rain-fed subsistence farming. The presence of Tsetse fly in the region prevents people from rearing livestock; the Masaai community being an exception. During lean agricultural periods, most households also engage in non-farm activities, either as wage laborers or as small businessmen. Due to the subsistence nature of the local household economy, most people show a high dependence on wildlife found in Gonabis. The most important of these is bushmeat, which is a major source of animal protein for the local people (Baldus et al., 2003). However, owing to logistical problems and limited purchasing power, the society is able to harvest only 30-80 % of the available quota.

Gonabis hunting block

The Gonabis hunting block is situated to the north of Selous, across river Mgeta. It is a part of the larger Mgeta River Buffer Zone and covers about 250-300 km^2 of vast alluvial plain, bounded by river Ruvu on the north, river Mgeta on the south and east, and river Mombwe to the west. During the wet season, which lasts from March to May, Gonabis turns into a seasonal wetland and rainwater starts receding only in the month of June. Most of Gonabis is covered by open woodland, with smaller areas of scrub, dense woodland, and riparian forest. These habitats support a high density of wildebeest, elephant, buffalo, zebra, giraffe, impala, waterbuck, reedbuck, and sable antelope. Among large carnivores, hyena and leopard are common, while lion, wild dog, and cheetah are seen occasionally.

Methodology

Criteria for attitudes towards wildlife

Allendorf et al. (2006) define attitude as: a human psychological tendency expressed by evaluating a particular object with favour or disfavour. Attitude consists of beliefs which are associations people establish between object and various attributes. Attitudes towards wildlife are influenced by several factors. Among them perceptions, wildlife costs, and wildlife benefits are considered important (Allendorf et al., 2006; Baral et al., 2007; Walpole et al., 2001). Of these, wildlife benefits were found to play an important role only when benefits were experienced at an individual level. Societal level benefits were found not to generate significant influence on attitudes. Similarly, negative attitudes towards wildlife were found to be associated with higher conservation costs in the form of higher forgone opportunities, higher crop, livestock, and human losses from wildlife (Boer et al., 1998; Baral et al., 2007; Walpole et al., 2001). For instance, Boer and Baquete (1998) found that local communities living on the fringe of Maputo Elephant Reserve in Mozambique had negative attitudes when they suffered crop damages by wildlife.

With the exception of a few studies (for instance Mehta et al., 1998), most studies find either weak or no significant association between socio-economic as well as demographic factors and attitudes (Boer et al., 1998; Heiner et al., 2007). Allendorf et al. (2006) argue that socio-economic variables affect attitudes indirectly by influencing perceptions. In this study, I consider people's perceptions, benefits, and losses in ascertaining the local community's attitude towards wildlife. In addition, I use only qualitative measures of costs and benefits.

Criteria for wildlife distribution

I use three key sources to study the effect of the new policy on wildlife: a) Systematic Reconnaissance Flight (SRF) Surveys, b) Interviews with JUKUMU Chairperson and Community Wildlife Officer, and c) Group discussion with village game scouts and local people at the selected villages.

In assessing the effect of a policy on wildlife, Lewis and Alpert (1997) recommend collecting information on trends in population of hunted species, such as wildlife densities, age structure, and reproductive rates. In the main thesis, a Distance Sampling method was used to report density estimates of frequently hunted species in Gonabis, such as wildebeest, impala, and zebra. But the results from this estimation are not discussed here. Instead, the paper relies on a review of four SRF Surveys conducted by Frankfurt Zoological Society in collaboration with the Tanzania Wildlife Conservation Monitoring. The purpose of these surveys was to identify the distribution of local and flagship species in Gonabis, which was covered as a part of the 'Outside North Buffer Zone'.[3] All four SRF surveys focused only on large herbivores and were conducted during the dry season. Despite this limitation,[4] the surveys provide a reliable means to monitor the distribution of herbivores over a decade.

Owing to the seasonal migration by wildlife between Gonabis and Selous, estimating wildlife densities through SRF surveys not only presents formidable challenges, but its interpretation also becomes weak. Novaro et al. (2000) argue that if non-hunted areas are typically adjacent to hunted areas, game dispersal into hunted areas could be a widespread process and may contribute significantly to the recruitment of wildlife in hunting areas. Consequently, dispersal and not just reproduction in hunted areas must be considered while examining the effect of a policy on wildlife populations. Because Gonabis borders the tourism zone of Selous, wildlife movement along the corridors between Selous and Gonabis is important in examining the

[3] Though Gonabis is covered in all the surveys as a part of the outside North, most animal sightings are reported from habitats located in Gonabis, with the adjoining areas reporting considerably lower densities of large herbivores. Therefore, the population estimates for the entire Outside North can be assumed as representing the population estimates for Gonabis.

[4] SRF surveys are limited by area coverage, reduction in visibility caused by vegetation, time of survey, high speed of the aircraft, and observer bias. These factors might lead to an underestimation of the survey results.

wildlife distribution. In addition, I also followed the recommendations by Ebregt and Greve (2000) and Gynne and Croze (2004) to identify key criteria for assessing wildlife distribution in Gonabis. These include: a) local and flagship species found in the area; b) distribution of flagship species in various ecosystem types; c) problematic species, such as crop and livestock raiding species, and d) corridor function of the area for migrating species. In line with the argument put forward by Ebregt and Greve (2000), a review of only the most important species is presented. Interviews and group discussions were used to achieve this.

Criteria for village selection

The study was administered in three of the seven villages in the village zone. The villages were selected using the following criteria:

a. <u>Ward location</u>: Villages surrounding Gonabis fall in three administrative wards, Selembala, Mvuha, and Bwakira. One village from each ward was selected to represent differences in socio-economic development, access to Gonabis, and wildlife related costs and benefits.

b. <u>Land contrbution to JWMA</u>: Table 2 shows that villages vary in their land contribution to JWMA. While in villages, such as Magogoni, per capita land contribution is as high as 15.99 ha, in others, such as Bwira Chini, it is very low. It is likely that this variation in land contribution affects people's attitudes towards wildlife.

Table 2: Village land under JMWA

Village	Ward	WMA %	WMA/C
Bonye	Bwakira	78.57	2.24
Mbwade	Bwakira	77.19	1.92
Kongwa	Mvuha	75.62	5.78
Tulo	Mvuha	80.72	4.24
Magogoni	Selembala	94.59	15.99
Bwira Chini	Selembala	32.52	0.36
Bwira Juu	Selembala	56.01	2.45

Source: Selous Management Plan, 1998.

Notes: WMA % = percentage of a village land; WMA/C = WMA land per capita in hectares.

Based on these criteria, three villages representing different wards and different levels of land contribution to the proposed JWMA were selected: Bonye, Tulo, and Magogoni.

Data collection

45 households, representing nearly five percent of the total households in the three villages, were interviewed using household surveys to assess: a) benefits and losses from wildlife; b) attitudes and perceptions towards wildlife; and c) wildlife distribution in Gonabis. Interviews were conducted in Swahili with the help of a Tanzanian field assistant. The study presents only an overview of costs, benefits, attitudes and wildlife distribution.

On an average, a typical respondent in household interviews was 42 years old, had a family size of 5.5 members, six years of education, and 3.9 acres of land. 18 % of the respondents were female. A Kruskal-Wallis test suggests that there were no differences in age ($\chi^2_2 = 1.391$, P = 0.499), household size ($\chi^2_2 = 1.505$, P = 0.471) and education ($\chi^2_2 = 0.975$, P = 0.614) across the three villages. However, land ownership varies highly and significantly across the three villages, with Bonye households having larger land (Kruskal-Wallis $\chi^2_2 = 18.537$, P = 0.0001).

Household Attitudes and Wildlife Distribution

Wildlife losses and household attitudes towards wildlife conservation

Before the attitudes of the respondent households were ascertained, they were interviewed for a number of wildlife related benefits and losses.

Table 3: Benefits derived from Gonabis (no. of households)

Village	Bushmeat	Fish	NTFP
Bonye	16	16	16
Tulo	20	20	20
Magogoni	9	0	0
Total	45 (100)	36 (80)	36 (80)

Note: Figures in parenthesis indicate percentages.

Wildlife related benefits differ substantially across villages (Fisher's exact test, $P = 0.000$). All respondent households reported consuming bushmeat procured by JWMA from Gonabis, with 80 % also harvesting fish and non-timber forest products (NTFP). Wildlife in Gonabis is the main source of animal protein for local households. Given the subsistence nature of the local household economy, this contribution is considered important. The respondents expressed their appreciation for the legalisation of access to bushmeat, but they also complained that despite a subsidized price (roughly Tsh. 300 per kg) meat remains expensive and the wildlife quota is never fulfilled. During a group discussion, village game scouts explained that lack of funds to buy ammunition was the chief reason for this. 80 % respondents also collected NTFP, such as *Milala* and *Nyasi* (raw material used for making ropes), and *kambala*, *borassus* and *charaka* for making wooden poles, and timber from *mikongo*, *mninga* and *mvule* trees. Respondents from Magogoni reported that they harvest neither fish nor NTFP from Gonabis.

Besides benefits, the local households also bear wildlife related losses, which can be grouped into three categories: crop, livestock, and human. The local communities were asked to rank the problem species in each category.

Table 4: Crop raiding species in Gonabis

Village	Rank 1	Rank 2	Rank 3	Rank 4
Bonye	Elephant	Bushpig	Buffalo	Vervet
Tulo	Bushpig	Vervet	Baboon	Hippo
Magogoni	Baboon	Bushpig	Vervet	Hippo

The pattern of crop raiding by wildlife varies across villages. Elephants were rated high for causing crop damage in Bonye, bushpig in Tulo, and baboons in Magogoni. In rare cases, crop damages were attributed to buffaloes and hippos, but only during the dry season, when these animals migrate locally to Mombwe river habitats. In most cases, however, common animals, such as bushpig, baboons, and vervet monkey, were found responsible for crop damages. Since these animals are not necessarily confined to Gonabis, but are also found locally in the study villages, the crop damage caused by them cannot be attributed to wildlife in Gonabis. This weakens compensation claims made by most people in the study villages. Ashley et al. (2001) and Gillinghem and Lee (1999) also report similar findings.

Table 5: Livestock raiding species in Gonabis

Village	Rank 1	Rank 2	Rank 3	Rank 4
Bonye	Leopard	Lion	Crocodile	-
Tulo	Hyena	Crocodile	Caracal	Serval
Magogoni	Leopard	Hyena	Lion	Caracal

Livestock losses also vary across villages. In all the villages, large carnivores were held responsible for livestock losses. In Bonye and Magogoni, leopards were considered as a major threat to livestock, but in Tulo, hyenas were held responsible for most livestock losses. In 2004, the Masaai community in Bonye lost seven cattle and several goats, and in defense, a lion and a leopard were killed. In Magogoni, hyenas killed a cow and several goats in the same year. Livestock losses were found to be more common during the wet season when grass is tall and carnivores find suitable cover to hide. This is also the season when Gonabis becomes a flood plain and most herbivores migrate back to Selous. It might be that a higher livestock loss in the wet season is associated with the scarcity of prey in Gonabis. Since large carnivores typically inhabit Gonabis, the villages should be able to claim compensations for livestock losses under the new policy.

Table 6: Species responsible for human losses

Village	Rank 1	Rank 2	Rank 3	Rank 4
Bonye	Crocodile	Leopard	Lion	Buffalo
Tulo	Crocodile	Lion	Leopard	-
Magogoni	Crocodile	Hippo	-	-

In all the villages, crocodiles were responsible for the loss of human lives, but households from Tulo and Magogoni suffered the most. In Magogoni, crocodiles were responsible for 46 deaths in 1999 and five deaths in 2003. In Tulo, 10 people were severely mauled by crocodiles from 2000-2003. In Bonye, leopards were responsible for five deaths in the 1980s. Further, in 2002, two people were reportedly killed in an encounter with a buffalo and a hippo in Tulo and Magogoni respectively. Since 1974 no case of human-lion conflict was reported. The human losses owing to crocodiles have declined since 2003 after JWMA was awarded the right to hunt a limited number of Tanzania's CITES (Convention on International Trade in Endangered Species) quota of crocodiles in 2001-2002. This enabled the society to keep the crocodile population in control and at the same time gain additional benefits from the sale of their skin (GTZ, 2003).

An overview of wildlife related costs and benefits suggests that these vary across the studied villages. For instance, while local households in Bonye derive higher wildlife related benefits they also bear a high burden of crop losses mainly caused by elephants. In Tulo, while benefits are similar, the loss of human life due to wildlife was relatively high. In Magogoni, wildlife related benefits are lower in relation to the other villages, but the loss of human life was also the highest. Consequently, there exists a multitude of positive as well as negative wildlife impact on local livelihoods.

Table 7 reports perceptions of the respondents towards wildlife conservation. Irrespective of the differences in costs and benefits, all respondents strongly agreed that wildlife has a right to live, it is their moral duty to protect wildlife in Gonabis, and that it is important to conserve wildlife in Gonabis, for reasons ranging from consumptive use benefits to existence values. Further, all respondents strongly disagreed with the construction of

Kidunda dam on river Ruvu, that would lead to the submergence of Gonabis under water.

Table 7: Perceptions of the respondents towards wildlife conservation (%)

Attitude variable	Very Important	Important	Not Important
Importance of Gonabis	100	0	0
Attitude Variable	Strongly agree	Partially agree	Disagree
Wildlife in Gonabis has a right to live.	100	0	0
Moral duty to protect wildlife in Gonabis.	100	0	0
Gonabis should be protected because it provides bushmeat, which is a valuable source of animal protein.	100	0	0
Gonabis should be converted to agricultural land.	20	7	73
Do you support the idea of a dam construction on Ruvu that would lead to the submergence of Gonabis?	0	0	100

The villages differ strongly in their response to the conversion of Gonabis to an agricultural land (Fishers Exact Test, P = 0.000). 20 % respondents, all from Magogoni, strongly agreed that Gonabis should be converted to an agricultural land. Three reasons were sited for this: a) higher land contribution than any other village to WMA, b) fewer benefits derived from Gonabis, and c) higher wildlife related losses. The local households in Magogoni are neither compensated for higher land contribution, nor for higher wildlife related costs, but are rather given a similar share in wildlife benefits as the remaining villages. Massai and older men from Bonye also partially supported the conversion of Gonabis. Because the Masaai community does not eat game meat, bears a higher share of livestock losses, and is not allowed to graze cattle in Gonabis, there is little incentive for them to support wildlife conservation in Gonabis. Gillingham and Lee (1999) also report a mixed response in this category.

Table 8 reports priority sectors for government spending from a respondent's perspective. A large majority identified health and education as a priority sector for government spending. A non-trivial share (29 %) considered Gonabis as the second most important sector, while a majority (71 %) rated Gonabis as the third priority for government spending. A Fisher's exact test shows that ratings differ across the three villages (P = 0.000) and that the respondents who support the conversion of Gonabis into agricultural land, also rated Gonabis as less important for government spending (P = 0.000). Overall, Gonabis appears to be a moderately important sector for government spending, next only to health and education, and agricultural development.

Table 8: Priority sectors for government spending

Sector	Rank 1	Rank 2	Rank 3
Health and Education	42	0	1
Conservation in Gonabis	0	13	32
Drinking water	3	0	10
Agricultural development	0	32	2
Electricity	0	0	0
Communication	0	0	0
Total	45	45	45

Most respondents identified poaching as the main threat (80 %) to wildlife (Table 9). Baldus (2006) also reports that poaching is again on a rise in the area. The remaining respondents (all from Magogoni) rated trophy hunting in Gonabis as the main threat. A few respondents (again all from Magogoni) also identified poor management as a threat. Trophy hunting is also considered as a cause behind wildlife depletion in the other two villages. Hunting decisions are taken exclusively at the Division level and the local communities are never consulted in the selection of hunting companies, species to be hunted, and the designation of a hunting quota. The hunting industry in Tanzania is strongly opposed to granting the local community any decision making power and puts considerable pressure on the Division not to grant such rights. This reflects well on apprehensions raised by many authors concerning active local participation in the decision-making process with respect to the management of wildlife in WMAs. The concern of the local communities is not unfounded, for in many places hunting quotas have indeed resulted in over-hunting. The Tapika-Nagarmbe pilot WMA is an example, where hunting quotas have resulted in a serious damage to several years of hard work involving the local communities (Baldus, 2006; IWDG, 2004). In Gonabis itself, it has led to a severe decline in the population of top carnivore species, such as lions.

Table 9: Threats to Gonabis

Threat	Rank 1	Rank 2	Rank 3
Poaching	36	9	0
Trophy hunting	9	36	0
Poor management	0	0	9

Like previous studies, I did not find an association between socio-economic variables (age, family size, land holding, gender and education) and attitudes towards the conversion of Gonabis into an agricultural land, rating of priority sectors for government spending, and threat perception of the communities (Mann-Whitney Test, $P > 0.05$).

Wildlife distribution and migration patterns in Gonabis

The key wildlife species found in Gonabis include: wildebeest, zebra, impala, elephant, buffalo, giraffe, and lion. The Systematic Reconnaissance Flight Surveys (SRF) of the Selous Game Reserve and the areas adjoining the reserve have been useful in studying the effect of the new policy on key herbivore populations. The details are given below:

<u>1989 Census Report</u>: The census was conducted shortly after the introduction of the new policy. It is therefore taken as the base year for monitoring subsequent changes in the distribution of herbivores in Gonabis. During the census, Gonabis recorded the highest density of large herbivores, with Mgeta habitats recording a density of greater than 600 animals per km^2. The census also reported a high density of herbivores in the vicinity of Gonabis. This was mainly due to a high concentration of wildebeest and zebra, which recorded densities as high as 600 and 200 animals per km^2. Gonabis was the only area in the Selous ecosystem to have such a high density. However, the density of buffaloes and impalas was reported to be low and no elephant sightings were listed.

<u>1994 Census Report</u>: Gonabis and Kilombero Game Controlled Area recorded the highest concentration of large herbivores in the Selous ecosystem. Again, wildebeest and zebra densities were high, with the former being still the highest. The density and distribution of buffaloes improved considerably in Gonabis and the adjoining areas. In fact, the buffalo population in Gonabis was next only to Selous and Kilombero Game Controlled Area. The density of impalas was also reported to be high, with population estimates next only to Selous. This time elephants were also sighted in Gonabis and their density was estimated at 20 animals per km^2.

<u>1998 Census Report</u>: Gonabis continued to have a high density of large herbivores. The density of wildebeest was reported to be high, higher than other areas in the Selous ecosystem. The population estimates for the entire Outside North were 30,000. The density of zebras was also reported to be high. Again, most wildebeest and zebra were observed in areas located along the boundary of Gonabis and Selous. Buffalo and impala densities also remained the same, with most sightings reported in the areas between Gona-

bis and Selous. The elephant population was reported to be stable as in 1994.

2002 Census Report: As in earlier surveys, Gonabis reported a high concentration of herbivores. The density of wildebeest, buffalo, impala, and zebra were again reported to be high. The estimates for wildebeest and impala were second only to Selous. Buffalo densities were again estimated to be high; in fact all areas outside Selous recorded higher densities. This was also the case with elephant, impala, wildebeest, and zebra population.

From the SRF surveys, it appears that the density of key wildlife species, such as wildebeest, zebra, impala, elephant, and buffalo has remained stable over the years. To further ascertain the status of wildlife in Gonabis, a group discussion with the village game scouts and an interview with the JUKUMU chairperson were also conducted. During the discussion, it was found that wildlife in Gonabis is mainly found in 21 critical habitats, most of which are located along the rivers bordering Gonabis (see Rustagi, 2005). The game scouts reported regular wildlife sighting in these areas. For instance, elephant population was reported to be stable, varying between 100-300 animals, and largely confined to habitats along river Mgeta. The buffalo population was reported across nine riparian habitats, with a resident population of 1500-2000 individuals in almost nine groups.[5]

A buffalo herd in the Baobab tree area

Among large carnivores, reliable estimates could be obtained only for lions. All sources consistently reported that due to excessive tourist hunting, the social structure of lion prides has been destroyed, leading to small prides varying in size from 2-3 individuals. The chairman of JUKUMU also reported that a decade ago almost 15-20 prides were found in Gonabis, but

[5] Given the fact that zebra, impala and wildebeest, occure in large numbers in Gonabis, such estimates could not be obtained for them.

today their number varies from zero to at the most two. It is not surprising therefore that most households also rated trophy hunting alongside poaching as the main threat to wildlife found in Gonabis. This is perhaps also the reason that lion related livestock and human loses have declined over the years. The population of other large carnivores, such as hyenas and leopards, was reported to be stable with frequent sightings. Wild dog sightings were rare, but this is because wild dogs are only occasionally found in Gonabis and are a wide-ranging species.

Given the importance of wildlife dispersal in estimating wildlife distribution, data was also collected on wildlife migration patterns. As mentioned earlier, wildlife distribution in Gonabis varies across seasons: wildlife move not only locally within Gonabis but also from Gonabis to Selous and vice versa. The village game scouts reported that wildlife uses five main migration routes: Niamigadou in the west, Fumbili, Mpera chapa and Lukengezua in the south, and Tangireni in the east. Migration occurs at least two times in a year: At the onset of the dry season in June, large herbivores migrate from Selous to Gonabis; the cycle is reversed with the onset of the wet season in March. During Distance Sampling transects in Gonabis, conducted just before the onset of the wet season, wildlife was seen migrating both to Gonabis and Selous. The village game scouts reported no disturbance in wildlife migration patterns.

Wildebeest migration from Selous to Gonabis

There is a link between wildlife migration patterns and wildlife related losses. It was found that wildlife migrates not only between Selous and Gonabis, but also across habitats within Gonabis. This movement is seasonal and occurs between habitats along rivers Mgeta and Mombwe. For instance, during the dry season, while buffaloes, wildebeest, zebra, and giraffe migrate from river Mombwe to Mgeta, elephants migrate in a reverse direction, from Mgeta to Mombwe and Duthumi, causing extensive crop damage along the route, especially in Bonye. Since carnivores follow prey species, livestock losses also tend to increase during this period.

Conclusions

The benefit sharing mechanisms under the new wildlife policy have led to mixed attitudes towards wildlife conservation among the local communities. Most respondents support wildlife conservation in Gonabis and oppose the construction of the Kidunda dam on river Ruvu, which will lead to the submergence of Gonabis under water. Gonabis also appears as the third most important sector for public spending. This positive change can be compared from the attitudes in the 1990s, when Selous authorities considered every local as a potential poacher and the locals considered wildlife conservation as a tool for oppression. Despite this, few respondents expressed negative attitudes as reflected by their support for the conversion of Gonabis into agricultural land. In general, a variation in the attitudes of the local communities reflects wildlife related costs and benefits. But, this difference is not reflected in the implementation of the new policy, which considers all 22 villages as equally eligible for wildlife related benefits.

Because Gonabis was created after pooling land from eight villages, the households in these villages bear costs at three levels: a) opportunity cost of land forgone, b) opportunity costs of benefits forgone from hunting wildlife, and c) agricultural, livestock and human losses from wildlife. Ipso facto, the people from the villages bordering Gonabis can claim compensation on these fronts. In contrast, since land from the remaining 16 villages that make up JWMA was neither appropriated, nor do they experience significant wildlife related losses, their compensation claim is relevant only in the context of forgone benefits from wildlife hunting. As a result of this egalitarian benefit sharing mechanism, there is a high level of dissatisfaction among the households from some of the villages bordering Gonabis, notably Magogoni. Further, owing to several reasons, bushmeat access benefits are low and will not be able to compensate these losses. That said, it could be argued that the residents of villages bordering Gonabis should be compensated on a different level.

Like attitudes, the impact of the new policy on wildlife found in Gonabis is also mixed. The population of key herbivores, such as wildebeest, zebra, buffalo, impala, and elephant, has remained fairly stable in the new policy period. However, the population of key carnivore species, as lions, has declined. It is, therefore not surprising that respondents identified trophy hunting alongside poaching as the main threats to wildlife. Since lions are a top carnivore species found in Gonabis and are also listed as a vulnerable species by the International Union for the Conservation of Nature and Natural Resources, low lion populations could have negative repercussions for the ecology of Gonabis. The wildlife migration patterns are stable and popular migration routes are still under use. The Selous management, which is responsible for issuing hunting quota in Gonabis, needs to undertake a regular census of the key carnivore species. The management needs to integrate local communities, especially their local knowledge on the distribution of several carnivore species, before allocating hunting quotas.

Overall, the impact of the new policy on both attitudes and wildlife distribution is mixed. Much better results can be obtained through, inter alia, designing compensation mechanisms on the basis of the distribution of wildlife related costs and benefits. The management needs to reconsider its criteria of allotting hunting permits in Gonabis so as not to interfere with the natural regeneration of the key carnivores in Gonabis. Active participation by the local communities in key areas, as designing benefit sharing and trophy hunting quotas, can improve these results. This will help the new policy in achieving its intended target of rural development as well as wildlife conservation.

Acknowledgement

The GTZ Wildlife Division in Tanzania supported this research through an internship position. I am especially thankful to Dr. Rolf D. Baldus who provided me with an opportunity and institutional support to conduct this study. I extend my gratitude to the Selous Park Manager - Mr. Benson Kibonde for his extended support throughout the study. My thanks also to Dr. habil. Tobias Haller, Mr. Semua Twaha, village game scouts, Charles Leonard, GTZ staff members, village residents, and the handsome wildlife of Gonabis.

References

Allendorf, T., Swe, K. K., Oo, T., Htut, Y., Aung, M., Aung, M., Allendorf, K., Hayek, A. A., Leimgruber, P., Wemmer, C. 2006. Community Attitudes towards Three Protected Areas in Myanmar (Burma). Environmental Conservation. 33/4: 344-352.

Ashley, C., Mdoe, N., Reynolds, L. 2002. Rethinking Wildlife for Livelihoods and Diversification in Rural Tanzania: A Case Study from Northern Selous. Ladder Working Paper 15. Overseas Development Institute.

Baldus, R., Kibonde, B., Siege, L. 2003. Seeking Conservation Partnerships in the Selous Game Reserve, Tanzania. Conservation Partnership in Africa. Parks. 13/1, 50-61.

Baldus, R. 2006. The Crucial Role of Governance in Ecosystem Management – Results and Conclusions of the Selous Conservation Program/ Tanzania 1987-2003. Serengeti Conference (May 2006) on Managing Africa's Natural Systems, TANAPA, FZS, Federal Ministry of Environment, Nature Conservation and Nuclear Safety.

Baral, N., Heinen, J. T. 2007. Resource Use, Conservation Attitudes, Management Intervention and People-Park Relations in the Western Terai Landscape of Nepal. Environmental Conservation. 34/1: 64-72.

Boer, W. D., Baquete, D. S. 1998. Natural Resource Use, Crop Damage and Attitudes of Rural People in the Vicinity of the Maputo Elephant Reserve. Mozambique. Environmental Conservation. 25/3: 208-218.

Brandon, K., Wells, M. 1992. Planning for People and Parks: Design Dilemmas. World Development. 20: 557-570.

Ebregt, A., Greve, P. 2000. Buffer Zones and their Management. Policy and Best Practices for Terrestrial Ecosystems in Developing Countries. Theme Studies Series 5. EC-LNV and IAC, Wageningen (the Netherlands).

Gillingham, S., Lee, P. C. 1999. The Impact of Wildlife-related Benefits on the Conservation Attitudes of Local People around the Selous Game Reserve, Tanzania. Environmental Conservation 26/3: 218-228.

Goldman, M. 2003. Partitioned Nature, Privileged Knowledge: Community-based Conservation in Tanzania. Development and Change 34/5: 835-862.

GTZ, 2003. Resource_Management Zoning Plan – JUKUMU, Morogoro. GTZ Wildlife Programme in Tanzania. Dar es Salaam.

Gynne, M. D., Croze, H. 2004. East African Habitat Monitoring Practice: A Review of Methods and Application. Nairobi.

IUCN, 2003. Message of the Vth IUCN World Parks Congress to the Convention on Biological Diversity. IUCN.

IWDG, 2004. WMA Implementation Issues for Discussion on 15/09/2004 with the Minister of Natural Resources and Tourism: Hon. Zakhia Hamdan Mehgji.

Lamb, R. (ed.) 1997. People and Parks: Wildlife, conservation and communities. Panos Media Briefing No. 25: pp 21.

Lewis, D. M., Alpert, P. 1997. Trophy Hunting and Wildlife Conservation in Zambia. Conservation Biology 11/1: 59-68.

Lewis, D., Kaweche, G.B., Mwenya, A. 1990. Wildlife Conservation Outside Protected Areas – Lessons from an Experiment in Zambia. Conservation Biology. 4/2: 171-180.

Mabugu, R., Mugoya, P. 2001. Financing, Revenue-Sharing, and Taxation Issues in Wildlife Management Areas. A Report submitted under Environmental Policy and Institutional Strengthening Indefinite Quantity (EPIQ) Contract to the Wildlife Division, Ministry of Natural Resources and Tourism, Tanzania.

Mehta, J. N., Kellert, S. R. 1998. Local Attitudes Towards Community Based Conservation Policy and Programmes in Nepal: A Case Study in the Makalu-Barun Conservation Area. Environmental Conservation 25/4: 320-333.

Murphree, M. W. 1996. Wildlife in Sustainable Development: Approaches to Community Participation. Unpublished Report to African Wildlife Policy Consultation. Sunningdale, U.K.

Neumann, R. P. 1997. Primitive Ideas: Protected Area Buffer Zones and the Politics of Land in Africa. Development and Change 28 /4: 559-582

Novaro, A. J., Redford, K. H., Bodmer, R. E. 2000. Effect of Hunting in Source-Sink Systems in the Neo-Tropics. Conservation Biology. 14/3: 713-721.

Nuding, M. 1996. The Potential of Wildlife Management for Development Cooperation. Tropical Ecology Support Program (TÖB), GTZ.

Rustagi, D. 2005. What Kidunda Dam Will Destroy: Ecological and Socio-economic Value of Gonabis, Selous Game Reserve, Tanzania. Tanzania Wildlife Discussion Paper 45. GTZ Wildlife Division.

Shauri, V. 1999. The New Wildlife Policy in Tanzania – Old Wine in a New Bottle? Lawyers Environmental Action Team, Tanzania.

Siege, L. 2000. From Decline to Recovery – The Elephants of the Selous. Tanzania Wildlife Discussion Paper No. 27. GTZ

Simon, J. 1983. Is it sensible to say that natural resources are finite in supply? World Development. 11/9: 825-834.

Simon, J. 1990. Population matters: People, Resources, Environment and Integration. New Brunswick, NJ. Transaction Publishers. Xiv-544.

Shyamsunder, P. 1996. Constraints on Socio-buffering Around the Mantadia National Park in Madagascar. Environmental Conservation 23/1: 67-73.

Songorwa, A. N. 1999. Community Based Wildlife Management (CWM) in Tanzania: Are the Communities Interested? World Development. 27/12: 2061-2079.

TWCM, 1991. Wildlife Census, Selous, June 1991. Frankfurt Zoological Society. Arusha, (Tanzania).

TWCM 1995. Aerial Survey of the Selous Game Reserve, Mikumi National Park and Surrounding Areas, Dry Season, 1994. Frankfurt Zoological Society. Arusha (Tanzania).

TWCM, 1998. Aerial Survey of the Selous Game Reserve, Mikumi National Park and Surrounding Areas, Dry Season, October 1998. TWCM, Arusha (Tanzania).

TWD, 1989. Selous Census. Frankfurt Zoological Society, Arusha (Tanzania).

TWCM, 2002. Aerial Survey of the Selous Game Reserve, Mikumi National Park and Surrounding Areas, Dry Season, October-November, 2002. Frankfurt Zoological Society, Arusha (Tanzania).

Walsch, M. T. 2000. The Development of Community Wildlife Management in Tanzania – Lessons from Ruaha Ecosystem. Paper presented at the Conference on African Wildlife Management in New Millenium in Mweka (Tanzania). College of African Wildlife Management.

Walpole, M. J., Goodwin, H. J. 2001. Local Attitudes towards Conservation and Tourism around Komodo National Park, Indonesia. Environmental Conservation. 28/2: 160-166.

WCMC, 2003. Selous Game Reserve, Tanzania. UNEP-WCMC. Internet source: www.unep-wcmc.org.

Weladji, R. B., Moe, S. R., Vedeld, P. 2003. Stakeholder Attitude towards Wildlife Policy and the Benoue Wildlife Conservation Area, North Cameroon. Environmental Conservation 30/4: 334-343.

Wells, M., Brandon, K. 1992. People and Parks: Linking Protected Area Management with Local Communities. World Bank, Washington D.C.

Chapter 7

Common-Pool Resources, Legal Pluralism and Governance from a New Institutionalist Perspective. Lessons from the African Floodplain Wetlands Research Project

Tobias Haller

Introduction

A brief look at the *Digital Library of the Commons* and state of the art publications (see Ostrom et. al., 2002; Agrawal, 2003) indicate that there is a large amount of literature on single cases of common-pool resource management but few qualitative comparisons. The *African Floodplain Wetlands Project* (AFWeP) tried to fill this gap and widen the theoretical perspective on collective action and institutional change by focussing on the enlarged neo-institutional approach proposed by Jean Ensminger (1992). AFWeP is a comparative study on common pool resource management and institutional change in similar ecological settings: African floodplains in semi-arid areas. We selected floodplains in Mali (Inner Niger Delta), Cameroon (Waza-Logone), Tanzania (Pangani and Rufiji Floodplain (Kafue Flats) and Botswana (Okavango Delta). We were interested in finding out how institutions for the management of common-pool resources such as fisheries, wildlife, pasture, forests and water have changed since colonial times. African floodplains are important areas for local livelihoods and of special interest to conservation organisations such as the World Conservation Union (IUCN) (Hughes et al., 1992; Jeffrey et al., 1992; Acreman et al., 1996; Loth et al., 2004). These ecosystems are interesting because inundations in an otherwise semi-arid environment make them resource-rich pockets. Most of these common-pool resources are managed through local institutions (rules, norms, customary laws and regulations). These institutions were developed in pre-colonial times and often continued to operate during the colonial era. Today, however, most of the local rules and regulations of CPR management have lost their effectiveness, as the state claims control of the common-pool resources. At the same time, common-pool resources have become more and more attractive to seasonal immigrants who are interested in their commercial use. The state legally and officially controls the common-pool resources but lacks the capacity to do so in practice. In many of the areas studied, immigrants and local people are competing over the extraction of common-pool resources that are now open access. As a consequence, signs of CPR degradation can now be observed. However, comparative research findings go beyond the analysis of open access situations and overuse of resources: Based on the framework of the New Institutionalism, I propose three major findings: *A)* There is a problem due to the loss of state control, because immigrants use the ideology of citizenship to get free access to common-pool resources, hindering local collective action *(the paradox of the present absence of the state hypothesis). B)* Traditional institutions that give a rent to powerful people will survive (*rent hypothesis*) and C) actors use legal pluralism in order to maximize their gains from existing and transformed institutional designs *(the forum shopping strategy hypothesis).* This latter point elaborates the enlargement of the New Institutionalist approach by including issues stemming more from post-modernist and political anthropological approaches such as power, ideology and discourses/narratives.

The paper will be structured as follows: I will first briefly outline the theoretical basis and methodology. Then I will present major findings and discuss these with some specific examples. Here we will focus on Mali, Cameroon and Zambia in order to illustrate the way in which legal pluralism affects governance of common-pool resources. The examples will show how important it is to come to a historical understanding of how institutions have changed from pre-colonial to the present times.

Theoretical basis and hypotheses

In the AFWeP we used the New Institutionalism in economics, anthropology and political science (North, 1990; Ostrom, 1990; Becker et al., 1995; Ensminger, 1992; 1998; Ensminger et al., 1997; Acheson, 1989; 2003) as a theoretical basis. Under this theoretical umbrella institutions (rules, regulations, norms, values and laws) not only regulate access to and use of common-pool resources,[1] they also make resource users and use predictable.[2] In

---

[1]Based on the work of Ostrom (1990) and McKean (2000) common-pool resources are defined as common-pool goods which are subtractable and where exclusion is difficult or costly. They are often, but not always, managed by common property regimes, where rights to flow or units of flow are parcelled to individuals but rights to stock are shared.

[2]According to Ostrom and other scholars working on the commons, there is no need for a *Tragedy of the Commons* (Hardin, 1968), predicting overuse of natural re-

addition, and of central importance, Ensminger applies a historical approach in order to analyse how institutions change and which factors trigger this change (Ensminger, 1992). According to her, institutional changes are triggered by external factors (the social and physical environment, including ecological, economic, socio-political; demographic, and technological aspects) that are changing so called relative prices. This means that prices for example for fish, wildlife and pasture rise in proportion to other prices (agricultural goods, salaries etc.) and as access to these resources is made less costly due to external factors (roads, better technology, lack of monitoring facilities) a major change is triggered within a community. Internal variables such as bargaining power, organisation, ideology and institutions are changed. For example, Ensminger shows that a rise in cattle prices among the Orma in Kenya leads to a switch by some previously nomadic Orma to a sedentary lifestyle. They wanted to profit from cattle trade and started to close the communal pastures needed for their cattle. Gains made from the cattle trade and from government backing favouring sedentary lifestyles increased the bargaining power of those who settled but there was division among them due to differing interests over the closing of the commons: Some of the settled Orma had close relationships with nomads and did not want to close the commons. Finally, a young chief using the ideology of modernity called in the police and forced the closing of the commons. Ensminger therefore highlights the process related to the distributional effects of institutional changes and the need to identify, who profits (Ensminger, 1992; Ensminger et al., 1997). The theoretical implication of this example is that external changes might affect relative prices, increase the profitability of the exploitation of floodplain common-pool resources and seriously affect the bargaining power of different actors who try to steer institutional change for their own benefit. In this process an increase in relative prices does not automatically lead to privatisation of resources; depending on power and ideology it can lead to a delay or to other outcomes in institutional change. This framework proved to be extremely useful in analysing the changes we looked at in the AFWeP. It can be shown from our data in Mali, Cameroon, Tanzania, Zambia and Botswana that external factors have been strongly shaping the use of common-pool resources, turning them from communal property to state property. But in most cases, as

---

sources held in common. Common-pool resources are often held in common property regimes, which are institutions that can reduce uncertainty effectively. This is especially the case if institutions reduce transaction costs (information, monitoring and sanctioning). Ostrom provided a set of eight design principles that characterize well-working institutions (see also debate and critical discussion by Agrawal, 2003)

states have been affected by economic crisis since the mid 1970's they lack the capacity to manage and monitor the commons, thus creating a de facto open access situation (see also Feeney, et al., 1990; Bierschenk et al., 1996; Ostrom et al., 2002). At the same time, local rules have been eroded or weakened and rendered inoperative. However, scholars such as Keebet and Franz von Benda-Beckmann have argued that there is seldom a total vacuum. Often traditional and modern legal norms co-exist at the same time. This is labelled legal pluralism because different legal forms such as customary norms and laws, colonial and post-colonial laws, and rules and regulations exist at the same time. Sometimes they overlap, other times they compete with each other (see Meinzen-Dick et al., 2002). In the 1980's, K. von Benda-Beckmann already indicated that actors pursue what she called forum shopping: In specific contexts, actors exploit the variety of legal possibilities to strategically choose the possibility that suits them best (K. von Benda-Beckmann, 1984; F. and K. von Benda-Beckmann, 1997; F. von Benda-Beckmann, 2002). Major contexts, in which this appears can be disputes:

Arab Choa with cattle

During disputes and negotiation, claims are justified by reference to legal rules. The disputants use different normative repertoires in different contexts or forums depending on which law or interpretation of law they believe is most likely to support their claims, a process known as forum shopping (K. von Benda-Beckmann, 1984). Which law is accepted and enforced depends on power and social relationships between the different claimants (Meinzen-Dick et al., 2002:5).

This highlights the way institutions are chosen, transformed or eradicated by different actors. In this context, Ensminger indicated that issues of bargaining power and ideology are relevant: it is important to see how people's dependency on and interest in a particular resource triggers the use of ideology in order to legitimize access and to increase their bargaining power. I therefore argue that this perception of ideology opens up our theoretical framework and allows us to integrate post-modern ideas about the relationships between nature and culture (see the work of Escobar, 1999). It also becomes possible to integrate approaches that focus on discourses and narratives (see Fairhead and Leach, 1996; Agrawal, 2005). Legal pluralist situations offer ample room for the construction and deconstruction of laws and regulations depending on bargaining power and interests. Studies of various land tenure regimes, for example in Niger by Lund (1998) illustrate this point as do legal court settings in Zambia studied by Cutshall (1980). What often matters is who has the power to decide which institutional framework is appropriate in a certain setting and which law is relevant in which context. However, new institutional arrangements can arise during "open moments" – moments in which governance and power relations have to be newly defined (Lund, 1998b). The new arrangements however, often draw upon already existing structures and create "twilight" situations (see Lund, 2007 on twilight institutions). The major findings of AFWeP contribute to this debate with a link to governance issues. In our studies of common-pool resources and the institutional transformation of common property regimes into de facto open access we found that three important differentiations have to be made:

A) *Problems exist in relation to the ideology of citizenship (present-absence of the state hypothesis)*. As citizens of the state, (seasonal) immigrants regard themselves as fully entitled to use common-pool resources as they wish. Local stakeholders are not empowered or backed by the state to prevent immigrants from unsustainable use of local common-pool resources by means of locally developed traditional institutions. The paradoxical situation therefore arises in which the state and in particular its enforcement agencies are absent, while the presence of the state's legislation creates constellations of permanent de facto open access.

B) *Rules that pay are going to stay (Rent hypothesis).* From the major trends of institutional change one could assume that traditional institutions will vanish. But not all traditional institutions are eroded by the management of common-pool resources through the state. Some of them remain, often transformed, because they grant access to resources and tradable CPR goods for powerful local elites.

C) *Importance of legal pluralism in order to assess governance (forum shopping hypothesis):* A peculiar institutional insecurity is evident in all the study settings because it is not clear, which rules are operational (state, local, NGO and international regulations) and at what level. In these heterogeneous legal frameworks, actors display strategic initiative, assessing and choosing ideologies, discourses and narratives that justify their use or appropriation of common-pool resources. The questions of who is entitled to use which resource, how and to what extent thus lead to conflicts. Forum shopping for governance purposes is therefore a process shaped by actors with different bargaining power using different ideologies in order to legitimize and formalise their actions based on a selection of possibilities and institutional opportunities, based on the whole spectrum from so called traditional up to modern institutional frameworks.

Note that the findings in this paper are based on a historical and political approach. We present findings from the different phases of change observed in the case studies.

The further parts of the paper are organised as follows: First I will give basic information on the research settings and methods before presenting the basic findings. These will then be related to the institutional changes taking place from pre-colonial and colonial to post-colonial times illustrating the evolution of open access constellations and overuse of common-pool resources. I will underscore them with the economic changes that create push and pull factors in the respective areas. These factors that are making the commercial use of common-pool resources more attractive are often actually damaging the resources themselves. In the third section I will discuss the three major findings outlined above and then come to the final conclusion.

Study background

Research set-up, research settings and methods

The following floodplains and ethnic groups were studied by the research group between 2002 and 2005 (see Table 1). Unless otherwise indicated, data mentioned in the text stems from MA, PhD or post-doctoral work by the respective researchers and from papers presented at an international conference held in Zurich in 2005.

We employed a qualitative comparative methodology (see Richie et al., 1994), and collected and analyzed the empirical data along core themes, provided by Ostrom (1990) Ensminger (1992) and Ruttan (1998) and further refined by Haller (2001): We have analysed how institutions were set up in pre-, colonial and postcolonial times by comparing the robustness of the institutions regarding territoriality and membership, monitoring and sanctioning devices and organisational aspects. We included the test of hypothesis on power relations and on economic change in the countries and the areas involved. Apart from participant observation, the most important methods used were structured and semi-structured interviews and the gathering of primary household data in a community or village (household surveys including budget data for 50 to 250 households per setting). The issues raised in this project also required the gathering of historical data by interviewing elderly people (oral history, biographies (10 to 15 per case, gender equal). We also collected data on the past state of the environment compared with the present situation (environmentally related oral history and indigenous local knowledge).

Table 1: Overview of floodplains, ethnic groups[3], researchers/ departments and main funding

Country/floodplain	Ethnic groups	Researchers	Funds and Programmes
Mali, Inner Niger Delta	Bozo and Somono fishermen	Sabrina Beeler (MA student) and Karin Frei (MA student),	Dept. of Social Anthropology, Zurich, Funds: Dept. of Social Anthropology, Zurich
Cameroon: Waza-Logone	Kotoko, Mousgum, Arab Choa, Fulbe	Gilbert Fokou (PhD student), Université Yaounde, Gabriela Landolt (MA student)	Dept. of Social Anthropology, Zurich.) Programme: NCCR North South, IP6[4]
Tanzania: Pangani River Basin	Pare and Maasai	Gimbage Mbeyale (PhD student) University Dar es Salaam	NCCR North South, IP 6 research programme
Tanzania: Rufiji Floodplain,	WaRufiji	Patrick Meroka (PhD student), Dept. of Social Anthropology, Zurich,	Programme: NCCR North South, IP6
Zambia: Kafue Flats,	Ila, Balundwe and Batwa	Tobias Haller (Post doc), Dept. of Social Anthropology, Zurich	Funds: Swiss National Science Foundation
Botswana, Okavango Delta	Hambukush, Bayei	Roland Saum (MA), Dept. of Social Anthropology, Zurich	Dept. of Social Anthropology, Zurich, Funds: Dept. of Social Anthropology, Zurich

[3] I use ethnic terms in this paper. However, I want to emphasize that the whole team is fully aware of the debate on ethnic denominations and on the construction of ethnicity. These names are often, but not always, names given by outsiders or terms from the colonial context. We still use the ethnic names for the sake of simplicity, while aware of the consequences. Nonetheless, when we are dealing with constructions of identity that shape ideologies and forum shopping strategies, we do mention it (see also Lund (ed.), 2007; Kuba et al. (eds.), 2006, Evers et al., 2005).

[4] NCCR means National Competence Centre in Research. The research programme referred to is the North-South NCCR with the title: Research Partnerships for Mitigating Syndromes of Global Change, led by the University of Bern, Centre for Environment and Development. The studies which are used here have been coordinated and supervised by the author in the subproject Nr. 6 (Livelihood strategies and institutions; Department of Geography, University of Zurich, Switzerland)

Characteristics of African Floodplain Ecosystems

African floodplain ecosystems are recognised important targets for conservation because they form resource-rich pockets, which are crucial for the livelihoods of local populations, especially in semi-arid environments (Adams, 1990; Hughes et al., 1992; Acreman et al., 1996; Stevenson et al., 1999; Haller, 2002a, b; Loth, 2004). Table 2 provides an overview of all the floodplain areas studied.

Table 2: Basic characteristics of the selected African floodplains

Country	Name	Floodplain area in km2	Local annual rainfall in mm
Mali	Inner Niger Delta	40'000	200-600
Cameroon	Waza-Logone	12'000	500-700
Tanzania	Pangani River Basin Pangani Mountains	1'000	500-800 3'000
	Rufiji Floodplain	10'000	1'000
Zambia	Kafue Flats	6'500	800
Botswana	Okavango Delta	16'000	400-600

Source: Research team, Hughes and Hughes, 1992; Acreman, 1996

Each floodplain has low average and erratic annual rainfall of between 500 and 1'000 mm. The water flooding these plains stems mainly from run-off from distant mountain areas. The floodplains are thus part of a larger river basin system and vulnerable to upstream changes. The annual cycle is as follows (see also Drijver et al., 1985 for the Kafue Flats in Zambia; Loth et al., 2004 for the Waza-Logone): After the dry season, when the rains begin, the filling of the tributaries leads to first small inundations. Some months later, towards the end of the rainy season, when larger amounts of run-off from the mountain areas reach the floodplains, river channels, tributaries, ponds and lagoons overflow. Now, vast areas adjacent to the rivers are inundated. After the floods, the water recedes, but leaves behind sediment that enhances the fertility of the agricultural areas and pastures that had been submerged. Many of the floodplains have depressions, which turn into lakes and ponds, meaning that water remains available even after the inundation. These water bodies are important for fisheries and wildlife (Drijver et al., 1985; Chooye et al., 1995; Ellenbroek, 1987; Chabwela, 1992).[5]

[5] Normally forests are not important issues in floodplains but in two of researches conducted in Tanzania forest in higher sometimes mountain zones are important for timber production and related to the floodplains studied.

Map 1: Location of floodplains studied in the AFWeP

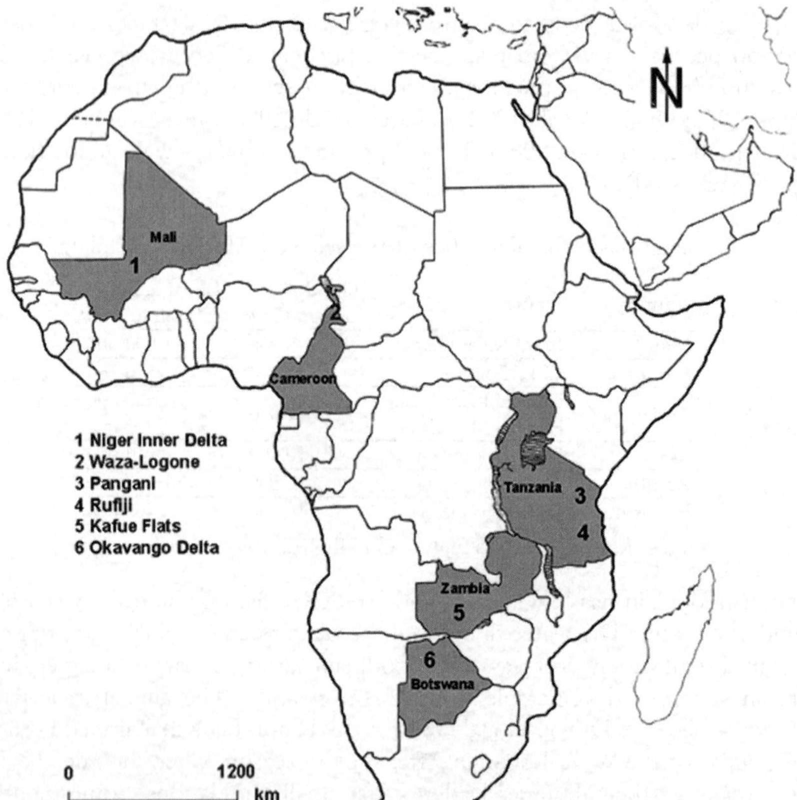

c. by C. Furrer, Dep. of Social Anthropology, University of Zurich, Switzerland

Basic findings from the research

Characteristics of traditional CPR institutions

In all the floodplain areas studied, the various ethnic groups have developed institutions for the management of common-pool resources (Moorehead, 1989; Loth et al., 2004; Chabwela, 1992). During periods of high flood, access to fisheries and wildlife is open, because resources are abundant and widely spread over the flooded area. It is therefore costly and difficult to exclude others from the use of resources. During the recession of the floods and at the beginning of the dry season, when fish is trapped in ponds and wildlife congregates in certain locations, common property regimes for mobile common-pool resources come into play. Resources are then treated as common pool goods and outsiders are excluded from their use. But it is difficult to regulate the resource subtraction by individual group members. During the dry season, highly localised common-pool resources become private property (see also Thomas, 1996). This institutional pattern of resource use does not only apply to fish and wildlife but also applies to water. This resembles the economic defendability model (Dyson-Hudson et al., 1978; Eggertson, 1996).[6] Pasture is another important resource in the floodplains, which is highly seasonal. During high floods, pasture is inaccessible. During the dry season pasture is managed under a common property regime. Apart from the resource regimes that largely depend on environmental patterns, additional factors are important to understand resource management in pre-colonial times. This will be illustrated in two of the cases, namely among the Ila and Batwa in the Kafue Flats, Zambia (referring to Haller, 2007) and the Bozo and Somono in the Inner Niger Delta in Mali (referring to Moorehead, 1989 and Beeler et al., 2005):

A) *Membership in ethno-professional groups* (Moorehead, 1989): Among the Ila and Batwa as among the groups in the Inner Niger Delta, access to common-pool resources was organised on the basis of membership in kin groups, villages or groupings of villages or clans claiming control over a certain territory. Particular ethnic groups often form so-called ethno-professional groups that specialize in the exploitation of certain resources and areas. The Batwa fishermen controlled the river section of the Kafue River, while the Ila agro-pastoralists controlled mainly pastoral areas in the Flats. The Ila also hunt and fish in tributaries. In the Inner Niger Delta, Mali, the indigenous Bozo defined themselves as fishermen using specific water-logged areas and river sections, while the Somono focused on fishing open river waters. Ethnic labels[7] were thus often linked to a particular use of resources. Membership of an ethnic group and subsection (as a member of fishermen, pastoralist or hunter-gatherer groups) meant having access to these common-pool resources. Most groups also defended their territories against

[6] This is related to issues of tenure and transaction costs: Eggertsson (1996) mentions variables that lead to exclusion and includes physical characteristics of a resource, techniques of enforcement, inputs for exclusion, etc.

[7] See footnote 3.

intruders. The Ila for example, took action against some late-comers who established themselves in their area (see also Kotoko fishermen and Arab Choa pastoralists in Cameroon[8]).

B) *Culturally embedded institutions (religion) and co-operation based on asymmetrical altruism* (Ruttan, 1998): The power of local authorities who controlled, monitored and sanctioned resource use were usually legitimised by religious ideology and linked with the spiritual world: For example, among the Ila, access to pastures and local fisheries is only allowed after the completion of ritual activities. At the direction of village leaders (*mwami*), ritual leaders perform rituals for ancestral spirits. These leaders see themselves as spiritual owners of the territories. In order to be able to use common-pool resources collectively, ancestral spirits or other spiritual beings linked to their ancestors have to be approached ritually, meaning that the individual use of common-pool resources has to wait until these activities had been completed. Otherwise, harm to humans and their livestock in the forms of sickness, attacks by wild animals (crocodiles etc.), bad catches and thunderstorms will result. For the Batwa, ritual offerings have to be made for ancestral sprits to avoid wild animal attacks and ensure successful fishing. In Mali, Bozo leaders stated that they are related to water spirits and therefore have the right - via specific rituals - to control the area by renewing a contract with the water sprits and by coordinating collective fishing events ritually. In both settings, there are also groups of men monitoring resource areas in critical times to prevent free riding. These examples show that physical control of common-pool resources were backed up by monitoring and sanctioning embedded in the respective religious system. In addition, these ritual activities often preceded collective use of resources and therefore acted as coordinating device.[9]

C) *Arrangements of reciprocal access between user groups* (Thomas, 1996): In most groups, first-comers claim more control and take more common-pool resources. On the other hand they also grant access to other groups. Among the Ila this means that first-comer groups

---

8 See Fokou (Fokou, 2005), different groups in Rufiji and Pangani in Tanzania (Meroka, 2006; Mbeyale, 2005) and Bayei and Hambukushu in the Okavango Delta Panhandle, Botswana (Saum, 2005).

9 See also Kotoko in Cameroon on collective fishing (Fokou, 2005), hunting and fishing events among the different Warufiji groups (Meroka, 2006)

claim to be the supervisors of an area and that groups who come later will have a lower status and will not be able to control the resources. One of the local Ila first-comer groups controlled and coordinated access to main pasture areas and hunting grounds in the Kafue Flats. These groups got the best pastures and larger meat cuts and the skins from collective hunting as well as first access to the fish ponds. Like the Bozo and Somono leaders, the Ila also claim spiritual ownership based on a close relationship with water spirits. They are able to tax outside users to give them a third of the catch, which they redistribute. Distribution is therefore not equal, but access is granted in an orderly manner by the more powerful (see also Ruttan, 1998 from a theoretical point of view; for Cameroon see Fokou, 2005; for Tanzania see Meroka, 2006 and Mbeyale, 2005). The political systems however vary widely: Whereas the Ila are organised in competitive groups on a big man system, the Batwa are acephalous and segementary i.e. they do not have formal leaders. In Mali the groups discussed have no central authority apart from the 'Masters of the Water'. What is important about leaders in this context is that they often invite people from other areas on a reciprocal basis. For example, among the Ila giving access to fishponds and pasture gives the leader prestige. On the other hand the leader's people can then claim reciprocal access to the common-pool resources of the foreign users.[10]

D) *Restraint for gain (and not for conservation)* (Ruttan, 1998): Rules are not implemented for the conservation of resources per se but are imposed to maximise the yield of common-pool resources: This principle is evident among the Ila: they wait for the most productive time for grazing, collective hunting and fishing in order to maximise gains. Rather than conservation, the motivation is a harvest of longer grass, larger fish and fatter antelopes. The same principle is seen among the Bozo and Somono, who also make fish available subject to good catches. Regulations also help to solve conflicts and often stem from institutionalised conflict resolution. The Ila system of grazing is a case in point: There were rules governing the time of the move to the main cattle camp. The spiritual owner-group of in the Kafue Flats area close to the main river, responded to violation of these rules with a new rule of access to different cattle camps

---

[10]Similar reciprocal access arrangements can be found in Cameroon (Fokou, 2005), Tanzania (Meroka, 2006; Mbeyale, 2005), Botswana (Saum, 2005).

granted to different local village groups. Users had to pay one head of cattle for a long-term hereditary usufruct right to the pastures. However, access based also on a co-ordinated move of cattle and the monitoring of cattle posts by a leader (*kuwila-kubola* transhumance-system). Rules are often about coordination and include timing and closure. This means that among the Ila the beginning and end of grazing, fishing, and hunting activities is clearly set. Collective hunting (*chila*) on lechwe antelope among the Ila was co-ordinated by spiritual owners of a territory, who set the start of the collective hunt, involving hundreds of people from neighbouring groups during three days. Hunting before and after these hunts were forbidden and severely punished. This hunt was extremely productive and was a kind of limited cull giving high gain with little effort, especially skins and meat for the spiritual owner group but also for neighbouring groups. These hunts were based on reciprocity and therefore the controlled access granted to neighbours also opened access to other territories (see Haller, 2007). For fisheries, the Ila, Batwa and other Inner Niger Delta groups specified permissible fishing gear (spears, long nets demanding co-operation or fishing with baskets). Violations are fined. But catch limits are not set. The set of rules also includes conflict resolution mechanisms to deal with disputes between resource users at the leader's level.[11]

Institutional change in colonial and post colonial times

Pre-colonial institutions were neither ideal nor static, but they seem to have been functional when compared to the institutional regimes governing many of the floodplains today. However, most of these institutions have been altered or abolished during the colonial rule, and after independence (see Table 3 for an overview). I will illustrate this process by referring to the Kafue Flats and the Inner Niger Delta Case in which also change in relative prices are illustrated:

Kafue Flats (Zambia): In the case of the Kafue Flats the British South Africa Company started to control and to pacify the area around 1900. It increasingly installed a system of taxation (inclusion in monetary system), and manipulated local power structures to create a collaborating local leadership. Among the Ila, they created chiefs to achieve this goal. Furthermore, new laws regulating fishing, hunting, the use of land and pastures, water and

[11] See Beeler et al., 2005; Fokou, 2005; Meroka, 2006; Mbeyale, 2005.

forests were introduced. This resulted in a complete alteration of the local land tenure systems, which regulated the use of common-pool resources of different parts of the ecosystem in response to changing inundation patterns. Fisheries were opened to commercial fishermen from other ethnic groups because the company and later on the British colonial rulers wanted to produce more food for the mining areas. At the same time the colonial masters started to control wildlife and forbade collective hunting events. Thus, they started to strip local people of their sense of ownership and the mechanism by which the common-pool resources were defended. At the same time, new demands were created and common-pool resources were opened up to other user groups under the protection of the colonial state (Haller, 2007; Haller, 2007b).

Kotoko fishtrap

Inner Niger Delta (Mali): Similar processes happened in Mali. The Bozo and Somono came under the control of the Fulbe groups in the 19th century who formalised the traditional fishing system integrating it into the Dina traditional grazing legislation. However, when the French started the colonial process by the end of that century, like the British, they created a administrative structure with new kinds of territories controlled by a *Chef du Canton*, installed to collect taxes. The French also started to put fisheries under colonial legislation and were very interested in commercial fishing. Nevertheless, the "Masters of the Water" managed to stay in power locally although under the control of the colonial administration. A further change was that new, more efficient equipment became available and attracted new fishermen. The equipment included were nylon nets, fishing hooks, lead weight, épervier (a mobile fishing net) and motorboats. The new equipment was easier to handle and could be used anywhere individually. The nylon nets, for example were lighter and therefore did not need many fishermen to pull. Motorboats made navigation easier and more intensive. But the motors and fuel actually chased away the fish, which was then difficult to catch with traditional techniques. While modern fishing techniques have been adopted universally, traditional techniques remain confined to their original sites. This implies that traditional knowledge of fishing techniques was no longer needed and lost its value. Access to fisheries was now more and more based on cash because money started to be the key to gaining access to fishing sites and equipment (Beeler et al., 2005).

General political changes after independence and rise in prices for common-pool resources: All countries in the study became independent between 1960 and 1966 and inherited a colonial system of statehood with the central notion of citizenship. But there were two distinct developments: In the former French colonies and in Botswana, capitalist systems, which had major anti-democratic and highly centralised tendencies, were established. Tanzania and Zambia, on the other hand, developed into African Socialist systems. But in both systems common-pool resources were managed by the state to a greater or lesser extent, depending on the effectiveness of local laws and regulations. This opened up the access to the floodplains for outsiders as well as for the state control of various resources:

In *Zambia,* for example, rules and regulations regarding the management of fisheries and wildlife were separated. While fishing was regulated as a highly commercial resource, collective hunting was forbidden and in certain areas only allowed with an expensive license. More and more National Parks were established, limiting access to resources for local people, especially for the Batwa but also the Ila. At the same time, common-pool resources were already being opened up for outsiders. As long as they had licences or titles, all citizens were permitted access to common-pool resources without local consultation. In addition, the planning and implementation of a large hydropower dam system downstream (Kafue Gorge) and upstream (Iteshiteshi) started. This new infrastructure altered flooding patterns and made the floodplain even more accessible during specific times for outsiders. In addition, reduced floods were leading to massive changes in pasture (weed invasion), changes in wildlife (better access for poachers) and in fisheries (disturbance of breeding patterns). After a major crisis in the copper-driven economy in the mid 1970's, Zambia's economy was performing badly and the country did not know how to face its international debts. The situation did not improve after a change of Presidents (including a political change from socialism to capitalism), with the adoption of market regulations and cuts in the state budgets since the 1990's in order to comply with structural adjustment programmes (lowered subsidies, reduction of formal employment etc). While agricultural production became less interesting due to low prices, prices for common-pool resources such as fish, wildlife and cattle was improving massively: Between 1980 and 2000, prices for fish increased 17-fold, game meat 20-fold and cattle 80-fold while staple food, minerals and wages increased much less or even decreased (Haller 2007, Haller et al., 2008). The countries' economic development was stagnating as can be seen from the Human Development Index for Zambia which remained on a low level of below 0,5 up to 1990s and then declined under 0,4.[12] Today Zambia is one of the poorest countries in the world. In 2000 - 2004 it had about 300 US$ of average annual income per capita (Haller, 2007).[13]

In Mali, after independence in 1960, the major trend was that common-pool resources such as fisheries remained under centralised state control while the government pushed cash crop production inherited by the French (peanuts and cotton). In addition, the government kept the colonial territorial structure (department and sub-department boundaries) and therefore movements between fishing areas by small groups with outboard motors and nylon nets increased. Furthermore, it claimed all natural resources (water, land and pastures) as state property[14] and introduced a tax system to get access to those resources under the ideology of fighting "traditional feudalities". The "Masters of the Water" were portrayed as feudal, archaic and elitist and said to control all the revenues from the fisheries. Thus the traditional fishing systems and rights were eroded. The *Service des Eaux et Forêts*, created during colonial times, was charged with the organisation and control of the fishery.[15] The state divided the river into administrative territories, whose boundaries did not correspond with the pre-colonial territorial divisions, and their management was transferred to villages on the riverbanks. A local person was put in charge by the administration. He represented the local people in the fishing committees and collected taxes at the village level.

---

[12] Source: Based on UNDP data, compiled by NCCR North South 2006, University of Bern (Data CD for NCCR use).

[13] With the rise of copper prices in the last two years the avarage income rose again.

[14] Law Nr. 63/7ANRM, 11. November 1963.

[15] This implies setting dates for the collective fishing prescribe the techniques and mesh size allowed to use and fining transgressors.

The new regulations overlapped the complex local rules of access. But as the new law was not able to totally displace customary laws, a system of cohabitation between the two developed and the use of resources became a source of conflict. After 1991, criticisms of the centralised state and its abuse of power, and calls for decentralisation were frequently heard.[16] In 1992/93 the National Assembly adopted a law on decentralisation. This law calls for some kind of co-operative management between the state and local communities by ceeding to the latter an independent management of their resources. But the tutelage of the state is still conserved, as the state defines specific goals in resource management. In addition, the lowest unit of decentralised government is the rural commune, that consist of between 11 and 45 villages and is therefore a rather large group. At the village level, decentralisation of state power is therefore not really felt. In other words, while most common-pool resource use happens at village level, decentralisation has not yet extended to village level (Benjaminsen, 1997; Benjamin, 2006). Today, the control of the fishery and trade is in the hands of a parastatal organisation called *Opération de Pêche*. Despite the decentralised management of natural resources, local traditional knowledge and experience related to seasonal variations and fish life cycles only play a minor role. Economically the country developed marginally. Mali faced several droughts and its income from cotton and other cash crops has been declining. The Human Development Index only rose by a small proportion from over 0,2 up to 0,3 but remains on this low level (1975-2002).[17] Therefore as prices for fish are rising (6-fold compared to twofold for food-crops and a decline in state salaries) more people get engaged in fisheries – especially during the drought years in the 1970's and 1980's. The Delta has seen an increase of fishermen since the 1950's from 80'000 to 300'000 in the 1990's. New fishery laws and new technologies enabled easy access to the fisheries and the only alternative for the younger generation was to migrate to the relatively rich Ivory Coast as migrant labourers.

In addition to these changes in the Mali and Zambian cases, there has been population growth in both floodplains, partly due to immigration. However, in the Zambian example, growth of the population in the Kafue Flats has decreased since the 1990's and is now at the 2% level.

---

[16] Also described as paradigm shift in Natural Resource Management. Sahel orthodoxies blaming local people causing natural resource degradation are now being replaced by alternative paradigms emerging paradigms in at least three areas: Range Science and Pastoral Development, Common Property Theory, and the Management of Fuel wood Resources (Benjaminsen, 1997: 122-123).

[17] UNDP data compiled by the NCCR North South 2004.

We found similar tendencies in the other floodplain cases of our study: In Tanzania and in Cameroon relative prices for common-pool resources have been rising compared to other goods and services and compared to major income sources of the state during the time of the study (cash crops such as cotton in Cameroon, coffee in Tanzania, see Meroka, 2006; Mbeyale, 2005; Fokou, 2005). Botswana is the major exception due to its income of diamonds and tourism and with a rather stable elite; some of the revenues generated are trickling down (Saum, 2005).[18]

Table 3, presents a summary of external institutional changes. In all areas, "pacification" and "taxation" were introduced with formal state ownership of common-pool resources. Often this led to a fragmentation of control and ownership of common-pool resources in various separate state departments. In addition, in both capitalist and socialist systems, there were strong tendencies to foster an anti-ethnic, one-nation ideology. An exception was Cameroon with a schism between English and French and Islamic and Christian divisions. All the areas under study have also seen one or more large development or infrastructural schemes, the introduction of protected areas (except Mali), and severe droughts or environmental stress that reduced access to common-pool resources.

---

[18] In the two cases in Tanzania there is a rise in the prices of cattle, wildlife and timber, with the difference that in the Pangani river Basin rice has a high rise in prices while as rise in prices for fish in Rufiji are extremely high (90-fold), especially if one compared to salaries and other cash crops (coffee, sisal) that have been decreasing up to 2002 (coffee is rising again since then). In Cameroon the figures are moderate but still cattle and fish have a higher rise than salaries and cash crops. The only exception is Botswana, where common-pool resources have little value compared to formal salaries and especially diamonds. As another factor to be added is the value of wildlife for tourism (trophy hunting and game viewing) that has now after income from diamonds the rise (ibid). There are extreme differences between these countries in terms of average annual income: After Mali, Tanzania has the lowest annual average income with 270 US$, while Cameroon had nearly double (560 US$). However these averages are very small compared to Botswana (4736) in 2002/3 (Nohlen, 2004).

Table 3: Institutional, ecological and demographic changes in various African wetlands

	Pacification, Taxation	CPR as state property/formal laws/licenses/ titles	Political system S=socialist, C=capitalist	Ecological changes	Development schemes and protected areas	Increase in demography, population densities
Internal Niger Delta, Mali	Yes	Yes (fisheries)	C, anti-ethnic notion	Yes (Droughts)	No	2%, 33 p/km2
Waza Logone. Cameroon	Yes	Yes (fisheries, taxation of pastoralists)	C	Yes (Droughts. Less water from major upstream rivers)	Yes (Maga dam, irrigation scheme), Waza Logone Park	3%, 5 p/km2
Pangani River Basin, Tanzania	Yes	Yes (state forests and state water management, pasture management)	S (Ujamaa) strong anti-ethnic notion	Yes (Droughts Less water from major upstream rivers)	Yes (many upstream dams for irrigation), Mkomazi Game Reserve	3%, 33 p/km2
Rufiji Floodplain, Tanzania	Yes	Yes (fisheries, wildlife, forests)	S (Ujamaa) Strong anti-ethnic notion	Yes (Large floods and droughts)	Yes (irrigation schemes, New roads, Selous Game Reseve	3%, 5 p/km2
Kafue Flats, Zambia	Yes	Yes, fisheries, wildlife, Later (land and pasture)	S (Humanism) Strong anti-ethnic notion	Yes (Droughts. Less water from major upstream rivers), cattle disease	Yes (dams for hydropower, irrigation schemes) three protected areas, ADMADE-system	2%, 17 p/km2
Okavango-Delta, Botswana	Yes	Yes (land zoning, wildlife)	C, anti ethnic notion	Yes, cattle disease	Yes New CBNRM[19] schemes	1,5%, 1 p/km2

Source: Haller, 2002; Haller (ed.), 2005; Beeler et al., 2005; Fokou, 2005; Landolt, 2005; Meroka, 2005; Mbeyale, 2005; Saum, 2005; Haller et al., 2005; Secondary sources: Mali: Moorehead, 1989; Kassibo, 2000; Fay, 2000; Cameroon: Loth et al., 2004; Zambia: Smith et al., 1968; Rennie, 1982; Jeffrey et al., 1992.

[19] Community Based Natrual Resource Management

Institutional change: open access and consequences for common-pool resources

These changes in relative prices and the general institutional changes following the creation of nation states had consequences that can be categorised as push and pull factors. Firstly some push factors: Due to the loss of income from state-dependent economies, people in urban and peri-urban areas, as well as people depending on agricultural subsidies were forced to seek alternative livelihood strategies. Therefore, outsiders, locals and administrators developed a stronger interest in common-pool resources as a source of income. One case in point is *Zambia* where after the fall of copper prices and cuts in the state budgets, unemployed people went into fisheries in massive numbers, making it become one of the most important informal sectors (Scudder pers. com 2003). Poaching also became one of the important sources of income (see Gibson, 1999). In the other study countries, more people are also engaging in commercial cattle husbandry, fishery, poaching, illegal logging, and irrigation agriculture.

Pull factors have generally been institutional incentives: Because local institutions have been rendered ineffective and the state is not able to adequately manage resources, costs for access to common-pool resources have fallen dramatically. Since there have been severe cuts in state budgets for several government departments (fisheries, wildlife, agriculture and veterinary), the state generally lacks the financial means to carry out the effective monitoring and sanctioning that would control access to common-pool resources in the floodplains (see Haller (ed.), 2005; Haller, 2007; Haller, 2007b; Gibson, 1999) so the access to the area become open. In the Kafue Flats in Zambia, for example, the local Department of Fisheries is understaffed and does not have the money to afford adequate transportation for monitoring and enforcement of the fishery laws. Therefore, access to fish has been very easy and due to high prices very interesting for commercial fishermen and for traders alike. One can, therefore, speak of permanent open access to fisheries in this area. The same pattern is evident with fisheries, wildlife, pasture and timber in all the study cases except Botswana. In Botswana, common-pool resources have a high value in connection with tourism.

Some developments towards privatisation: On the other hand there are cases, for example in Cameroon, Tanzania and Zambia where a contrary process was also observed: Former common-pool resources become informal private property: In the Waza Logone area, people plant crops and trees in former pastures and on pastoral migration routes in order to mark private

Table 4: Degradation of CPRs in 6 African floodplains since the 1980s

Floodplain	Status of fisheries	Wildlife	Pasture	Water	Forests
Kafue Flats	Catch size declines 25%-75% (local survey). Annual catch falls from 10 to 2 Metric Tonnes (DoF, local DoF)	From 100'000 to 20'000 lechwe antelopes	Loss of 25-50%. Loss of most nutritional grass species (own research)	Less flooding	-
Rufiji	50% loss of fish (local estimations, no catch data)	50% loss of wildlife (Stephenson1987, since 1999 increase in Selous (protection for tourism)	-	-	Loss due to logging (unspecified)
Pangani:	-	-	Loss of pastures. 25%-50%,	Less water downstream (upstream farming, logging)	Loss 50%, due to logging
Waza-Logone	Less catches 50% (local estimations). Smaller fish size)	Loss of wildlife	Loss of pasture. (Amount unknown)	Less flooding (dam)	-
Inner Niger Delta	Less catches, smaller size	-	(No data - study focussed on fisheries)	-	-
Okavango Delta	No reduction	Increase in wildlife (good monitoring)	Reduction due to protected areas rather than overuse.	-	-

Source: Own research between 2002 and 2005 (based on village surveys, interviews with local resource users and administrators, see Beeler et al., 2005; Fokou, 2005; Haller, 2007; Mbeyale, 2005; Meroka, 2005; Saum, 2006); official data from fishery, wildlife and forestry departments of local national universities and on expert reports and publications in Zambia (Kapongwe, 1993), Tanzania (Stevenson, 1987; Meroka, 2006; Cameroon (Loth et al., 2004).

ownership and to call for compensation, or they privatise fish ponds (Fokou, 2005). In the Pangani floodplain area, in Tanzania, people from the Pare mountains move into the Pangani floodplain and claim private ownership of agricultural land on previous dry season pastures of the Maasai (Mbeyale, 2005). In the Kafue Flats local powerfull people increasingly privatise pastures, demanding cattle as payment for each season's grazing rights (Haller, 2007). This means these common-pool resources can be controlled by powerful individuals, who exclude former commoners (see also Woodhouse et al., 2000).

The *consequences* on the resource side have been difficult to asses due to lack of long term reliable quantitative data as the respective governments lack funding to effectively measure and monitor the state of resources. However, older data and estimates have been available and evidence from local users and local administrators could be obtained. Table 4 summarises the findings. It is apparent that in most cases, there has been a considerable decline in the status of common-pool resources with the exception of Botswana (Okavango Delta).

The changes happening in 4 out of the 5 wetlands studied can be attributed not only to man-made large-scale changes in infrastructure such as dams, irrigation schemes and roads and their environmental consequences, but also to the institutional weakness of open-access constellations. Botswana constitutes a special case due to its wealth in diamonds and tourism and a peculiar elite structure. This elite is very stable and despite its rigidity allows substantial revenues that do trickle down to make a small difference at the local level compared to the other cases. Local people profit from government aid grants and from remittances that people who are employed in the formal sectors send back home. In addition, some states invest more into infrastructure in remote areas such as roads and much better equipped schools and health centres than in others (Saum, 2005, 2006; Samatar, 2006).

Intermediary conclusions: Up to this point one can summarize the findings as follows: In all the cases studied and especially in the Kafue Flats and Inner Niger Delta, we have a general decline of common-pool resources stemming from their high value and a peculiar path of an institutional change from common property regimes to open access or on rare occasions to privatisation. This situation is the consequence of various state interventions, directly through the control of common-pool resources and the management difficulties states have experienced during their crisis. Botswana is an exception because common-pool resources are not of major economic interest. However, we cannot stop at this analysis, for a New Institutionalist analysis has to go deeper in order to explain our findings of the particular paths of institutional change and the role ideology and power of different actors have played. The next section ,therefore, will discuss examples from all the case studies in order to verify the three major hypotheses which are A) the paradox of the present absence of the state hypothesis, B) the rent hypothesis in order to explain why some traditional rules remain in place and C) the legal pluralism and forum shopping hypothesis where I will provide evidence of how legal pluralism and forum shopping influences ideology used by actors in order to legitimate the way they want to shape the institutional setting for their benefit. In order to better illustrate this, an example of how such strategies are used in a situation of conflict in Zambia is added.

Major findings and lessons

In this and in the next chapters not only the Malian and Zambian but also findings from Cameroon, two cases in Tanzania (Pangani River Basin and Rufiji Floodplain) will be presented in order to discuss the three hypothesis.

Open access and citizenship: The paradox of the present absence of the state

Examples of erosion of traditional institutions:

There are many examples of traditional rules being violated, eroded and ignored since the state took control and introduced *de facto* open access. In Cameroon (Waza Logone) most of the collective fishing rules and rituals as well as the traditional coordination of access to pasture among the indigenous Kotoko fishermen had been in the hands of a traditional coordinating body lead by a *Sultan* and by village authorities: there was a pasture coordinator called *ngalway*, responsible for local coordination of access to fisheries and for pasture also on the village level. Fishing activities were coordinated on village level by ritual specialists. All these institutions have been completely eroded from late colonial times to the present. Since independence, immigrants from the ethnic Mousgoum group, who came in the late 19th century, increasingly pushed the citizen ideology. Since the political changes of the 1990s, the Mousgoum are the majority population and therefore no longer feel obliged to follow the rules of the Kotoko, who had been the first-comers controlling the area before. Therefore, fishing and herding activities can no longer be coordinated by the Kotoko. Pastoralist groups of the Arab Choa and of the Fulbe pay a tax to state officials and then feel free to do what they want. They have - as they put it - "bought" the pasture areas by making these tax payments (Fokou, 2005).

In both Tanzanian cases (Rujiji and Pangani River basins), local resource regimes based on ethno-professional groups and ritual coordination have been eroded since the areas have been administratively divided into different provinces and districts and resources are managed by several different departments. But the villagisation programmes (*Ujamaa*), were even more disruptive. These were designed to structure villages equally and mix different resource users in order to level ethnic divisions. This process opened up access to formerly controlled resource areas without regulations for the state did not manage these resources appropriately. Additionally ecosystem contexts were ignored leading to overuse of resources and resource degradation as well as disrupting livelihoods: In the *Pangani* case in Tanzania, disrupting water-use regulations, based on the concept of unity of a territory including mountain and plane areas have eroded water management institutions and created upstream-downstream conflicts. These conflicts was further intensified by the fact that logging in upstream state forests became a vital alternative to coffee production, affected by low coffee prices. In the lowlands, new rice irrigation schemes gave profit only to richer townsmen and lead to the loss of land for local people (Mbeyale 2005). In the Rujiji floodplain, in south-eastern Tanzania, villagisation and control of resources in different departments have lead to a erosion of local institutions. This is especially true closer to commercial centres where fisheries, forests and wildlife have become open-access-based on the citizen argument. In the hinterland poaching had been a serious problem due to high prices for trophy and game meat in the 1980's and due to a poaching network operating close to the Selous Game Reserve. Poaching problems can be mainly attributed to the state's inability to police National Parks during the mid 1990's (Meroka, 2006).

In the *Kafue Flats of Zambia*, traditional closing periods and rules regarding collective fishing and gender-related types of equipment are no longer respected. The Batwa's institution forbidding fishing at sacred spots in the river where bream (*tilapia*) breed, and restrictions on types of equipment are now disregarded. Since the economic crisis in the mid 1970s, people from all parts of Zambia come to the Kafue Flats in order to fish; all year round and with very fine-meshed nets. The Department of Fisheries lacks the finance and the capacity to control the river sections. In the tributaries of the same area, collective fishing events that were still respected six years ago are now being violated by young men, who fish ponds with nets before collective fishing takes place. Also, wildlife has become state property resource since the colonial administration began suppressing collective hunting (*chila*) in the 1950's. Political poaching was important before independence as a protest against the colonial government, but then declined massively due to big conservation investments made up to the mid 1970's (see Gibson, 1999; Haller, 2007). But the copper crisis triggered cuts in the conservation budget making wildlife in National Parks and Game Management Areas a *de facto* open-access resource. The effect for local people was especially painful effects. In order to mitigate the problems, the wildlife department (today called Zambian Wildlife Authority (ZAWA)) was trying to set up a participatory wildlife management scheme called ADMADE (see also Gibson, 1999). The initiative that was designed to organise people in Community Resource Boards (CRBs) and give financial incentives to three chiefs and some local scouts, failed to stop poaching in the area because the benefits for the local people were too small (Haller et al., 2005, 2006; Haller, 2007).

Problems for collective action: If we are indeed facing an open-access problem, the main question we have to answer is: Why are local actors not able to solve this problem and act collectively if according to Mancur Olson's theory of collective action, good conditions for solving common-pool management problems are i) absence of higher-level control and ii) small-scale groups (see Olson, 1965). The main answer is that these "local" groups are not just acting alone. They compete with outside commercial interests. Since independence, the state system was meant to balance outside and local interests. Although this system was never been perfect, it was to a certain degree operational. In Zambia for example, the Department of Fisheries had much more staff and much more equipment than today. Conservation was achieved by providing funds for scouts and military infrastructure (cars, planes, weapons etc). Now this imposed management system is imploding and the demand for co-management or local community management is rising. But people on the local level are often unable to act collectively in this situation, because the actors have become very heterogeneous and some outside actors are now very powerful. They often argue that as citizens of the state, they are empowered to use common-pool resources as they want, by virtue of their citizenship. At the same, time the state is absent. We have labelled this situation the paradox of "present absence of the state". In effect, it means that outsiders desiring access to common-pool resources can subscribe to the existence of the state and its institutions to justify gaining access to resources. But because the state is only virtually present (see also Berry, 2006 and Chaveau, 2006) for similar cases in Western Africa), the same people can violate state rules at will, without any reaction from the state. The state is not present to monitor and sanction misuse and therefore creates an open-access situation. The paradox of the "present absence of the state" gives these actors a tremendous bargaining power over local people for they define their legality themselves (Haller, 2007; Haller et al., 2008). On the other hand, the identity of being local, often linked with ethnic names in contrast to other names is used by people viewing themselves as being indigenous or autochthonous to the area (see also Lund (2007), Berry (2006), Chaveau (2006) on similar issues on how under decentralisation autochthony is newly constructed). However, in many of the cases we have studied claiming to be indigenous does often not pay in this constellation:

The case of fishing in Zambia illustrates this situation. Local people in the Kafue Flats are very aware of and angry about the fact that immigrant fishermen are using destructive techniques such as mosquito nets and that they are fishing during closed periods between December and February when fishing is prohibited to conserve fish in breeding areas in the river sections. But if Ila, Balundwe and Batwa groups, who claim to be the indigenous "sons of the soil", want to take action against seasonal commercial fishermen, these tell the "locals" that as citizens of the state they are not to be told what to do. "We are Zambians – Don't tell us how to fish" is a standard response of immigrated commercial fishermen to local collective action. One option for the different Ila and Batwa groups would be to use violence, but the seasonal fishermen are sometimes highly aggressive young men. So when such a conflict breaks out, it often turns violent and is perceived as an ethnic conflict. Because the use of force by locals is prohibited by law it leads to rapid military intervention – unlike a violation of the fishery rules. Therefore, local collective action is hindered by state agencies, which, nevertheless, fail to enforce official rules for the management of the fisheries of the Kafue Flats, while local rules have been dismantled or disregarded by outsiders (Haller et al., 2008).[20]

Similar situations occur in all the settings we have studied: In Mali democratisation and decentralisation have allowed a wider group of people who are citizens of the state newly created districts or communes to claim access to common-pool resources as they please (Benjaminsen, 1997; Benjamin, 2006; Beeler et al., 2005; Landolt, 2005; Fokou, 2005). Belonging to a newly created administrative unit and being a citizen in Mali enables young men with their motorboats and nylon nets to move wherever they want (Beeler et al.,

[20] Referring to such examples, it is not the authors' intention to take sides and claim that "outsiders" do not have the right to use these resources. Outside users have always been part of common property regimes but local people had control over common-pool resources.

2005). In Cameroon, the Mousgoum agro-pastoralists and fishermen now argue from the position of a democratic majority that they will no longer subscribe to Kotoko fishery regulations dictated by an undemocratic minority. Similarly nomadic pastoralists, after paying the state tax, move wherever they want to and justify access and free use of resources by the tax they paid to the government. The same happened in Tanzania: during *Ujamaa* villagisation, set up units against ethnic identity and fostered the idea that all the resources in Tanzania are for all the Tanzanians. Old institutions or regulations by locals were unwelcome hindrances to the ideology that all resources are for Tanzanians (Meroka, 2006; Mbeyale, 2005). While "locals", who often stay in an area for longer time, would like to craft rules in order to regulate access to resources, try to act collectively, they are hindered by the paradox of the present absence of the state while immigrants are given a free hand.[21]

Differential change in local institutions: Rules which pay are going to stay

We have shown above that state law has replaced local traditional institutions, and that local users often lost their sense of ownership of common-pool resources. While this is generally true in many constellations of the wetlands studied, we encountered cases in which traditional institutions or transformed versions of such institutions are still in place, or where traditional institutions still operate in areas with little pressure on common-pool resources.

In some cases, manipulated traditional institutions can become the source of rents for local powerful people, some of them deriving their power from rituals. These actors have an interest in upholding traditional institutions in ways that generate rent. They do not exclude outsiders in their attempts to use the common-pool resource.

In the case of the Inner Niger Delta in Mali, for example, traditional institutions have been transformed in ways that serve local administrators. The "Masters of the Water" of the Bozo and Somono continue to perform im-

---

[21] This is no contradiction with some of the new literature on identity processes of autochthonous and seasonal immigrants (Evers (ed.), 2006; Kuba et al., 2005; Lund (ed.), 2007). We are fully aware that when resource values rise, locals do start referring to them being the first and using a variety of strategies and ideologies with discourses and narratives to legitimize this claim. However, in most of the cases studied here making reference to being local and using a specific ethnic name does not challenge the high bargaining power of the seasonal immigrants.

portant rituals and still initiate collective fishery activities. However, while the control and coordination that the traditional institutional regime used to provide has been eroded, the distributional rule called *manga ji*, that allows the "Masters of the Water" to appropriate one third of the catch from outsiders remains valid. The *manga ji* is now regarded as a form of rent by these masters. Local administrators, who should actually enforce state regulations and should prohibit this traditional rule, profit from this situation. They support the "old rules" informally, because they enable them to receive payment from the masters (Fay, 2000; Beeler et al., 2005).[22]

In another case, traditional rules are regulating access to pastoral areas among the Ila in the Kafue Flats, Zambia. In one of the chiefdoms studied, old rules giving access to cattle camps (*matanga rule*) to local first-comer groups are maintained because of the future interests of a local opponent of a chief. He has opted to keep this rule as a traditional way of handling pasture management in the hope of future profit. In the old system, an extended Ila family had to give one head of cattle in return for a long-term usufruct right of access to a cattle camp and therefore to pasture. However, the opposition leader wants to change the rule of paying one head of cattle (usufruct right fee) into a rent of one head of cattle per family *per season*.

In *Cameroon*, fishing is traditionally done in special canals and the local Kotoko fishery groups are seemingly still in control of assigning rights to construct canals. But research among the Kotoko in two villages, showed that the Sultan and local ritual masters, who coordinated fishing activities are no longer really in control of fishing activities (Landolt, 2005; Fokou, 2005). The drastic increase in the number of fishing canals is caused by powerful people and leaders in the villages of the Kotoko, who assign rights to others to build canals and who are legitimizing this old institution historically. However, there is no regulation anymore of how many canals are made and how use is coordinated. The traditional institution remains to maintain the technology and issue the right to dig canals because it generates great profit and is easily accessible by outsiders (Fokou, 2005).

In conclusion, we argue here that rules that remain do so, not because of their benefit for sustainable resource management, but because powerful actors see them as an easy means of generating a rent. As the institution is understood locally, even if it exists in a transformed way, the basic reference

---

[22] As the 'Masters of the Water' were getting one third of the catch, formally given to them in kind and later in cash by outsiders, some areas are seen as being fully controlled by the administration, while the money is still collected by the 'Masters of the Water' (see Fay, 2000; Beeler et al., 2005).

to the old rule in this context helps to capture gains in a locally legitimate way. This is the case because transaction costs are considerably lowered by using a legitimate institutional reference. This enables resource or rent extraction with lower costs than if new rules had to be established. Such dynamics are linked to local elites, who allude to the traditional institutions for easy personal gain.

In remote areas, traditional institutions sometimes continue to persist because they are too far away from commercial centres and the influence of the state. Therefore commercial immigrants are not (yet) interested in these common-pool resources, and local communities are still relatively homogeneous. Among the Rufiji groups in Tanzania, which are far away from commercial centres, fisheries in a lake that is connected to the floodplain and is close to the Selous Game Reserve, are still regulated by traditional institutions, because the villages are homogeneous enough to protect their lake and still perform rituals intended to appease crocodiles but which actually coordinate the use of the fisheries in that lake (Meroka, 2006). Similarly, the fisheries in the tributary sections of the Kafue Flats in Zambia also continued to be managed according to local traditional rules up to six years ago, when the commercial fishery concentrated on the main river and the tributaries were still controlled and regulated by ritual specialists. However this changed after interest in commercial fishing in the tributaries started to grow due to rise in prices and scarcity of fish (see above, Haller et al., 2005, 2006; Haller, 2007, 2008).

Legal Pluralism, forum shopping, resource governance and conflict

As we outlined above, all regions display a major heterogeneity of legal frameworks. Resource regimes that have been formerly oriented to manage different resources inclusively within one territory or one ethnic group have become overlaid with different normative orders after various wetlands came under colonial and post-colonial control. Apart from different regulations emanating from the historical phases, regulations vary for each resource, sometimes overlapping within the same formal legal framework: In all the wetlands studied, wildlife and fisheries as well as land and water management are controlled by separate authorities or departments.

The case of Kafue Flats in Zambia illustrates this: Fisheries fall under the agricultural department, while wildlife is under the Zambian Wildlife Authority (ZAWA). The latter has a much more a military-like structure than the former. Water is regulated by yet another department and law set, while forest management is under a different office with its own regulations. If, for instance, fishing communities and agro-pastoralists develop an interest in fishing in the Kafue River Basin, all these departments and their respective formal laws and regulations are relevant: The area is close to National Parks and Game Management Areas within the Kafue River basin, which is also used for hydropower. This means that all these state parties are involved but act under different and contradicting jurisdictions. For example, in National Parks and Game Management Areas, the Departments of Fisheries and Wildlife often contradict each other. The same is true with water management in where different departments are involved with different interests (water affairs for hydropower, environmental departments, wildlife and fisheries, veterinary department, agricultural departments etc.). This often creates conflicts because jurisdictions are not coordinated and do not take customary law into account. But apart from this plurality of overlapping and competing traditional and modern laws and the pluralism within modern law, overlapping claims on the level of customary or "pseudo customary law" exist (see Cutshall, 1980). What is customary is a contested issue and often relates to the rights of being the first immigrants to an area (see also debates in Kuba et al. (eds.), 2006; Evers (ed.), 2005 and Lund (ed.), 2007). This is the case with the management of pastures in Zambia among the Ila of the Chiefdom Nalubamba, where in the context of a proposed irrigation scheme, a conflict about which customary law determines different stakeholder claims to control the use and allocation of pastoral lands develped (Haller, 2007, see below). To add to the complexity, we not only have customary laws and their interpretation, and formal legal pluralism, but there are several international environmental and development regulations and laws (protected areas, RAMSAR sites, different conventions etc.). To complete this complicated picture, we have international rules for economic cooperation and structural adjustment programmes. Aid such as poverty reduction programmes and new credit facilities are often made subject to conditions that influence national regulations on governance, agricultural and health policies. Foreign NGOs and governmental development organisations also intervene: On the national and local level there are regulations set up by NGOs or legal frameworks set up by the state, but supported by NGOs in a way that enact or interpret formal laws in a specific way. We therefore have sorts of semi-autonomous fields (Moore, 1978) and polycentric constellations (Ostrom, 1999) of often overlapping and contradicting levels (see Meinzen-Dick et al., 2002). One case in point is in Zambia, where inheritance laws were created that should prevent widows being „robbed" of the late husband's cattle by his relatives. This has especially involved the Ila and Balundwe groups of cattle owners and their traditional inheritance regulations. Traditionally at funerals, cattle of the late leader of an extended family will be widely distributed among relatives and some of it kept by the new head of the family, who takes the position of the deceased. This was done in order to keep this part of the herd as a collective property of the extended family. The new inheritance law labelled these distribution and social security mechanisms as robbery of individual property of cattle that shall be given to the widows and the children (sons). The possibility now to claim cattle as private property triggered a shift in the perception of ownership from kin and extended family group to individuals, and this had an impact on the demand of pastoral areas: As cattle are no longer a group property, more individuals hold their personal cattle and want their own cattle camp, leading to more pressure on pastoral areas, as more camps have to be assigned. This case illustrates the complexity of institutions and the possibilities for forum shopping that this provides. Widows and sons often try to get individual cattle via this law, while older men and more traditionally oriented younger men who profit form the control of larger herds try to argue for the traditional rules of group ownership in cattle by making reference to the traditional system of social security (Haller, 2007).

This means that generally in conflict situations, and often these are situations when access, use and distribution of common-pool resources are contested because they become scarce or economically more interesting, different actors use different legal frameworks and related ideologies. In addition, such constellations can also be labelled as „open moments" (Lund, 1998b), in which actors try to control important resources are worth considering because of special a situation, in which formal and informal institutions do not operate and new ones emerge in "twighlight" (Lund, 2007). Such moments could be situations of crisis (hunger, drought or war) as well as new laws bringing about opportunities for change. Since the 1980's, legal frameworks in Africa have often changed in connection with structural adjustment programmes geared to decentralisation and privatisation (see Woodhouse et al., 2000; Ribot, 1999; Ferguson, 1999; Ribot et al., 2006; Haller, 2007; Haller, 2007b). All these contexts make for often unpredictable changes in governance, because different actors have a huge array of tools at their disposal or legitimizing the way in which things are accomplished, and for controlling common-pool resources for their own use. All these elements within the legal framework fuel specific forum shopping as they not only provide impressions of legality but deliver the discourses and narratives underscoring actor's positions or undermining the positions of adversaries.

Contesting the floodplain: The case of the Mbeza irrigation project, Kafue Flats in Zambia: Such processes of legal pluralism do create conflict situations when different leaders fight for the recognition of their way of using the floodplain. This is best illustrated by a conflict over an irrigation project in the

Kafue Flats in Zambia, among the Ila people. A local chief wanted to introduce an irrigation project in the best parts of the pastoral area after a series of droughts and loss of 50 to 80% cattle due to a *theilerosis* epidemic.[23] He argued that the people of the area have rich soils and enough water to produce enough food. An opposition leader then challenged him, arguing in favour of the richer pastoralists, claiming that "the local Ila people" are still cattle herders and that irrigation agriculture would destroy their way of life, and their social security based on cattle. During the dispute, the chief was using a modernist ideology and a class discourse (the rich want the pastures for themselves), and the narrative that hunger was due to extensive production systems, and that intensive agriculture would solve the problem, thus fitting nicely into the governmental poverty reduction scheme. The opposition used "traditionalist" ideology with an ethnic identity discourse. A narrative claimed that the chief was not the son of the soil, that he did too little to fight the epidemic, and that he was dismantling the Ila social security system and the cultural pride based on cattle. In addition, he was accused of selling out the land to foreign investors. The dispute was fought on several levels: locally with rallies and counter rallies and meetings, direct confrontations, fight for representation in print and radio media, as well as the fight for recognition of politicians and members of government and administrators and last but not least in court. Behind the dispute some hidden agendas could be seen: The chief was fighting for recognition, as he did not have a material basis to be recognised "culturally". He wanted to control more land based on the new land act in Zambia in order to attract NGOs that would have brought him (and his followers) wealth from donor money. The opposition leader himself was trying to control the people that previously were in charge of pastoral areas in order to privatise the pastures. This privatisation was also fostered by the new land act of 1995 that makes it possible to receive leasehold titles for 99 years acknowledged by the President of the Nation and a local chief. As the opposition leader holds such titles but fears to lose them through conflicts with the local chief, he favours the old regulation because it allows him to control the land and generate future gains more effectively than through direct privatisation. It also helps him to mobilise people against the chief because on the "on stage level" he is seen as a defender of the traditional common property regime, while he is opting for a major transformation on a "back stage level" which suits his own interest. He therefore helped local richer cattle owners to organise the protest against the chief. Both actors – the chief and the opposition leader - tried to hide

---

[23] This cattle sickness is transmitted by ticks and is locally know as denkete or East-Coast Fever (see Haller, 2007).

their individual agendas by using arguments, taken from specific legal frameworks and based on norms and values rooted in different ideologies, discourses and narratives used to strengthen their respective bargaining powers (Haller, 2007).

Conclusion and lessons learned

Such processes need to be analysed carefully when lessons need to be drawn for the governance of common-pool resources. The cases presented here comparatively, indicate that local institutions for the management of common-pool resources existed and operated to reduce transaction costs for a co-ordinated use. Often, sustainable use has been a by-product of the control over resources, that powerful groups or individuals within the communities defending their interests in order to profit from the long-term distribution of access to resources. Interestingly, this kind of control is often embedded in religious rituals. The belief that resource controllers have connections to spirits is a worldview, which is used to strengthen the monitoring and sanctioning devices. In the process of institutional change, transfer to state ownership and crisis in the national economies fostered the change from a common property regime to *de facto* open access or, in some cases to informal privatization. The fact that on the national level control is reduced due to lack of financial means and that at the same time, relative prices for common-pool resources such as fish, wildlife, timber, pasture (in connection with cattle), compared to agricultural products, salaries and cash crop/mining products, are rising, makes the common-pool resources economically attractive. As Ensminger illustrates, the New Institutionalism predicts that those changes that are based on external changes and linked to internal changes within a community will also lead to changes in bargaining power, ideologies and institutions. Economic theory would predict that privatisation of resources that are in high demand would trigger institutions of private property. New Institutionalism tells us however, and this is illustrated by the examples, that this path is indirect or can lead to other directions: A rise in relative prices does not lead directly to privatisation but to de facto open access and to the retention of old common property institutions, often in a new form.

In order to understand these processes it is vital to identify how resources have been managed in the past and how the evolution of institutions for the management of common-pool resources were linked with the notion of local control, identity and belonging. However, there is also the need to analyse whether and how these institutions have been dismantled and to find out when and under which conditions of political and economic interest it happened. The African states from our case studies have often taken over control of common-pool resources to be managed under sectorial state laws (water, fisheries, wildlife, land, agricultural and veterinary services etc.). But because they often lacked means for monitoring and sanctioning (problems of state economies and crisis) they often created open-access constellations. External factors and changes in relative prices are leading to push and pull dynamics and increased interest in common-pool resources for "immigrants" and "locals". The exception, which however underlines this hypothesis is the case of Botswana, where due to the good economic performance there is no crisis of common-pool resource overuse as in the other cases because there is less commercial interest in common-pool resources compared to aid, remittance and salaries.

The most interesting level, where I see the possibility to enlarge the analysis of the New Institutionalism by incorporating new tendencies of more recent developments in anthropology and sociology, is the aspect of ideology and (bargaining) power: Institutional change to open access is often pushed by seasonal users of the common-pool resources who gain most by purely extractive use of the resources. For them the ideology of citizenship strengthens their bargaining power and prevents local interest groups from acting collectively. In such constellations collective action is difficult due to the paradox of the "present absence of the state" and in such constellations most often locally developed common property regimes most often collapse because collective action is rendered difficult. However in some cases "traditional" institutions or what is remaining of them, persist because they give powerful people the possibility and the legitimacy to extract a rent. Both constellations can lead to conflicts and in such conflicts are often linked to legal pluralism. Legal pluralism enables the different actors to refer to different legal formal and informal forums. This level of analysis helps to understand why people, according to their power, choose one option and not another. In some cases, it pays to push traditional institutions, while in others state law or NGO law pays better. Again, such constellations are linked externally with the economic situation of a nation state, but as well with the meso-level of administration, and finally the local level. However, if such a kind of analysis is pursued it also addresses the need to have a close look at what is understood by "local community" and identify the interests of the members of a often heterogeneous community (see Cleaver, 2001). When trying to involve local people in the management of natural resources (see Ribot, 1999; Hulmes et al., 2001), it is too easy to assume that a chief is able to lead local action peacefully. There is the need to address all stakeholders and to understand what motives and incentives they have and on what legal resources they draw upon based on these interests.

Therefore, the contribution of our comparative study is to show that there is a possibility to link economic and actor-driven approaches with more post-modern developments in social and cultural anthropology with a focus on power and ideology issues. The case studies illustrate that it is vital to be able to understand issues of changing power and distribution in the context of macro- and meso-level changes (economic, political and environmental), and how power and distribution are rooted in ideologies, discourses and narratives of identity and of belonging. The case of the Kafue Flats is a nice illustration of that issue and similar processes can be seen in other floodplain cases, where immigrants claim access to resources as citizens of the state, and refer to the notion of democracy and of modernity in order to justify free access (this happens the same way when the Mousgoum try to get access to fisheries in Cameroon and young men seek access to fish in Mali and Tanzania). The evolution of resource-use patterns, be it open access or hidden privatisation and rent seeking, is often anchored in the array of existing "traditional" and "modern" laws and regulations. This array is again linked to ideology in order to legitimize (free) access to use and use of common-pool resources and to strengthen the power of different actors and groups. It is our task to detect who has what interests on what levels, why claims are performed in a specific way, and why which aspect of the legal pluralistic setting provides an ideologically legitimate resource base in order to construct legitimacy. This is exactly what the enlarged framework of the Neo Institutional approach can do.

Acknowledgements:

The author wishes to thank all the research team of AFWeP for their contributions to the conference held in Zurich, Switzerland in 2005, on which much of this paper's data is based. We also thank Elinor Ostrom and Frank Van Laerhoven for their important and useful comments. We equally thank the National Competence Centre in Research North South programme for their support relating to the research done by three African students (Patrick Meroka, Gimbage Mbeyale and Gilbert Fokou), who were part of this programme (NCCR North South, IP6: Institutional Change and Livelihood Strategies). We further thank the Swiss National Science Foundation (funds Tobias Haller) and the Department of Social Anthropology (partly funding research of Sabrina Beeler, Karin Frei, Gabriela Landolt and Roland Saum). I especially thank Beeler and Frei for their valuable work on Mali, which is used in more detail in some of the chapters of this paper. I also thank Elinor Ostrom and Jean Ensminger, who supported this comparative research project. All errors are, however, the sole responsibility of the author.

References:

Acheson, J. A. 1989. Management of Common Property Resources. In: Plattner, S. (ed.): Economic Anthropology. Stanford University Press. Stanford: 78-351.

Acheson, J. A. 2003. Capturing the Commons. Devising Institutions to Manage the Maine Lobster Industry. University Press of New England. Lebabon.

Acreman, M. C., Hollis, G. E. (eds.) 1996. Water Management and Wetlands in Sub-Saharan Africa. IUCN, Gland (Switzerland).

Adams, W. M. 1990. Green Development. Environment and Sustainability in the Third World. Routledge, London.

Agrawal, A. 2002. Common Resources and Institutional Sustainability. In: Ostrom, E. et al.: The Drama of the Commons. National Research Council. National Academy Press, Washington D.C.

Agrawal, A. 2003. Sustainable Governance of Common Pool Resources: Context, Methods and Policy. Annual Review of Anthropology. 32: 243-262.

Agarwal, A. 2005. Environmentality. Technologies of Government and the Making of Subjects. Duke University Press. Durham and London.

Agrawal, A., Ribot, J. 1999. Accountability in Decentralisation: A Framework with South Asian and African cases. Journal of Developing Areas 33: 473-502.

Becker, D. C., Ostrom, E. 1995. Human Ecology and Resource Sustainability: The Importance of Institutional Diversity. Annual Review of Ecology. 26: 113-33.

Beeler, S., Frei, K. 2005. Collective Resources and Institutional Change in the Niger Inland Delta (Mali): The cases of the Somono and Bozo Fishermen of Wandiaka and Daga Womina. Presented at the Conference (February 2005) and workshop on CPR-Institutions in African Floodplain Wetlands, Department of Social Anthropology, University of Zurich, Switzerland.

Benda-Beckmann, K. von 1984. The broken stairs to consensus: Village justice and state courts in Manangkabau. Dordrecht (the Netherlands). Foris.

Benda-Beckmann, F. and K. von 1997. Natural Resources, Environment and Legal Pluralism: An introduction. In: Benda Beckmann, F. and K. von, Kuppe, R., Potz, R. (eds.): Natural Resources, Environment, and Legal Pluralism. Law and Anthropology. International Yearbook for Legal Anthropology 9. Martinus Nijhoff Publishers. The Hague/Boston/London: Pp.: I-XII.

Benda-Beckmann, F. von 2002. Who is afraid of legal pluralism? Paper presented at the XIIIth Conference of the Commission on Folk Law and Legal Pluralism, Chianmei, Thailand. www.jlp.bham.ac.uk/alphabetic.htm

Benjamin, C. 2006. Decentralisation and Livelihoods in the Malian Sahel: Challenges of Legal Pluralism in Decentralized Natural Resource Management. Paper presented at the 11th Biennal Conference of the International Association for the Study of Common Property, Bali, Indonesia.

Benjaminsen, T. A. 1997. Natural Resource Management. Paradigm Shifts, and the Decentralization Reform in Mali. Human Ecology. 25/1: 121-143.

Berry, S. 2006. Privatisation and the Politics of Belonging in West-Africa. In: Kuba, R., Lentz, C. (eds): Land and the Politics of Belonging in West-Africa. Brill. Leiden/Boston: 241-264.

Bierschenk, T., Olivier de Sardan, J.-P. 1996. Les pouvoir en absence de l'état. Configuration de pouvoir politique locale et rapport à l'Etat en milieu rurale en centre african. Working Papers on African Societies. Schiler. Berlin.

Chabwela, H. N. 1992 The ecology and resource use of the Bangweulu Basin and the Kafue Flats. In: Jeffrey, R. C. V.; Chabwela, H. N.; Howard, G.; Dugan, P. J. (eds.): Managing the Wetlands of Kafue Flats and Bangweulu Bassin. IUCN. Gland (Switzerland): 11-24.

Chaveau, J.-P. 2006. How does an Institution Evolve? Land, Politics, Intergenerational Relations and the Institutions of the tutorat among Authochtones and Immigrants (Gnab region, Ivory Coast). In: Kuba, R.; Lentz, C. (eds): Land and the Politics of Belonging in West-Africa. Brill. Leiden/Boston: 213-240.

Chooye, P. M., Drijver, C. A. 1995. Changing Views on the Development of the Kafue Flats in Zambia. In: Roggeri, H. (ed.): Tropical Freshwater Wetlands. A guide to Currents Knowledge and Sustainable Management. Luwer Academic Publishers. Dordrecht/Boston/London: 137-143.

Cleaver, F. 2001. Institutions, Agency and the Limitations of Participatory Approaches to Development. In: Cooke, B.; Kothari, U. (eds.): Participation: the new tyranny. Zed Books. New York: 36-55.

Cutshall, C. 1980. Disputing for Power: Elites and the Law among the Ila of Zambia. University Microfilms International. London.

Drijver, C. A., Marchand, M. 1985. Taming the floods: Environmental aspects of floodplain development in Africa. Centre for Environmental Studies. Leiden University. Leiden.

Dyson-Hudson, R., Alden Smith, E. 1978. Human territoriality: an ecological reassessment. American Anthropologist. 80: 21-41

Eggertsson, T. 1996. The economics of control and the cost of property rights. In: Hanna, S.; Folke, C.; Mähler, K.-G. (eds.): Rights to Nature Ecological, Economic, Culture, and Political Principles of Institutions for the Environment. Island Press. Washington DC: 157-175.

Ellenbroek, G. A. 1987. Ecology and productivity of an African wetland system: The Kafue Flats, Zambia. Geobotany 9. Leiden University. Leiden.

Ensminger, J. 1992. Making a Market. The Institutional Transformation of an African Society. Cambridge University Press. Cambridge.

Ensminger, J., Knight, J. 1997. Changing Social Norms: Common Property, Bridewealth, and Clan Exogamy. Current Anthropology 38/1: 1-24.

Emsminger, J., 1998. Anthropology and the New Institutionalism. Journal of Institutional and Theoretical Economics 154: 774-789.

Escobar, A. 1999. After Nature: Steps to an Antiessentialist Political Ecology. Current Anthropology. 40/1: 1-30.

Evers, S. et al. (eds.) 2005. Competing Jurisdictions. Settling Land Claims in Africa. Brill. Leiden/Boston.

Fairhead, J., Leach, M. 1996. Misreading the African Landscape. Society and ecology in a forest-savanna mosaic. Cambridge University Press. Cambridge.

Feeney, D., Berkes, F., McCay, B., Acheson, J. 1990: The Tragedy of the Commons: Twenty-Two Years Later. Human Ecology. 18/1: 1-13.

Fay, C. 2000. Des poissons et des hommes: pêcheurs, chercheurs et administrateurs face à la pêche au Maasina (Mali). In: Chauveau, J.-P. et al. (eds.): Les pêches piroguières en Afrique de l'Ouest. CMI, IRD, Karthala: Pages 125-166.

Ferguson, J. 1999. Expectations of Modernity: Myths and Meanings of Urban Life on the Zambian Copperbelt. University of California Press. California.

Fokou, G. 2005. Common Pool Resource Management, Power Relations and Conflicts between Fishermen, Peasants and Pastoralists in the Waza-Logone floodplain, North of Cameroon. Presented at the Conference and workshop on CPR-Institutions in African Floodplain Wetlands, Department of Social Anthropology, University of Zurich, Switzerland. February 14.-16, 2005.

Fokou, G. 2006. Common Pool Resource Management Institutions and Conflicts in the Waza-Logone-Floodplain. Submitted PhD Thesis, University of Yaounde, Cameroon.

Gibson, C. C. 1999 Politicians and Poachers. The Political Economy of Wildlife Policy in Africa. Cambridge University Press. Cambridge.

Haller, T. 2001. Common Property Institutions and Relations of Power: Resource-Management, Change and Conflicts in African Floodplain Wetlands Project submitted to the Swiss National Science Foundation in May 2001 Accepted in August 2001.

Haller, T. 2002a. Common Property Resource Management, Institutional Change and Conflicts in African Floodplain Wetlands: Presentation of a research project and reflections on institutional change and conflicts. The African Anthropologist. 9/1: 25-35

Haller, T. 2002b. The Understanding of Institutions and their link to resource management from a New Institutionalism Perspective. Working Paper No.1, IP 6 Institutional Change and Livelihood Strategies. NCCR North South www.nccr-north-south.unibe.ch/document/document.asp?ID=586&refTitle=the%20NCCR%20North-South&Context=NCCR.

Haller, T. (ed.) 2005. African Floodplain Wetlands Project, The Common Property Resource Digest. Quarterly Publication of the International Association for the Study of Common Property (IASCP), Bloomington, Indiana: Indiana University Issue No 74.
www.indiana.edu/~iascp/digest.html

Haller, T., Merten, S. 2005. Common Pool Resource Management, Institutional Change and Conflicts among the Ila, Balundwe-Tonga and Batwa, Kafue Flats, Zambia. Presented at the Conference and workshop on CPR-Institutions in African Floodplain Wetlands, Department of Social Anthropology, University of Zurich, Switzerland. February 14.-16, 2005.

Haller, T., Merten, S. 2006. "No capital needed". De facto open access to Common Pool Resources, Poverty and Conservation in the Kafue Flats, Zambia. Policy Matters. 14: 103-113.

Haller, T. 2007. The Contested Floodplain. The Institutional Change of Common Pool Resource Management and Conflicts among the Ila, Tonga and Batwa, Kafue Flats (Southern Province) Zambia. Department of Social Anthropology, University of Zurich. Zurich (Switzerland).

Haller, T. 2007b. Is there a culture of sustainability? What social and cultural anthropology has to offer 15 years after Rio. In: Kaufmann-Hayoz, R.; Burger, P.: Nachhaltige Entwicklung: Nachhaltigkeitsforschung – Perspektiven der Sozial- und Geisteswissenschaften. Akademie der Geistes –und Sozialwissenschaften. Bern (Schweiz).

Haller, T., Merten, S. 2008. "We are Zambians – don't tell us how to fish!" Institutional change, power relations and conflicts in the kafue flats fisheries in Zambia. Human Ecology. 36/5: 699-715.

Hulme, D.; Murphree, M. 2001. African Wildlife and Livelihoods: The Promise and performance of Community Conservation. James Curry Publishers. London, New York, Harare.

Hardin, G. 1968. The Tragedy of the Commons. Science. 162: 1243-1248.

Hughes, R. H.; Hughes, J. S. (eds.) 1992. A directory of African wetlands. IUCN. Gland.

Jeffrey, R. C. V., Chabwela, H. N., Howard, G., Dugan, P.J. (eds.) 1992. Managing the Wetlands of Kafue Flats and Bangweulu Bassin. IUCN, Gland (Switzerland).

Kassibo, B. 2000. Pêche continental et migration: contrôle politique et social des migrations de pêche dans le Delta central du Niger. In: Chaveau, J.-P. et al. (ed.): Les pêches piroguières en Afrique de l'Ouest. CMI, IRD. Karthala, Paris: 231-246.

Kuba, R., Lentz, C. (eds). 2006. Land and the Politics of Belonging in West-Africa. Brill. Leiden/Boston.

Landolt, G. 2005. Changing Institutions among the Mousgoum and Kotoko of the Village Lahai in the Waza-Logone Floodplain. Presented at the Conference and workshop on CPR-Institutions in African Floodplain Wetlands, Department of Social Anthropology, University of Zurich, Switzerland. February 14.-16, 2005.

Lentz, C. 2005. First Comers and Late Comers: The Role of Narratives in Land Claims. In: Evers, S. et al (eds): Competing Jurisdictions. Settling Land Claims in Africa. Brill. Leiden/Boston: 157-180.

Loth, P. (ed.) 2004. The return of the water. Restoring the Waza Logone floodplain in Cameroon. IUCN Wetlands and Water Resources Programme, Blue Series. IUCN. Gland.

Lund, C. 1998. Law, Power and Politics in Niger. Land struggles and the rural Code. APAD. LIT publishers. Hamburg.

Lund, C. 1998b. Struggles for Land and Political Power. On the Politicization of Land Tenure and Disputes. Journal of Legal Pluralism. 40: 1-22.

Lund, C. 2007. Twilight Institutions: Public Authority and Local Politics in Africa. Blackwell Publishing. London.

Mbeyale, G. 2005. Common Pool Institutions and Power Relations: Resource Management Change in Pangani River Basin, Tanzania. Presented at the Conference and workshop on CPR-Institutions in African Floodplain Wetlands, Department of Social Anthropology, University of Zurich, Switzerland. February 14.-16, 2005.

McKean, M. 2000. Common Property: What It Is, What It Is Good For, and What Makes It Work? In: Gibson, C.; McKean, M.; Ostrom, E. (eds.): People and forests: Communities, Institutions, and Governance. MIT Press. Cambridge.

Meinzen-Dick, R., Pradhan, R. 2002. Legal Pluralism and Dynamic Property Rights. CAPRi-Working Paper no. 22. IFPRI. Washington. www.capri.cgiar.org/wp/capriwp22.asp

Meroka, P. 2005. Common Pool Resource Management, Institutional Change and Conflicts among Rufiji people in the Rufiji Floodplain, Tanzania. Presented at the Conference and workshop on CPR-Institutions in African Floodplain Wetlands, Department of Social Anthropology, University of Zurich, Switzerland. February 14.-16, 2005.

Meroka, Patrick. 2006. Common Pool Resource Management and Conflict Resolution in Rufiji Floodplain, Tanzania. Dep. of Social Anthropology. University of Zurich. Zurich (Switzerland).

Moore, S. F. 2000. Law As Process. An Anthropological Approach (1978) LIT-publishers. Münster/London.

Moorehead, R. 1989. Changes Taking Place in Common-Property Resource Management in the Inland Niger Delta of Mali. In: Berkes, F. (ed.) Common Property Resources. Belhaven Press. London: 256-272.

Nohlen, D. 2004. Taschenwörterbuch der Dritten Welt. Rororo-Verlag. Hamburg.

North, D. 1990. Institutions, Institutional Change and Economic Performance. Cambridge University Press. Cambridge.

Olson, M. 1965. The Logic of collective action. Public Goods and the Theory of Groups. Harvard University. Cambridge.

Ostrom, E. 1990. Governing the Commons. The Evolution of Institutions for Collective Action. Cambridge University Press. Cambridge.

Ostrom, E. 1999. Coping with the Tragedy of the Commons. Annual Review of Political Science 2: 493-535.

Ostrom, E. et. al. 2002. The Drama of the Commons. National Research Council. National Academy Press. Washington D.C.

Rennie, J. K. 1982. Traditional Society and Modern Developments in Namwala District. In: Williams, G.; Howard, G. W. (eds.): Proceedings of the National Seminar on Environment and Change. The Kafue Basin Research Committee of the University of Zambia, Lusaka: Pages 35-46.

Ribot, J. C. 1999. Decentralisation, Participation, and Accountability in the Sahelian Forestry. Legal Instruments of political-administrative control. Africa 69/1: 23-65.

Ribot, J. C.; Oyono, P. R. 2006. The Politics of Decentralisation. In: Wisner, B. et al. (eds). Towards a New Map of Africa. Earthscan. London: 205-228.

Ritchie, J., Spencer, L. 1994. Qualitative data analysis for applied policy research. In: Bryman, A.; Burgess, R. G.: Analysing Qualitative Data. Routledge. London: 173-194.

Ruttan, L. M. 1998. Closing the Commons: Cooperation for Gain or Restraint? Human Ecology. 26/1: 43-66

Saum, R. 2005. Common Pool Resource Use and Change in Ikoga, Okavango Delta, Botswana. Presented at the Conference and workshop on CPR-Institutions in African Floodplain Wetlands, Department of Social Anthropology, University of Zurich, Switzerland. February 14.-16, 2005.

Saum, R. 2006. How to Make a Living in Ikoga Common Pool Resource Use and Change in the Okavango Delta in Botswana: A Case Study. Department of Social Anthropology. University of Zurich. Zurich (Switzerland).

Samatar, A. I. 2006. National Institutions for Development: The Case of Botswana. In: Wisner, B. et al. (eds): Towards a New Map of Africa. Earthscan. London.

Sorensen, F. L. 2003. Community-Based Tourism and Prospects for Sustainable Livelihoods: The Case of the Okavango Polers Trust in Botswana. University of Copenhagen. Copenhagen.

Stephenson, J. 1987. Rehabilitation of the Selous Game reserve. Final Report. Frankfurt Zoological Society. Frankfurt am Main.

Stevenson L., Frazier, F. 1999. Review of wetland inventory information in Africa. In: Finlayson, C.M.; Spiers, A. G. (eds.): Global Review of Wetland Resources and Priorites for Wetland Inventory. Supervising Scientist Report 144. Canberra (Australia).

Smith E. W., Dale, A. M. 1968. The Ila-speaking Peoples of Northern Rhodesia (First edition 1920). University Books New York. New York: Vol I. and II.

Thomas, D. H. L. 1996. Fisheries Tenure in an African Floodplain Village and the Implications for Management. Human Ecology 24/3: 287-313.

Woodhouse, P., Bernstein, H., Hulme, D. 2000. African Enclosures. The Social Dynamics of Wetlands in Drylands. Africa World Press. Trenton, Asmara.

Chapter 8

The illusion of establishing control by legal definition: Water rights, principles and power in canal irrigation systems of the Kunduz River basin, Afghanistan.

Katja Mielke, Iskandar Abdullayev and Usman Shah

Introduction

The Kunduz River Basin area, with its catchment in northeastern Afghanistan, is one of the country's main agricultural production areas, and has been since the 1930s, when the swamps were drained and converted into an irrigated plain for rice and cotton production. After more than 25 years of war, efforts are now being made by the Government of Afghanistan, with the assistance of the international community, to restore Afghanistan's agricultural potential. Because farming is heavily dependent on irrigation water, due to climate and soil characteristics, one important element of this intervention is the rehabilitation of irrigation management capacities. The inefficient implementation and subsequent breakdown of state governance structures in the course of the last several decades ascribed customary irrigation management a central role for food provision for the subsistence of the rural population. Ongoing reform attempts in the irrigation sector in the context of the *Kunduz River Basin Program* (KRBP) aim to enhance food security in the short term, and provide poverty reduction in the longer term. From an economic perspective, this involves greater productivity of agricultural land by means of improved irrigation management. There seems to be scope for improvements as the current distribution and allocation practices are not efficient and it is believed that this can be remedied by means of technical, institutional and social engineering. Viewed from a social perspective, poverty reduction would have to tackle social inequalities as they are expressed in inequalities in water distribution and landownership among the rural population.

Against this background, this article sheds light on ongoing developments in Afghanistan's irrigation sector by investigating the current structure of property rights in water management in five canal areas of the Kunduz

River Basin. In academia it is generally assumed that secure property rights provide prospective certainty in the fulfillment of mutual expectations of stakeholders, thus, reducing conflict over water and shaping incentives for sustainable water management through long-term investments. Therefore, the questions that requires clarification for the systems studied is how, and how well, are rights defined in the respective irrigation systems? Further, it needs to be analysed what the likely effects of more clear-cut definitions of water rights with regard to effectiveness and agricultural productivity are. The bundle of rights perspective (following Ostrom (2000), Meinzen-Dick (2002) and Schlager/Ostrom (1992)) is chosen as an analytical tool to help decipher how and in what types of situations water users are involved in irrigation management issues, and how the entitlement system works given varying perceptions regarding customary rights in absence of statutory regulations in the water sector. It will be shown that local water management involves a complex system of individual and collective entitlements, the legitimacy of which is contested due to different constructions of local law by stakeholders and water users. To understand the current functioning of canal irrigation systems and their evolution, i.e., the technical as well as social dimensions involved, it is crucial to assess the potential impact of ongoing alterations in the systems. Current reforms aim at the formalization of so far local, customary management patterns, by defining statutory use and control rights over irrigation water. Nowadays, water rights in Afghanistan are only loosely defined. A new water law has been in the process of being drafted for a number of years now, but has yet to be reviewed in parliament. The delay in ratification is at least in part due to the close conjunction of water rights with land rights. The latter are highly contested due to illegal land appropriation practices during the decade-long conflict, population growth and return migration from Pakistan. The efficient management of scarce natural resources is viewed as a strategic component of the state-building agenda in Afghanistan, with the formalization of property rights in all natural resource sectors given high priority by the state and international donors. It can be viewed as one element of the wider political agenda to create a new national identity as the current irrigation-centered development efforts resemble a property-creating process (Coward 1986: 492).

Background of the project

Research for this study was conducted in the framework of the *Social Management of Water in Afghanistan* (SMWA) project, implemented by *German Agro Action/Deutsche Welthungerhilfe* (GAA) in five irrigation systems in Kunduz and Takhar Provinces. SMWA is one component of the *Kunduz River Basin Program* (KRBP), an EC-funded pilot program that aims at overhauling the traditional water management system via the implementation of a river basin approach aimed at the more efficient management and enhanced sustainability of water resources.[1] The Kunduz River Basin encompasses a swath of territory in northeastern Afghanistan.[2] The KRBP aims to reorder the human-environment relationship around the notion of the river basin as a hydro-spatial unit. Accordingly, the Kunduz River Basin's key institutional bodies[3] will be the provincial irrigation departments in Baghlan (Pul-i Khumri), Kunduz (Kunduz City) and Takhar (Taloqan). SMWA commenced work in February 2006 and was based in Kunduz until September 2007, after which it shifted its operational center to Taloqan. As a project partner, the Center for Development Research (ZEF) provided research on different aspects of the SMWA canal systems since March 2006 (Shah, 2006; Mielke, 2007/2008).

SMWA's objectives can be summarized, on a macro-scale, as aiming to contribute to poverty alleviation via the improvement of food security[4], which is ought to be achieved through more efficient and equitable irrigation management and system maintenance. The central issue in this regard is the attempt to implement bottom-up-stakeholder participation of all user

---

[1] River Basin Management has evolved as mainstream development approach for irrigation management during the last years. It encompasses a holistic perspective on water catchment areas on the one hand and foresees decentralization of water governance on the other hand. In the framework of the persisting participatory development paradigm, empowerment, ownership and equity are claimed to be the key tools for poverty reduction and the implementation of sustainable resource management structures.

[2] According to the SMWA Grant Application Form, the total command area of the five target canals of SMWA amounts to 31.564 ha. See Deutsche Welthungerhilfe 2005.

[3] The KRBP-approach to water management reform in north Afghanistan foresees the establishment of hierarchical institutional structures based on hydrological networks and boundaries as is mirrored in the hydrological unit river basin and its respective sub-units. This conforms to the latest international development imperatives, which have been elaborated and implemented after recognizing that water sources are under pressure and shortages due to unsustainable management bear a considerable potential for large-scale food insecurity and future conflicts among water users on global, international and local scale. In accordance with the concept of *Integrated Water Resources Management* (IMWR), reforms aim to create management bodies at basin, sub-basin and irrigation-canal levels which will take over management competencies from current top-down-organized line agencies at different administrative levels (i.e. province/*velayat* and district/*wuluswali*).

[4] Deutsche Welthungerhilfe, 2005: 4.

groups and institutional bodies. GAA facilitated the establishment of Water User Groups (WUGs) on a sub-canal basis in the autumn of 2006 in all five irrigation systems within its mandate. By the end of 2006, twenty-four WUGs had been created encompassing an area of approximately 17,000 ha, with an estimated population of 80,500 water users.[5] At the same time, all WUGs in each canal system were provided with a superstructure of a canal committee. In the following phase, the reform agenda will oversee the establishment of Water User Associations (WUAs) according to the main hydrological unit at the local level – the irrigation canal, i.e. one WUA per canal system.

Farmer-Managed Irrigation: The Property Rights-Perspective

Irrigation systems and the management thereof, involve complex interlinked relationships among different stakeholders, as well as multi-level linkages between water users and property rights assigned to, or claimed by individual persons and groups. In the framework of the wider Natural Resource Management (NRM)-debate, irrigation water is believed to be one of the more complex and difficult resources to be dealt with, because it "is mobile over space and variable over time" (Meinzen-Dick, 2002: 224).

Before entering the property rights analysis, a brief definition of property rights shall be given. According to Commons (1968), a property right is the authority to take actions in a specific area or domain. The property right delineates one's actions against others with regard to a specific resource that one can then legitimately exploit. Ostrom (2000) pointed out that property rights are always relational, and that it takes somebody to acknowledge the right/s of another actor in order to have the property right fully established in all its dimensions. This situation can be captured with the "bundle of rights" concept (Schlager/Ostrom 1992). The bundle consists of five types of property rights governing common pool resources (CPRs): access, withdrawal, management or modification, exclusion and alienation rights. Whereas access and withdrawal rights can be summarized as use rights, the latter three categories are understood as control rights (Schlager/Ostrom 1992). The heuristical value of this perspective lies in the fact that the extent to which a stakeholder – whether it is an individual or collective actor – possesses water rights and exercises control, can be made visible by analyz-

[5] Interim Narrative Report SMWA of January 2007, 5; Annex A, 37, unpublished. All numbers are mere estimates and need to be taken with scepticism because reliable measurement did not take place throughout the last decades and the capacity to conduct large-scale land surveys and a population census is still not built up.

ing which of the five rights categories the particular actor lays claim to and actually holds. To give an example, the large number of absentee landlords in the Kunduz oasis[6], and in five the irrigation systems studied, implies that sharecroppers cultivate the fields of landholders in different kind of tenancy arrangements. In this case, the sharecropper-as-farmer gets the withdrawal right for a certain amount of water, but does not possess any control rights, i.e. he is not authorized to rent out and to pass on allocation rights to a third party. To what extent the landholder exercises control rights, fully depends on the documents he has and the power of the one who challenges his rights. In some cases, in accordance with the duration and circumstances of the landholder's absence, the sharecropper – who may also be a landless relative of the landholder – might be authorized to enforce limited control rights, e.g. modify the water course. This empirical example, by deciphering resource access, withdrawal and control rights, demonstrates quite well how notions of "ownership", usage, and rights intertwine. Water rights, as such, might be claimed by different stakeholders who all share parts in the bundle of rights. This instance also demonstrates how water rights are linked to, and are dependent on, land rights.

Thus, property rights differ to the extent of the different dimensions which a right over a resource might include (e.g. access versus withdrawal versus alienation et cetera). It has been noted that property rights are subject to interpretation under different legal regimes, and how people translate these rules into daily practice or not (von Benda-Beckmann et al., 1998). This allows an interpretation of property rights as an outcome of negotiation and bargaining processes. Researchers on legal pluralism (von Benda-Beckmann et al., 1998) have derived a useful distinction between principles and fixed rules (e.g. in water law), which becomes especially visible under scarcity conditions. In times of shortages, resource allocation does not follow fixed formal or informal rules that are codified and "normally" shared by a certain user community. Distribution results rather from *ad-hoc* decisions in the particular situation. The "reality test" – effective water distribution in times of severe irrigation water shortage – also shows that the distinction between different rights is merely an analytical tool that we, as researchers, construct in terms of our (non-local/'western'/outsider) understanding of rights and legal concepts, whereas meanings of Afghan local law and concepts differ in a way that we find difficult to grasp.

---

[6] The Kunduz oasis is the fertile stretch of irrigated agricultural land receiving water from the Kunduz River.

By distinguishing three main dimensions of complexity specific to irrigation water management, the following paragraphs give an introductory overview of the property rights debate in water resource management, and provide the conceptual cornerstones for the subsequent sections of the paper.

1) At a general level, the main reason for the complexity of irrigation water management lies in the nature of irrigation systems, i.e. the fact that irrigation water is a natural resource, the efficient provision of which is not only dependent on availability and allocation practices, but also upon adequate maintenance of irrigation infrastructure (Meinzen-Dick, 2002). This, in turn, requires taking into consideration the question: who is in charge of maintenance, and in exchange for which services or payment? Furthermore, the proprietorship of irrigation infrastructure needs to be clarified. It is this characteristic that makes the application of the bundle of rights-perspective especially valuable for deciphering actual property rights and complexities related to irrigation management.

2) Irrigation water is a typical common-pool resource (CPR), with the need to assign (via entitlements, rights) and measure the resource flow in water portions to a group of individual or collective users (Ostrom, 2000: 338). Though water is commonly thought to be managed collectively, the bundle of rights perspective offers insight into the wooly rights holding patterns, and allows distinctions on a case by case basis about whether property rights are privately held by individuals or by collective actors (users, "communities"), organizations and/or the state. In many cases, single rights out of the bundle (mostly for access and subtraction) might be owned privately, while others may be subject to collective proprietorship and decision-making (control right types). In addition, water rights in northeastern Afghanistan have been found to be in close conjunction with land rights. In general, the latter are more strongly defined because of actual title deeds landholders may possess. Yet, at the same time even land proprietorship is commonly based on customary and local use rights and not legally defined. Furthermore, over the past 20 years masses of agricultural land have been illegally appropriated in Afghanistan, thus adding a further dimension of 'disorder' to current property relations in rural areas.

3) Generally speaking, property rights in Afghanistan are only weakly – if at all – defined. This relates to statutory law and the formalization of property rights in the country's legal codes. As a consequence of regime break-ups in the previous decades of war and conflict, laws are not in place or are contested by amendments and different legal systems which were established under the various semi-legitimate political regimes that rose and vanished.

Given the dynamic political changes, is it justified to ask how far attempts to change rights relations formally affected local laws and practices? Did redefinitions of property rights by various regimes touch upon local law at all? Effective practices can be labeled "deviating" if a narrow understanding of rights is applied, or these practices can be viewed as concrete outcome of a certain interpretation of property-regulating principles.

Consequently, for actual practices of water allocation and distribution, informal customary rules have played a vital role and compensate for the absence of a formal water rights system. But even in the sphere of informal, customary rights, competing claims exist and actual use and exclusion patterns in critical times of resource scarcity may be different from customary principles. The strength and enforcement capacity of customary rights like water withdrawal, access, modification or exclusion depends on several factors, the quality and strength of the authority of the issuing institution to the user's authority, and finally from all stakeholders' perceptions regarding claims and ownership. Subsequently, on a theoretical level, both, a quasi-*de jure* and *de facto* dimension can be distinguished for the non-state or informal irrigation management sector (Meinzen-Dick, 2002: 229). The customary *de jure*-dimension relates to customary law as such, which reflects an acknowledged norm that is codified, but not necessarily written. For example, there is the widespread notion of the "right to thirst" (Llewellyn, 2003), an element of Islamic law that functions like a principle in customary water law. However, the actual practice, whether this "right to thirst" is always granted in times of drought and scarcity, is subject to negotiation and interpretation. *De facto*-practices or effective stakeholders' behavior might contradict or bend customary principles (*de jure* dimension) when water is scarce. Further examples for customary principles and rules are the notion that the *mirab* (local water manager, literally: 'water lord') should be appointed from the tail end of the canal system, or that upstream riparian users have prior irrigation rights.[7]

Thus, one guiding assumption of the paper is that in water management, principles can be distinguished from more steadfast rules of water allocation on the one hand, and effective practices on the other hand (Benda-Beckmann et al., 1998: 80). As the notion of principles allows manifold

---

[7] Llewellyn gives a basic overview over Muslim juridical expertise in the allocation of water rights. In a hierarchy of water uses he mentions access to drinking water ('right to thirst') as highest priority, followed by water rights for domestic purposes and the right to water livestock. Irrigation needs figure only on fourth rank. See Llewellyn, 2003: 203ff.

interpretations of rules depending on the situation and the actors involved in a decision, it creates fuzzy overlaps between the two poles of 'hard' water rights (being agreed upon *de jure*) and situations when the latter are abandoned in effect (*de facto*) in times of water shortage.

Data base and methodology

The data presented in this analysis was collected in structured and semi-structured interviews, systematic observations, transect-walks, and also through repeated discussions with various stakeholders involved in water management at the project sites between 2006 and 2007. As stakeholders, we define all water users and other individual or collective actors with an interest ("stake") in irrigation water management in the respective sites. In addition to farmers and other water users (mills, households etc.) they include government officials and project (GAA) staff. Secondary sources, such as documents and academic literature on water management issues in Afghanistan further added to the data base.

Figure 1: Map of the five canal systems covered by the SMWA project

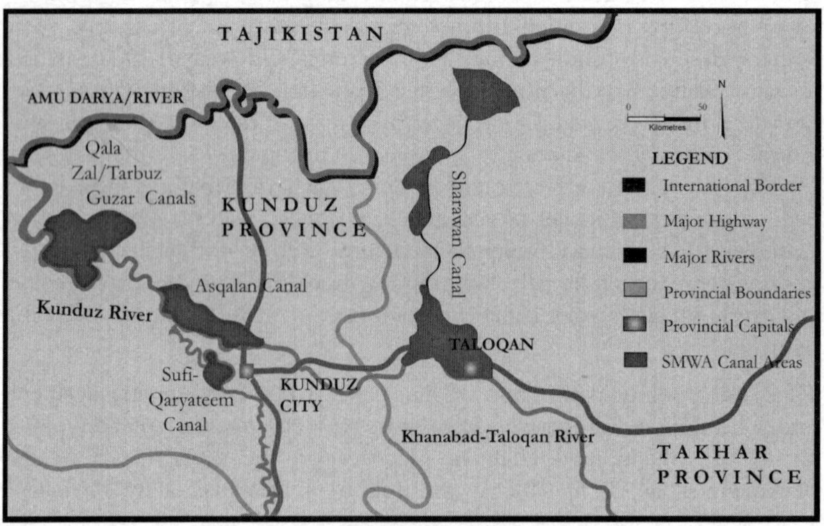

(Copyright U. Shah)

The five canals covered by SMWA and investigated by the researchers were: Asqalan, Sufi-Qaryateem, Qala Zal, Tarbuz Guzar and Sharawan. Whereas research in the Sufi-Qaryateem canal area was constrained due to security concerns for local and international staff in 2007, the researchers covered all other irrigation systems throughout at least one irrigation season. The following table gives a basic overview over the size of the four canal systems studied:

Table 1: Technical indicators of the systems studied

Types	Canals	Length (km)	Command area[8] (*jerib*[9])	Number of off-takes (registered)
Large	**Sharawan**	145	150.000	48
Medium	**Qala Zal**	39	48.000	28
Small	**Asqalan**	21	14.500	18
	Tarbuz Guzar	18	7.000	14

(Source: Abdullayev et al., 2007)

Agricultural production and cropping choices vary to a large extent according to water availability. Consequently, water-intensive rice is cultivated mostly in the head end of the canals where water is more readily available. Cotton, vegetables and fruits are cultivated in the middle reaches. Less water-intensive mungbeans and fodder crops are grown in the comparatively water-scarce tail ends of the systems. As a rule, winter wheat is grown in all parts of the canal systems. Agricultural activities in the study areas depend on irrigation. Except for some rain-fed wheat and pea cultivation in Sharawan, crop cultivation without irrigation is largely impossible.

[8] We define a command area as the acreage irrigated with water from one canal system, e.g. the Tarbuz Guzar command area (estimated 7.000 *jerib*) encompasses all cultivated land which lies within reach of the secondary and tertiary canals of the main Tarbuz Guzar canal and is supposed to get water thereof. Exact measurement and obtaining accurate data is difficult, since local farmers and single water users are reluctant to give information about land ownership in fear of future taxation by government authorities. Consequently most data constantly vary depending on who is asked. For practitioners as well as researchers it is important to keep in mind the limited reliability of quantitative data in the context of Afghanistan.

[9] The local square measure of one *jerib* equals 0.2 ha or 2,000 sqm; thus one hectare consists of 5 *jerib*. Before 1950 (year 1371 according to the Afghan solar calendar) one *jerib* actually amounted to 1,936 sqm.

Water rights, principles and control: Who benefits from proposed reforms?

Initially, after the ousting of the Taliban regime by the U.S.-backed Northern Alliance forces at the end of 2001, Afghanistan became to be perceived as a post-conflict country. Despite ongoing violent conflicts in its southern and eastern provinces reconstruction and rehabilitation efforts were kicked off by the international donor community. Development organizations with rural portfolios started setting up larger-scale projects in the northern part of the country from about 2003-2004 as the security situation then still allowed engagement with local target groups. For a discussion on property rights it is important to take into account the lack of formal or state-defined property rights due to previous breakdowns of political regimes and respective legal frameworks. In addition, the extent to which 'formal' property rights were well-defined prior to the outbreak of violent conflict at the end of 1978 remains unclear. It is widely assumed that the state did not establish full control of all spheres of social and economic life of its citizenry in the past. Underdevelopment, limited bureaucratic and governance capacity, and high dependency on external aid characterized the two decades before 1980. Knowledge about natural resource management, or even the consciousness for a need for resource management was largely absent among the bureaucratic elite.

Thus, a property rights analysis of irrigation water needs to tackle the statutory dimension as well as the two non-statutory ("customary") dimensions at which water rights and the rules and regulations they imply are enforced.

A legal framework for natural resources in general and for irrigation or water management specifically, is still absent in Afghanistan. The pro-communist government under Soviet occupation issued a Water Act in 1360 (1981). Alone, the provisions could not be enforced and the Water Act as such hardly had any effect. Given the virtual absence of a legal framework for water governance in Afghanistan, officially established water rights and any notion thereof are meaningless until a respective legal framework with strong institutional backing are installed (Meinzen-Dick, 2002).

Whose rights? – backed by which institution?

The five SMWA-project sites resemble canal irrigation systems constructed from intakes at different locations along the Kunduz River.[10] Historically the Kunduz oasis was known to be a poorly inhabited large swamp area, the

[10] The Kunduz River is 480 km in total length (Dupree, 1973: 35).

drainage of which started only in the 1920s after an influx of refugees from Soviet-occupied Central Asia. In response to the immigration of mainly Uzbeks, Tajiks, and Turkmen families, the Afghan government initiated an internal colonization scheme to counterbalance their ethnic domination along its northern border with the resettlement of Pashtuns, Pashai, and Hazara from other parts of the country in the 1930s. Though partly forced into resettlement by decree of the King, most newcomers were attracted by the land made available for them if they agreed to put it into agricultural production. As a consequence the swamps were reclaimed; canals were dug and extended depending on the settlement flow of different population groups and their intermixing over decades. The land title documentation for these irrigation land allocations was not begun until the mid-1950s and not finished before the outbreak of political turmoil and subsequent war in 1978.

Since there is no public water supply system in Afghanistan, self-supply of water for consumptive and productive purposes is common practice. Accordingly, though dug for agricultural irrigation, the canal streams do not only provide irrigation water, but at the same time the water is used for other purposes, such as household consumption (washing, small gardening, cooking, ablution), milling, construction, brick-making, and animal watering.[11] Given the various uses of canal water, the user groups are very heterogeneous and can be broadly generalized to include all groups of people and individuals living in the command area of the irrigation canal.

In the subsequent parts of this paper the authors focus on water distribution and issues related to water rights for irrigation purposes. The stakeholders involved in irrigation matters are usually farmers, i.e. large (*zamindar*) and small landholders (*kamzamin*), and sharecroppers/tenants (*nesfakar*). The existing irrigation management patterns are thus best described as farmer-managed irrigation systems. In the literature on water management in Afghanistan, and South Asia in general, the trend is to speak of community-based or collective irrigation management, though neither the whole community, as a collective actor, nor a homogeneous collective group of farmers or individual farmers hold "total" property rights in most cases. In this re-

[11] Few wells exist in the settlements along the stream. A considerable amount of inhabitants of the respective command areas, especially if they live in the vicinity of the irrigation canal, supplies themselves with drinking water from the open canal. Only few people own a pump-well for irrigation and domestic purposes, because electricity is a major problem. Generator use is very expensive due to high and steadily rising fuel prices.

gard the "bundle of rights"-perspective helps to decipher the intermixing of private and collective rights and to determine who holds which rights over what. Adding to the complexity is the fact that rights in irrigation management are not only embodied in allocated water. Water flow units (portions) in conjunction with land rights and infrastructure are manifestations of property rights as well.

The *mirab* (literally: water lord) is at the heart of the customary water management in the irrigation canals studied. He is selected by the landowners and traditional leaders of a community to take care of the canal infrastructure and to organize maintenance activities like intake repair or desiltation works. But, more importantly, the *mirab* has the official (customary) authority to distribute water in times of scarcity. Usually this implies elaborating and being in charge of a rotation schedule to assure an equitable amount of water according to agreed-upon turns for the different farmers. This institution or post, not the individual person, with the respective profile, embodies the official customary "rules of the game" that govern water management in irrigation systems throughout northeastern Afghanistan. As will be shown below, the *mirab* functions as the prolonged arm of the large landowners, and can thus be described as a manifestation of the latter's vested authority.

In institutional terms the *mirab* has the formal authority to implement water rights: Depending on the strength and extent of power and authority a respective *mirab* possesses, different rights of single individual or single collective users can be enforced effectively. Indicators of the *mirab*'s authority are his ability to mobilize people for maintenance works, his service in equal water distribution; his ability to collect money for maintenance expenditures and to collect his own salary. However, this somewhat ideal mandate of the *mirab* requires that the claims of the water users are legitimate and that the *mirab* post is appointed with an unselfish and altruistic individual who fulfills his duty objectively and does not follow his own interests, or the collective interests of his wider family and social exchange network (*qaum*), not to mention the interests of large landowners. However, this is hardly ever the case, because one of the selection criteria for the *mirab*-job is that he himself owns land. Reportedly, the *mirab* was traditionally selected from the tail end of the canal though, out of the five canal systems investigated only the two *mirab*s in Tarbuz Guzar and Qala Zal met this criterion in two subsequent irrigation seasons.

The practical dimension of water rights: On allocation theory…

Apart from irrigation purposes, the access regime for irrigation water throughout the canal systems studied can be described as open-access because withdrawal for domestic use is customarily guaranteed for every user group and not subject to fees, sanctions or limitations by the state or land owners. According to accounts of different respondents in all five canal systems, the withdrawal rights for water of all residents for household consumption, including water needs for animals, has never been questioned and was viewed as negligible, even in times of water shortage and rotation.[12] This can be explained with the acknowledgement of the Islamic "right to thirst" – a norm which grants every command area inhabitant the right to use water for basic needs. When it comes to subtraction for irrigation purposes, though, use rights are individualized and distinguished in accordance with land ownership. This means water rights are connected to the size of the agricultural area under cultivation of the individual water user. The conjunction of water rights with arable land implies, in a narrow reading, that anyone not possessing land does not dispose of any automatic withdrawal rights, whereas the landed have customary withdrawal rights to the extent that they own land. The underlying water rights principle is similar to other irrigation management patterns in South Asia, where those endowed with a greater area of land are entitled to a greater share of water (Mollinga, 2008).

However, the legacy of regime changes and violent conflict over the last decades also accounts for poorly defined land rights. Though private individual land ownership is a widely used and acknowledged concept, the breakdown of cadastre services and a traditionally large sphere of customary land inheritance practices have resulted in a plurality of land rights where legal and customary forms of proprietorship intermix. Most people in the rural areas of northeastern Afghanistan have no title deeds (*sharai*-documents), but their land ownership is mostly fixed in local customary agreements (*orufi*) granted to a third or second generation inheritor. More than weakly defined water rights, land rights are regularly contested by different claimants. Furthermore, "land grabbing", the illegal appropriation of land by powerful people through the threat of or actual use of force has evolved as a common practice during the last two decades. As a result, water allocation is highly dependent on the strength of land rights, and how well the latter are defined. This ranges from private title deeds that are acknowledged by contemporary law and other people on the one hand, to (at one time) illegally appropriated land (by force or because the title holder is away)

---

12 Whether this information is true could not be verified, in order to find out long-term observation in the residential areas adjoining the canal and during times of rotation (water scarcity) would be necessary. Increasingly, households make use of privately owned bore wells, but need electricity, e.g. generators, for pumping the water up.

without documents or to powerless smallholders with *orufi*-documents (inofficial, local, unregistered documents) on the other hand. The 'strength' or robustness (Meinzen-Dick et al., 2000: 6) of land rights is understood to be increasing with the institutionalization of originally unlawful land appropriations over time.

For the five canal systems studied, the need to organize water distribution usually arises when scarcity cannot meet general demand for water. As long as water flows in the canal in abundance, no rules apply, and irrigation water is treated as a collective resource. Water withdrawal rights become an issue as soon as water availability is limited for some reason and rotation schedules should apply. This occurs regularly; late snowmelt, little precipitation, extraordinary heat or damaged intake constructions are frequent causes for irrigation water scarcity at field level.

When applied, water rights are not only linked to land, but contribution to canal maintenance is an equally determinate factor for legitimate and practical water allocation. The link between withdrawal rights and maintenance oblications is reflected in the distinct notions of *bel* and *qulba*. In each irrigation system, the agricultural command area is virtually structured into *bel* or *qulba*-parcels. Thus, first of all, *bel* and *qulba* resemble measurement units for water allocation reflecting size and quality of farmland. One *qulba* for example always equals 40 *jerib* (9 ha) in one irrigation system, but – given size of the land and the maintenance contribution remaining equal – actual irrigation takes place in accordance with location, i.e. quality of the land. This means longer time intervals for watering if the land is higher, or less water/shorter intervals if the agricultural land lies below the water level. In addition, *bel* and *qulba* embody units according to which irrigation water users have to contribute to maintenance works. The following two cases highlight the inter-linkage of subtraction rights with maintenance obligations. By exposing the difference in the *qulba* and *bel*-systems (fixed versus flexible units) which are behind the claimed and effective rights to subtraction, the existing gap in-between is illustrated.

> **Case 1**: *bel* in Qala Zal and Tarbuz Guzar canals: "Flexible" water rights
>
> In both canals, a *bel* defines the water right which consists of two elements: of a time interval for the irrigation of an agricultural plot (the size of which is flexibly determined according to quality/location of this particular plot) and the number of persons to be assigned for canal maintenance works. The size of a *bel* in *jerib* depends on location

and (related) quality or agricultural productivity of the land.[13] Land plots located higher than the water level in the canal need to be irrigated longer and are thus assigned less *jerib* per *bel* (e.g. 10 *jerib* is equal to one *bel*). Fields located below the water table have less *bel* per *jerib* (e.g. one *bel* equals 30 *jerib*) as they are more easily, i.e. faster irrigated. This flexible application of bel-units allows a balanced contribution scheme for maintenance if it is considered that farmers usually have to send one person per *bel* for intake repair in spring before the start of the irrigation season.

Moreover, the label 'flexible water rights' does apply, because the *bel*-system leaves scope for interpretation regarding the soil quality and thus can be adjusted according to wishes of a landowner. If the latter wants to have the *jerib* per *bel*-ratio reduced he can consult with the *mirab* or his assistant (*kokbashi*) in charge of the particular part of the canal where the land in question is located. For example, if a farmer is not satisfied with the amount of time for which his plot gets irrigation water (allocated according to a certain *bel*-size following a *bel-jerib*-ratio following *jerib*-units), he can claim more hours by re-registering with a higher *bel*-amount (in effect reducing the *jerib-bel*-ratio) which means he has to contribute more workforce for maintenance. In the contrary case, if a water user cannot meet his contribution for canal maintenance from his family's workforce and also cannot hire somebody, he can ask to have the *jerib* per *bel*-ratio increased which reduces both his obligation for maintenance contribution, and also the water portion to be allocated (time span for irrigation).

Case 2: *qulba* in Asqalan canal: "Fixed" water rights

In Asqalan *qulba* is the respective unit for water rights. It resembles the irrigation claim in a time interval based on plot size and the obli-

---

[13] The fixing or flexibility of water rights is not linked to the 'label', i.e. not only '*bel*' is flexible, but '*qulba*' as well, though apparently not in Asqalan as Case 2 shows. There are variations in *qulba*-size in other canals, for instance one *qulba* equals 20 *jerib* in some parts of Chahar Dara (Sufi-Qaryateem) or the upper end of Sharawan canal. And even within one canal system different *qulba*-sizes may be practiced for different locations. Reportedly this is due to the availability of water in the respective (parts of the) system. If the water is less, one *qulba* tends to include more *jerib*; if water is available in abundance, the *qulba-jerib*-ratio is small (one *qulba* less *jerib*), but the same workforce contribution has to be mobilized. To give an example: In the Sufi-Qaryateem system, one *qulba* equals 20 *jerib* on higher land and 40 *jerib* on lower lying land in Uzbekha (interviews, May 8, 2006).

gation to contribute to maintenance. One *qulba* equals 40 *jerib* as a fixed unit of land. In Asqalan there are no variations in *qulba*-size throughout the entire canal command area.[14] Yet what both, *bel*- and *qulba*-system have in common, is that one laborer per unit is usually sent for construction or maintenance works. The water allocation-*qulba* ratio varies in accordance with the location of the land from 4 to 12 hours of water per one *qulba*. As such the ratio is fixed and formally not adjustable to changing cropping situations. This implies that if farmers at the head end of the canal engage heavily in rice growing, water availability for the middle and tail parts of the canal is severely limited. As a consequence, while contributing to maintenance works to the same extent as head-end landowners, tail end water users receive considerably less water, if any (see Table 2 gives an overview over the different water allocation regimes according to the *qulba*-system).

Table 2: *qulba*-based water rights

Canals	**Number of hours per 1 *qulba***		
	High water[15]	Normal water	Low water
Asqalan (1 *qulba*- 40 *jerib*)	12	8	6
Qala Zal (1 *qulba*- 20 *jerib*)	8	6	4
Upper Sharawan (1 *qulba*- 20 *jerib*)	12	5	2

Each farmer is aware of the number of *qulba* or *bel* he farms and the corresponding number of workers (*mardikar*) he is obliged to send for maintenance and construction works to sites throughout the irrigation canal. Even if the *qulba* is not always getting full water rights (especially during the water-short periods), the landowner is obliged to contribute *mardikar* according to *qulba* upon request of the *mirab*.

When it comes to contesting claims and conflict over water distribution during times of scarcity, the *qulba*- and *bel*-system is relied on as a reference. Oral agreements and pre-arranged schedules are usually elaborated in advance of shortages, often at the beginning of the irrigation season when it is not yet predictable whether shortages will actually occur or not. However, if

[14] The fixed *qulba-jerib* relation throughout the Asqalan-canal system could be taken as indicator mirroring the established power stalemate along the canal with the tail-enders being deprived of water in times of shortages and the head-end settlers growing rice on expense of the former.

[15] High, normal and low water is approximately >100%, 90 to 80% and <50% of expected water flow into the area.

water scarcity is rampant, water is distributed in an ad-hoc manner in most cases, and power turns out to be a decisive factor in who gets water and whose crops die.

To sum up the findings on withdrawal rights so far, the main conclusion is that *qulba* as well as *bel* units provide for a reference system that regulates irrigation water governance under the supervision of the *mirab*. This *de jure*-customary water management pattern needs to be mirrored with the effective (*de facto*) customary practice, because in spite of all principles and regulations, when it comes to water shortages, power factors determine emergency irrigation practices.

... and allocation practice: Power and social difference in user communities

To give an example, Asqalan canal annually has two *mirab*s appointed, one for the head end, with mainly non-Pashtun farmers, one for the tail end with an almost exclusively Pashtun population. The ethnic dimension is being emphasized here because it is an indigenous self-depiction and felt as such by the people inhabiting the command area. For several years, tension and subtle conflicts have existed between the upstream and downstream water user factions. Such conflicts and tensions originate from settlement history and the recent Afghan past of violent national conflict, with non-Pashtuns claiming that all Pashtuns joined the Taliban. The downstream *mirab* is said to be subordinate to the one from upstream, although in effect, both have the same obligations to serve their communities.

In interviews, water users as well as *mirab*s mentioned the local principle according to which a *mirab* would always have to be recruited from the lower reaches of an irrigation canal in order to ensure equitable water allocation for the users along the canal. In reality this principle is not observed by many water user communities; as mentioned above, the *mirab* of the canals studied was most often from the upstream area. The Asqalan-case could be interpreted as a compromise of upstream and downstream communities to have two *mirab*s appointed. Yet, the apparent effort to go along with the principle of recruiting the water manager from downstream, most likely has to do with a stalemate of power between the settlers in the different sections of Asqalan canal.

Besides the shared obligations – both *mirab*s mobilize laborers for intake construction works and *lukh puli* (money to buy sacks to dam up water) – upstream and downstream *mirabs* are selected for the job by their constituent farmers for the following reasons: First, because they are not the poorest and have land. For example, one *mirab*'s brother was a famous commander in the *jihad*, another was a commander himself during the recent civil war, a period when arbitrary appropriations and re-appropriations of land were common practice. Second, their status and authority is not so high that they could make and enforce decisions in disregard of more powerful farmers along the canal. These characteristics of the water managers ensured that 'people with a beard' – a metaphor for elders and powerful community members – who would take water illegally, cannot be stopped by the *mirab*s. The latter are not in the position to say anything in such a case because they are appointed by the same powerful figures. Thus, the *mirab*s' actual enforcement capacity against the powerful is quite weak. As many former and currently acting *mirabs* interviewed stated, they were chosen because they close their eyes and remain silent when 'elders' abuse customary water distribution rules.

Perhaps this understanding of sharing the same destiny as being appointed by more powerful landlords and the need to be subservient to them, coupled with face-to-face interactions common to social life in the local arena, has caused good cooperation between both *mirabs* of the Asqalan canal during times when water is plentiful. The conflict potential is quite high though if the crops of downstream farmers are about to fail because upstream users do not grant them their 'share' of water as is fixed in rotation schedules jointly agreed upon by the *mirab*s at the beginning of the irrigation season. In times of water shortage, the *mirab-e kalan* (upstream 'chief'-*mirab*) first and foremost serves upstream water users, and as a result, fights between both *mirab*s consequently break out regularly because tail end users do not get enough water. The conflicts are mainly expressed verbally between the *mirab*s, a fact that can most likely be ascribed to the individual *mirab*'s temper. Thus, conflicts can be contained and prevented from turning violent most of the time, except for rotation periods when violent escalations are quite common among water users: They mostly take place at offtake-sites at nighttime and at dawn, when some landowners get caught stealing other users' water, i.e. irrigating their fields out of turn. The water rights and distribution issue is further exacerbated by the trend of increasing rice cultivation at the head sections of the canals studied. Rice is more and more replacing wheat and cotton as staple food and cash crop in many irrigation systems in North Afghanistan, despite the fact that rice growing is especially water intensive. As a result, rice cultivation is becoming a major factor that influences the revision of water rights.

It must be considered that the dichotomy of upstream and downstream is artificial to a certain extent, because neither community is homogeneous. To be more precise, small and large farmers and tenants/sharecroppers live in both head end and tail end parts of the canal. Thus, if it is acknowledged that scarcity and drought have different meanings to large and small landholders it becomes obvious that the impact of water scarcity is mitigated mainly by wealth. Because richer tail-end farmers could afford to water their fields with pump wells during emergencies, their poorer neighbors are much more vulnerable to drought conditions because they do not have this possibility. Besides economic wealth, power originating from a certain social status, acts of violence or the mere availability of guns and their potential use determines allocation rights in a way that it can impede or facilitate access to an offtake in order to irrigate a particular field. It would be only slightly exaggerated to claim that those who have guns (even secretly) effectively determine water allocation or – put in institutional terms – are able to "flexibly" define their water rights.

This argument is further supported by evidence in the Sharawan canal, where there is a pronounced and enduring influence of local *qomandans*[16] on determining water rights. They continue to exert power and pressure to their advantage, largely with impunity, and in doing so, prevent the rehabilitation of the institutions governing water resource management in Sharawan. At the tail end, in Khwaja Ghar, it was alleged by interviewees that powerful landowners continue to extract irrigation water by force, and with little scope for recourse. Importantly, investigations showed that they could flexibly define their own water rights with impunity due to the institutional weakness of the Water Management Department[17], the local elders' councils and the *mirab*, whom are as powerless as the poor farmers in preventing the illegal extraction and use of water from the irrigation system. In the Mullah Yusuf area, located in the mid-section of the Sharawan canal, respondents stated that *qumandans* are only now being challenged, under the newly established WUGs, to cease over-extraction of water and restore the previous system of water rights. These 'men with guns', despite superficial compliance with gun buy-back schemes (DDR/DIAG) and the adoption of a rhetoric of 'freedom and democracy', continue to define, through the influence and legitimacy they wield, the shape of the water rights regime. Perhaps

[16] Strongmen, who had been fighting in the war against Soviet occupation and/or the ensuing civil war, thus gained power in the course of violent conflict and, still today, they are able to gather followers who can be armed any time and are loyal to them.

[17] The Ministry of Energy and Water of Afghanistan is represented in each each district and province of North Afghanistan by respective Water Management Departments.

the most telling instances of this phenomenon exist in the head reaches of the Sharawan canal, where powerful *qomandan*s have altered the entire shape of water resource use and management by augmenting, with force, the definition of their right to irrigation water. Respondents argued that by virtue of their upstream status, and with the institutional weight of their armed factions behind them, *qomandan*s were entitled to more water than those users downstream.

The examples above illustrate, that issues of water allocation and property rights in general are not limited to institutional considerations, but instead illustrate that local communities' histories, cultural backgrounds and group dynamics must be also taken into account equally, in order to better understand the make-up and structure of practiced property relations. Accordingly, if water rights are to be formalized, as foreseen in the impending National Water Law of Afghanistan, allocation rights would, on the one hand, gain a statutory legal base, whilst, on the other hand, the fixing of water rights can generate conflicts itself, as much of the flexibility of modes of local governance will be lost if the law is to be strictly enforced. Thus, a law articulating principles for water governance would be suited best for the individual organization of water allocation among users on the ground, because it could still be negotiated on the basis of different stakeholders' perceptions and in line with local values and norms.

Who sets the agenda locally, and also crafts norms and modes of life is a different matter. The popular assumption of outsiders, that 'indigenous' norms are democratic and just *per se*, is not valid in many cases (Benda-Beckmann, 1998: 93). In Afghanistan, social relations are characterized by high inequalities and intra-communal social differences. These are especially visible in distinct social strata the group members of which dispose of different assets. Land, for example, is quite unevenly distributed. Nevertheless, due to the close conjunction of land rights with water rights the latter reinforce unjust land relations and vice-versa. The establishment of statutory law would only help to change these conditions if enforcement of land titles and water rights could be guaranteed. Since this is rather unlikely because of the high transaction costs, the implementation of a water act or a new land law is being delayed and – should respective decrees be issued – will meet resistance by local stakeholders.

In the absence of state authority – who is in control?

Whereas use rights are shown to be quite flexible and should be seen as outcomes of social negotiations between groups and individuals, control rights often rest with one particular actor – whether individual or collective.

In this context of use rights versus control rights, especially what Schlager/Ostrom (1992) called the right to manage a resource should be seen as the collective right of all irrigators because it encompasses construction, maintenance and authoritative decisions to limit the water flow in particular canal sections and also to restrict cropping choices of farmers upstream, for instance, water-intensive rice cropping in dry seasons. However, despite the fact that all water users are concerned, here again arises the question as to whether the collective-choice customary rights are effectively implemented. Empirical observations allow the conclusion that it depends on the type of management action put into effect. As we have seen, construction work and maintenance contribution obligations are linked to withdrawal rights in accordance with *bel* and *qulba* – which relate to size and quality of land owned by a farmer. Deviating behavior in maintenance contribution was witnessed in few cases with approval of the *mirab*. While, for once, normal non-compliance with construction obligations is being sued and sanctioned by the *mirab* through the issuing of a fine and/or alleged reporting of the farmer to the local police, there are, secondly, cases when the *mirab* – though heavily involved himself – endorses his kin, relatives or clientele unsanctioned absence and non-contribution in maintenance works. Thirdly, the principle of "buying laborers" applies as a component of local water management rules. In this situation, the landowners and the *mirab* they appointed agree that for an equivalent of up to five laborers, the large landowners reimburse the *mirab* with cash which he does not have to invest in construction and maintenance activities of the irrigation canal, but which counts as part of his personal salary. In effect, the maintenance contribution of the collective group of landowners who are not part of the deal has to compensate this manpower.[18]

The second element of control rights – the right to determine who is excluded from allocation rights and irrigation water benefits – belongs *de jure* (customary) to the *mirab* as representative of the farmer community which appointed him. *De facto* or in effect, since the *mirab* is the extended arm of large landowners with their own specific interests and because the *mirab*'s actual enforcement capacity is not strong enough, the larger landowners exercise and enforce exclusion rights in practice. Baluchha[19], the most up-

---

[18] It remained unclear which landowner is entitled to 'buy laborers' – whether there exists an underlying rotation system or the power traditionally rests with a fixed group of landowners or it is decided ad hoc each season.

[19] Baluchha is the name of a settlement, but the word as such literally means 'the Baluch' (people). To avoid confusion the inhabitants of Baluchha will be called 'Baluch' in subsequent paragraphs.

stream community in Asqalan, provides a good example for exclusion of a whole group of people from water allocation for irrigation purposes through the redefinition of water rights despite the Islamic norm that water should not be denied. According to Baluch accounts, their water rights originate in long-time settlement and water use practices upstream. They settled in the upstream area before the Torbrakash Pashtuns' arrived and established their homesteads and fields downstream. The Baluch even helped the newly arrived in the extension of the canal. During the years of turmoil, a combination of factors led to the deprivation of withdrawal rights and subsequent loss of the Baluch's stakes in Asqalan's water management. The flight and evacuation of the Baluch due to Soviet bombardment coalesced with a shifting river course in one of the following years and the rise of a local Turkmen commander who had an 'illegal' spillway built below Baluchha. By the time the Baluch returned, the water user communities in Asqalan and Torbrakash used the new status to fix the water allocation system at the expense of the Baluch by denying them water withdrawal for irrigation purposes and participation in the system management.

The example of Baluchha demonstrates a case of collective exclusion – a community is denied water rights by another community. Individual exclusion is also practiced in times of shortages, but only by single individuals who, through the act of offtake opening to irrigate their fields, capture other users' rights. While force is sometimes involved, the general pattern seems to be that illegal water withdrawal is not contested, but is instead put up with in cases when the illegal taker is powerful - may this power rest in authority, wealth, force or, most likely, a mix of all of these factors.

Empirical observations indicate that big landowners, more than any other stakeholder control rights. Smaller landholders can plant trees, for example, if their land is located in direct vicinity of the irrigation canal, but they are not in the position to decide about cropping choices of others or changes in the canal's shape etc. The same is true for excluding water users – in this regard the small landowners and sharecroppers with small own land plots, and landless *(bezamin)* are comparably powerless. On the land that is being farmed in by sharecroppers, sharecroppers have individual use rights and share collective management responsibilities as far as maintenance and construction obligations are concerned. But they do usually not exercise any kind of further control rights. In the case of rich absentee landlords, with only one or two sharecroppers taking care of big plots of land, the reality might be that these sharecroppers also take water illegally, and thus exclude others. The opening of off-takes by force in times of shortage by the sharecropper, results in the exclusion of the 'rightful' water users and equal distribution. Besides this exceptional scenario, control rights of sharecroppers are very much limited. Sharecropping relations might be inherited, though, and carried on in a family over decades.

Table 3 summarizes the peculiarities of different control rights of actors who are traditionally involved in water management. The local water manager (*mirab*), his assistant (*kokbashi*), landowners (*zamindar*) and government agencies make up the main stakeholders in irrigation water management as it is practised at this time. Of course, *mirab*s and *kokbashi*s themselves represent the big landowner-category, but in addition *mirab* and *kokbashi* – as a rule – always serve the biggest landholders, thus *zamindar* are listed separately to show how their rights are embedded and structured in comparison to the rights of government agencies. The split-up of each of the control rights into *de facto* and *de jure* rights follows this papers' conceptual point of departure with the distinction of three levels of rights, whereas formal rights are excluded since a water law is not in place. Here *de jure* relates always to customary practices as they are claimed, *de facto* to rights in use as they are effectively practiced.

Table 3: Empirically observed control rights of actors involved in water management (highlighted) (*potentially statutory, according to future state law)

Control rights of actors involved in water management	**Management: Change resource**		**Exclusion**		**Alienation: Transfer resource to others**	
non-statutory ("customary")	de facto	de jure	de facto	de jure	de facto	de jure
mirab	yes	yes	yes	yes	yes	yes
kokbashi	-	-	-	-	-	-
zamindar	yes	-	yes	-	yes	-
government agencies*	-	yes*	-	yes*	-	yes*

The conceptual category of "alienation", i.e. the right to transfer a resource to others, is very much disconnected from the empirical water management context in Afghanistan, because no market for water trading exists, and water rights as such are not sold or inherited detached from land use rights. Thus, inheritance or sale goes along with the quality of land rights relations – as mentioned above in close conjunction to the type of title deed a landowner possesses (*sharai* vs. *orufi*). The property relations for hydraulic property – which is next to non-existent so far – are not clarified, though the common perception is that technical and infrastructure devices are owned by the respective user community. It is usually not subject to sale or inheritance, but perceived to be common or collective property. Islamic law provides that irrigation canals are the joint property of the individuals who built them. This hints at the fact that the collective alienation rights (and control rights in general) are not only confined to the actual farmer group but can be rightfully claimed by families whose ancestors or members were involved in canal digging but are not using water for farm irrigation purposes at the moment – either because the landowners fled in the course of violent conflict, or because they lost their land (for some other reason).

What then becomes clear is that traditional water management is carried out in accordance with local law – a mix of Islamic norms, situational interpretations of water rights principles and fixed irrigation rules that evolved in the respective command areas over decades, and were altered by changing power relations among all involved stakeholders. Thus, property relations, i.e. water rights, are not only dependent on rights and respective negotiation processes in a narrow sense, but are also to a large extent depend on the historical and political conditions the water users are embedded in, and which have nothing to do with Natural Resources Management in the first place. Even if government agencies like the irrigation department[20] traditionally had *de jure* control rights to some extent in the past, these could not be enforced in practice because enforcement capacities were always lacking in financial and human capital terms. The actual power and control in irrigation management thus lies with the *mirab* and the landowners. While the former executes *de jure* and *de facto* control rights because he is appointed by the landowners, the latter disposes of hard *de facto* rights regarding irrigation water due to the fact that the large landowners appoint the *mirab* on an annual basis who cannot be seen as neutral a mediator, but as fulfilling the interests of this particular constituency. The same is true for *kokbashi*s, who, if at all, can influence modifications of the irrigation system, to the exclusion of water users or alienation in coordination and agreement with the *mirab*.[21] Table 3 visualizes that irrigation canals are in the hands of *zamindar* whose influence rests on the rule 'the more power, the more land, the more rights – to water and land'. The imbalance in irrigation water management and control over resources is thus inherent in the customary system.

As the preceding discussion focused on individual water rights and not obligations towards canal maintenance and intake construction, it can be con-

---

[20] At the time of writing the irrigation department is a subdivision of the Ministry of Energy and Water.

[21] The *kokbashi*'s competencies are higher in regard to withdrawal rights, but since the discussion here focuses on control rights these are all displayed as negative.

cluded that the state does not play any decisive role in irrigation water management. Recently, since the new Government of Afghanistan under Karzai has taken on reforms in all sectors, and water has been declared a strategic resource, the government has for the first time ever taken heightened interest in questions of water and irrigation management that do not only include technical fixes, but also tackle governance questions. This interest is mainly stimulated by foreign aid and external support provided for the government, which is conditioned to irrigation sector reform in the IWRM-framework. Accordingly, grants of the large international donors like the EC are given to NGOs, who act as facilitating partners to implement river basin programs in partnership with government agencies.

Conclusion

As has been shown for allocation (use and access) rights above, control rights also range from effective control to mere claims of control by different stakeholders. However, control rights are even more obviously vested in social institutions of authority and power relations. In the absence of statutory law and weak irrigation departments which largely lack enforcement capacities, large landowners and the *mirab*s played a central role in irrigation management, and as representatives of farmers' interests in outside relations. Following this line of reasoning, it comes as no surprise that local irrigation systems remained intact despite the fact that decades of turmoil and war put the canal infrastructure and social relations under heightened pressure.

Pluralistic local law, i.e. customary norms and practices based on and mixed with religious principles and social norms, allocation, management and exclusion rights, has always been regulated by, and at times heavily influenced by, actual power vested in individual members of the user community. The concepts of principles and negotiation provide alternatives to statutory law and normatively fixed definitions of rights. As a consequence, practically, this allows all stakeholders to select the one mechanism for solving water rights problems which fits their interest in a particular situation best. Such purposeful selection of one institution out of a wider range available to the actors can be described as institutional shopping (Bierschenk et al., 2003).

The empirical examples confirm that water rights are embedded in both land tenure and social relations. In this context, the acknowledgement of social differences among water users is of utmost importance for the understanding of effective irrigation practices. Projects that assume communities to be homogeneous entities are likely to reproduce existing inequalities with their activities. Nevertheless, in addition, water availability and the geographical location of the farmland (upstream vs. downstream) are basic independent variables that structure and constrain water users' possibilities for action in the irrigation system.

Rural Afghanistan's water economy is predominantly informal because water rights were only weakly, if at all, defined over the course of the previous decades. With the attempt to reform the traditional irrigation management system, water rights are currently in the process of being statutorily defined, yet customary structures do, and will continue to parallel *de jure* notions of water rights. This paper attempted to illustrate the gap between local, normative water rights and effective practice. The important point to note is that current interventions which aim to create new water management bodies (water users groups and water users associations) will have an irreversible impact on existing water rights, because they touch upon already contested domains of power (Li, 1996; Mosse, 1998). International agencies promoting new water management institutions at the community level are likely to support one of several contesting stakeholders – intentional or not – and thus form a challenge for competing water users which might potentially cause instability and lead to conflict escalation (Mosse, 1995).

Outlook

For the current institutional changes to gain ground, i.e. to bring about more transparent and accountable water management bodies and distribution patterns at the local level, initially undesirable developments which were caused by the program's intervention so far, for example the further strengthening of unequal power relations, will have to be corrected. This could only happen through commitment and persuasion during a long-term engagement and interest of donors, NGOs and the Afghan government in irrigation management reform. The prospects of such developments are rather bleak as exactly the latter three stakeholder groups commonly form a stratum that is far detached from local rural realities and dependent upon external framework conditions of programs like project tenure and performance pressures (i.e. to spend money, to show results, to report success).

On the contrary, an optimistic scenario would assume the will and dedication of the same groups. On these grounds the introduction of water user groups and associations could be positively interpreted as first stepping stones for the establishment of effective and equitable irrigation management patterns. As a consequence, the experiences and intervention activities implemented so far would have to be accepted as givens and used to reflect on the functioning of the current water management system, power distribution, and rights and obligations of all involved stakeholders. In this regard the facilitating NGO plays a key role in order to approximate the mutual understanding of irrigators' needs and implementers' capacities and management visions in further discussions and meetings. Yet it requires as a prerequisite the adequate training of the NGO's field staff that works on the interface between the program and the water users as the main target group. Only after the local staff's capacities have been built up, the provision of information, education and consultation activities could set in to enable local people to understand the aims and benefits of water management reforms and – most importantly – to enable all of them to make claims and represent their interests in a self-contained manner. Such developments would ideally lead to an overhaul of existing power structures in the long run and subsequently the achievement of irrigation reforms as envisaged in the program documents. Time and commitment are crucial in this process and as such likely pose decisive constraints for success, constraints that do not even have much to do with the particular situation in Afghanistan yet.

In addition, for the more realistic scenario, the local context has to be taken into account, i.e. factors like the average mindset and attitudes of rural Afghan society, that tend to be overlooked by programme writers and aid strategists. In the case of Afghanistan decades of turmoil and war resulted in deep distrust towards any kind of outside intervention. This largely conditions that the overhaul of local power relations and changes towards more equity in water distribution are not likely to materialize any time soon, let alone within the project's extended time frame.

References

Abdullayev, I., Shah, U., Mielke, K., Schetter, C., Mollinga, P., Subramanian, S. 2007. Social Management of Water in Afghanistan. Consolidated Field Report, July-August 2007. SMWA Field Report Series No. 3. Bonn/Kunduz: ZEF.

Benda-Beckmann, F. von, Benda-Beckmann, K. von, Spiertz, H. L. J. 1996. Water Rights and Policy. In: Spiertz, J., Wiber, M. G. (eds.): The Role of Law in Natural Resource Management, Special number: Recht der Werkelijkheid 1996/2: 77-100.

Bierschenk, T., Olivier de Sardan, J.-P., 2003. Powers in the Village. Rural Benin Between Democratisation and Decentralisation. In: Africa. 73/2: 145-173.

Commons, J. R. 1968: Legal Foundations of Capitalism. University of Wisconsin Press. Madison.

Coward Jr., E. W. 1986. State and Locality in Asian Irrigation Development. The Property Factor. In: Nobe, K. C., Sampath, R. K. (eds.): Irrigation Management in Developing Countries. Current Issues and Approaches. Boulder (USA). Westview Press: 491-508.

Deutsche Welthungerhilfe, 2005. Social Management of Water in Afghanistan. Kunduz River Basin Programme, Europeaid/121165/C/G/AF, Grant Application Form, May 2005.

Dupree, L. 1973. Afghanistan. Princeton University Press. Princeton.

Li, T. M. 1996. Images of community: discourse and strategy in property relations. Development and Change 27: 501-527.

Llewellyn, Othman Abd-ar-Rahman 2003. The Basis for a Discipline of Islamic Environmental Law. In: Foltz, R. C., Denny, F. M.; Baharuddin, Azizan (eds.): Islam and Ecology. A Bestowed Trust. Harvard University Press. Cambridge: 185-248.

Meinzen-Dick, R. 2002. Property Rights and Maintenance of Irrigation Systems. Journal of Applied Irrigation Science. 37/2: 219-235.

Meinzen-Dick, R., Bakker, M. 2000. Water Rights and Multiple Water Uses. Framework and Application to Kirindi Oya Irrigation System, Sri Lanka. EPTD Discussion Paper No. 59 (March 2000). Washington: International Food Policy Research Institute (IFPRI).

Mielke, K. 2008. Social Management of Water in Afghanistan (SMWA). Report on Community Governance Structures. Unpublished Report, 31 January 2008.

Mielke, K. 2007. On the Concept of 'Village' in Northeastern Afghanistan. Explorations from Kunduz and Takhar Provinces. ZEF-Amu Darya Series Paper No. 6, SMWA-Paper No. III.

Mollinga, P. 2008. Water Rights in Farmer Managed Irrigation Systems in India. Equity, Rule Making, Hydraulic Property and the Ecology. Paper presented at the Conference on "Water Rights in South and Central Asia", Bonn, Germany, 21st January, 2008.

Mollinga, P., Meinzen-Dick, R., Merrey, D. J. 2007. Politics, Plurality and Problemsheds. A Strategic Approach for Reform of Agricultural Water Resources Management. Development Policy Review: 25/6: 699-719.

Mosse, D. 1995. Local institutions and power: The history and practice of community management in the development of tank irrigation systems in south India. In: Wright, S., Nelson, N. (eds.): Power and participatory development: Theory and practice. Intermediate Technologies. London.

Mosse, D. 1998. Colonial and contemporary ideologies of community management: the case of tank irrigation development in south India. Modern Asian Studies 13.

Ostrom, E. 2000. Private and Common Property Rights. In: Encyclopedia of Law and Economics, Vol. II: Civil Law and Economics. University of Ghent. Ghent: 332-379.

Schlager, E., Ostrom, E. 1992. Property-Rights Regimes and Natural Resources. A Conceptual Analysis. Land Economics. 68/3: 249-262.

Shah, U. 2006. Livelihoods in the Asqalan and Sufi-Qaryateem Canal Irrigation Systems in the Kunduz River Basin. ZEF Amudarya Research Series. Social Management of Water in Afghanistan Paper I. Bonn: ZEF.

Chapter 9

Compensation crisis, *adat* law and unresolved land issues in Sarawak, Malaysia

Welyne Jehom Jeffreys

Introduction

This paper discusses the consequences of poor governance of compensation claims on *adat* land, on both sides of the Sarawak state government and the natives, when Bakun dam was implemented in September, 1993[1], on a vast native land in Upper Belaga, Sarawak, Malaysia. The implementation of the dam has displaced more than 9000 natives from 15 longhouses (villages). The main problems highlighted in this paper with relation to the poor governance of claims on compensation are: inadequate information for the natives to work on their claims, and non-transparent action of the Sarawak state government in handling the resettlement and claims on compensation. Both problems are illustrated in the case studies presented in this paper.

Theoretical frame and working concepts

> "Good governance systems are built on (1) participation as the foundation of legitimacy in all democratic systems; transparency; accountability; effectiveness and efficiency; responsiveness to the need of all stakeholders, (2) the rule of law; and gender equity. Good governance puts people first. It is indispensable for building peaceful, prosperous and democratic societies." (Hemmati et al., 2002: 28)

Governance can be used in several contexts such as corporate governance, international governance, national governance and local governance. The concept of governance, like development, is both a political and a technical term. This concept of governance conflates the normative and prescriptive with the descriptive and analytical, and consequently refers to both an end

---

[1] For more illustration and discussion on the history of Bakun Hydro-electric project, refer to Welyne Jeffrey Jehom, 2008, Development and Displacement: Kenyah-Badeng in Bakun Resettlement Malaysia, ZEF (Bonn).

state and a process (Agrawal et al., 1999). Governance can be conceptualised in many ways – including structural constructions, dynamic approaches and objective-driven strategies (Pierre et al., 2000). Alternatively, as argued in this paper, governance may be thought of as the relationship between the state and individual citizens, i.e. natives, which refers to local governance, and is thus fundamentally different from the concept of government. Therefore, governance, as used here, covers the whole range of institutions and relationships involved in the process of governing (Pierre et al., 2000).

> "Good governance depends on transparency, accountability and equality in ways that are responsive to the needs of people. It is composed of the mechanisms, processes and institutions, through which citizens and groups can articulate their interests, exercise their legal rights, meet their obligations and mediate their differences." [2]

Good governance, however, is an ideal which is very difficult to achieve[3], particularly in relation to the issue of resettlement. This paper shares the view of Dolores Koenig[4] that "resettlement impoverishes the natives by taking away their political power, notably to decide how and where to live. It disrupts the control that a local social group has over its social institutions, and increases their political marginalisation". In this paper, drawing on Koenig's view, it is argued that by implementing resettlement with a package of 'top-down development' by the state has implies all but good governance, particularly referring to the case of the natives' involuntarily relocated by the implementation of the Bakun hydroelectric project in Sarawak. One of the findings in the study on the implementation of the Bakun hydroelectric project in Sarawak is that there were weaknesses in the chain of communication between the state and the natives. There were problems of transparency, accountability and equality in the way the state responded to the needs of the native settlers (Jehom, 2008).

The local officials who acted as the mediator between the state and natives could be the easiest target for major problems in communications and the problem of dissemination of information. They are the front runners dealing with the natives. Perhaps, it was likely that the local officials exercised con-

---

[2] Cited from http://www.developmentgateway.com.au/jahia/Jahia/pid/192

[3] Refer more details on good governance and the eights characteristics of good governance at http://www.unescap.org/pdd/prs/ProjectActivities/Ongoing/gg/governance.asp

[4] "Improving Outcome of Development Induced-displacement and Resettlement Projects." Compiled by Chris de Wet Cited from http://www.fmreview.org/FMRpdfs/FMR12/fmr12.2.pdf

siderable discretion, as they developed operational routines where cutting corners and corruption are possible. And for the affected natives, local officials are the 'government' (at least the representative of the state), and any decisions made are those authorised by the state. For this matter, the state's credibility is in the hand of the government officials who basically represents the state for the image of good governance or otherwise.

Background of the natives and Bakun Hydro electric project

The Kenyah-Badeng is listed as one of the native peoples in Sarawak, Malaysia in the Interpretation Ordinance of 1958 (Hooker, 1999). The Kenyah-Badeng is a variation of the Kenyah community categorised under the 'Other Bumiputras' in the population census as shown in Table 1. Sarawak has a population of 2.31 million as of 2005. There are more than 40 ethnic groups with their own distinct language and culture. The major ethnic groups are the Malays, Iban, Chinese, Bidayuh, Melanau, Orang Ulu, Indian and other indigenaous groups. In the census as shown in Figure 1, Orang Ulu and other indigenous groups are categorised as 'Other Bumiputras'. This category includes the Kayan, Kenyah, Penan, Kelabit, Bisaya, Kajang, Sembop etc. The Kenyah-Badeng of Long Geng, who are one of the five communities relocated to the resettlement in Sg. Asap, are presently living in their new village known as Uma Badang at the resettlement since September 1999 because of the implementation of the Bakun hydroelectric project. Since 1998, five native communities including the Kenyah-Badeng, from 15 longhouses have moved to the resettlement. The relocation and move to Sg. Asap was carried out through an operation conducted by a few government agencies led by the Belaga District Office. In mid-1999, all the 15 longhouses officially moved to Sg. Asap. Currently, Sg. Asap consists of five different ethnic groups which are the Kayan, Kenyah, Ukit, Penan Talun and Kajang. There were 9428 inhabitants or 1639 households in Sg. Asap by 2001 and with many births (no written documents except health records at the Sungai Asap Clinic) by 2005, the inhabitants have increased.

The settlers are comprised of people with various economic backgrounds, who work in the area of education, health, public administration and private companies. However, the majority of the population in the resettlement area is made up of farmers and unskilled labourers. Their skills are mostly related to subsistence agriculture, hunting, fishing and collecting jungle products. Unskilled labourers work on the oil palm plantations and at timber camps. Since employment at the resettlement is very scarce, they have to migrate to other regions for employment.

Figure 1: Sarawak total population by ethnic group, 2000

Ethnic group	Population
Malay	462270
Iban	603735
Bidayuh	166756
Melanau	112934
Other Bumiputras	117690
Chinese	527230
Others	8103
Non-Malaysian citizen	62738
TOTAL	2071506

Note: This table has been modified to simplify its presentation.
Source: Yearbook of Statistic Sarawak, 2005.

The natives considered their relocation to the resettlement as involuntary on the basis that they were not consulted about the choice of place to live. They also claimed that they were not consulted about the value of the compensations for their *adat* land and properties (Jehom, 2008).

It is a well known fact, one confirmed in the United Nations discussion in the forum of Commission On Human Rights (Fifty-ninth session: Item 15 of the provisional agenda, dated 21 January 2003), that "in the case of the Bakun project, rights to indigenous common land in the Ulu Belaga site were not recognized or properly assessed".[5] In this study, the interviews with the households confirmed the inefficient assessment on their land and property. All of the households interviewed claimed that the major portion of their land had not been surveyed. They stated that only relatively small areas in the vicinity of their longhouse were taken into account.

Methodology

Most of the information for the case studies presented in this paper is derived from informal interviews. As the Kenyah-Badeng people like to reminisce and speak about their life in Long Geng, their former village where they said food was in abundance, it was not difficult to conduct the inter-

[5] Cited from http://www.hri.ca/fortherecord2003/documentation/commission/c-cn4-2003-90htm

views. Certainly, from their description on how life was in Long Geng before they moved to the resettlement in Sg. Asap in 1998, life in Long Geng was much easier and natural resources were readily available. The forest was their ´supermarket´.

Who are the natives?

As stated by Hooker (1999), "we have to be careful as to what we mean by law, native, *adat* and especially land and land rights. These terms are all loaded with history, preconceptions, and contemporary government policy."[6]

'Native' refers to the indigenous groups who inhabit the state, as listed in the schedule to the Sarawak Interpretation Ordinance and Article 161A, Clause 6 of the Federal Constitution. However, it is notable that the constitutional definition of natives in Sarawak includes the Malays. While the Malay-Melanau groups are coastal dwellers, the other natives are typically longhouse dwellers whose livelihood depends on the jungle and on shifting agriculture. Occupying the intermediate zones and the interior areas of Sarawak, their geographical locations and dependence on the land clearly determine the way that land administration affects them (Bulan, 1999; Hooker, 2000).

In this paper, the major questions guiding the interviews were how much the households knew about their rights to land claims, and whether they clearly understood what they should claim and how much they could claim. In addition, the objective of the research was to determine if there was an understanding amongst the Kenyah-Badeng of the *adat* system as it supports traditional land tenure. It is well understood by the Sarawak government and all agencies as well as NGOs who are directly and indirectly involved in the implementation fo the Bakun hydroelectric project that the Kenyah Badeng at Long Geng were claiming compensation based on their rights on land under Native Customary Land Rights. Nevertheless, they were not clearly informed as to what to claim and, even worse, they did not know how far they could go to claim the land or how much land they had rights to. The impression given was that although they knew they possessed ancestral land designated under native customary right, they did not understand the amendments on the rights towards the land they claimed to own.

---

[6] Hooker, M.B. 1999. A note on native land tenure in Sarawak (Research Notes), *Borneo Research Bulletin.* Available on http://www.highbeam.com

The definition of *adat* land and Native Customary Law

Sarawak has a unique history as a former British colony where Sarawak was under a British protectorate in 1888, and was only annexed to British dominion in 1946. Sarawak became independent upon joining Malaysia in 1963. From 1841 to 1946, Sarawak was ruled by the Brooke family who were British. This historical legacy has shaped, and continues to influence the development of the law and policies relating to native customary land. Prior to James Brooke's arrival in Sarawak there was a system of land tenure in existence based on *adat* (native customary law) which remained virtually the same over the following century.

The landscape of a place is a historical record of the activities of past generations, "woven like a tapestry from the lives of its inhabitants" (Ingold, 2000: 15). Indigenous people's control over a territory operates through informal rules embedded in their customs and traditions, and most of these rules have never been codified in formal laws. Therefore, in Sarawak, the Brooke land administration gave due recognition to an intimate relationship between *adat* and traditional land tenure.

Referring to Porter (1967: 18), within Sarawak, the term *adat* is used to describe this body of Native Customary Law or Native Customary Rights. As Porter (1967: 10) further states that:

> "At the time of James Brooke´s arrival in Sarawak there had been for centuries in existence in Borneo and throughout the eastern archipelago a system of land tenure originating in and supported by customary law. This body is known by the generic term "Indonesian adat." Within Sarawak the term "adat", without qualification, is used to describe this body of customary rules or laws; the English equivalent is usually "native customary law" or "native customary rights."

Native customary rights to land consisted of rights to cultivate the land, rights to the produce of the jungle, hunting and fishing rights, rights to use the land for burial and ceremonial purposes, and rights of inheritance and transfer. According to the native ideas, the clearing and cultivation of virgin land confers permanent rights on the original clearer (Geddes, 1954; Freeman, 1955; Richards, 1961). *Adat* is still widely practiced among the native communities in which it is under the custodianship of the village headmen in every community. Generally, the *adat* system constitutes an informal constraint, which regulates and structures social relations. The validity of the *adat* system is generally accepted by community members; it is accessible to all and it costs very little to administer (Ngidang, 2005).

Following the Secretariat Circular 12/1939 on Forestry and Land Use, in 1939 *adat* land tenure via the settlement process was codified in which it explicitly recognized the need for more rational forest policy to eliminate shifting cultivation. Due to WWII, the plan was not fully implemented; however, it left a significant impact. Village councils were officially appointed as custodians of *adat* to deal with land tenure and inheritance in each community (Richards, 1961; Hong, 1987). The responsibility of these councils was to demarcate village boundaries in order to determine the limit and extent of customary land. These lands, which were acquired via native customary law, would become Native Communal Reserves under the Land Orders. Natives were only permitted to claim additional farmland if approval was given by the District Officer (Ngidang, 2005: 59).

The Kenyah-Badeng and *adat*

"Adet" (*adat* in the way the Kenyah-Badeng pronounce it) includes a way of life, basic values, culture, accepted code of conduct, manners, conventions, and customary laws (quoted from Majlis Adat Istiadat Sarawak).[7] However, it is not known how much in reality do the Kenyah-Badeng understands the meaning of *adat* as defined and stated in the document by the Majlis Adat Istiadat Sarawak. In this study, through observation and interviews with key informants, particularly individuals who are seen as important in the Kenyah-Badeng community, there is great doubt about the real practice of the *adat* system within the political structure of the community. Although *adat* is understood as a convention and customary law by all native communities in Sarawak, the practice of the *adat* system in the Kenyah-Badeng community seems to be less visible. It is possible that the ineffective role of the headman (*tua uma'*) of the Kenyah-Badeng in administering the community particularly with issues related to *adat* land was due to the lack of knowledge of the *adat* system of their own community.

As pointed out by Richards (1961) and Porter (1967), the crucial definition of *adat* system is the rules of access and right of ownership to land and other natural resources within a longhouse domain. It dictates law of land inheritance and transferability of land from the pioneering ancestors to the present generation. Langub (1998) noted that every longhouse community used informal governance to regulate social relations and its farming as well as economic activities. Ngidang (2005) further added that *adat* is also a collective community framework for regulating resource utilization and manage-

---

[7] http://www.nativescustoms.sarawak.gov.my/web/rit3.html

ment in a sustainable manner for the common good. However, amongst the Kenyah-Badeng community, many examples exhibit the inefficiency of the community leader in implementing the *adat* system, particularly prominent during the process of claiming compensation over *adat* land. There were many overlapping claims on *adat* land within the Kenyah-Badeng community because most of them do not have the clear knowledge about the boundaries of their land. In the study, there are many aspects discovered within the Kenyah-Badeng community where the community leader could show his leadership in settling dispute related to land claims, according to the main informants. The major aspect is on overlapping claims on *adat* land. As *adat* land owned by a family within the community can be lend to another family for farming, there has been a major problem in deciding the rightful owner of the land. By the time Bakun hydroelectric project was announced and process for evaluating *adat* land for compensation began, many families who have used other families land claimed rights toward that land they were utilizing. By right as in *adat*, the original clearer of the land have the full rights over the land, and the user of the land has no right to claim the land as theirs. Matters related to this unrightfully claim were forwarded to the community leader. However, the community leader who has no absolute knowledge regarding the *adat* lands that were claimed, was unable to settle the dispute. By right, as a community leader with the responsibility clearly as the guardian of the *adat* system, he was supposed to be able to clear the matters.

The history of the enforcement of the land regulations and amendments in Sarawak

Porter (1967) explains that under the Land Regulation of 1863, James Brooke instituted private land ownership in Sarawak in two ways: (1) instituting private land ownership by leasing "state" land to individuals and companies for a duration of 999 years; (2) the practice of instituting private land ownership was done by giving land grants in perpetuity only to natives under the Land Settlement Order of 1933, in which customary rights had been established on state land. In James Brooke´s definition, private ownership referred strictly to registered land ownership with a document of title. As stated by Appell (1971), this codification system was in conflict with the inheritance system of the native community where both landed and non-landed properties are held under a customary rights system. Under the *adat* system, the freedom to exercise property rights is traditionally bestowed upon individual households and communities under the informal governance structure of the *adat*. These rights, however, were seen as a threat by the Brooke administration because they interfered with the regime´s political and economic goals to control natural resources in Sarawak. Therefore, the Brooke administration proclaimed that all lands not codified or privately owned, belonged to the state. The colonial government of Sarawak also imposed the same ruling, stating that all lands belonged to the Crown when Sarawak was ceded to the British colony in 1946. In addition, in order to control land use,"the Brooke administration" and colonial rule labelled customary rights usufruct, rather than acknowledge the possessor rights of natives. By invoking the policy that all lands belong to the state and that state lands are free from claims of ownership, natives are seen only as licensees of state or Crown lands. Crown land means "all lands for which no document of title has been issued" (Porter 1967:84). A major source of ambiguity in the Land Code is that a title without a document is not defined; however, there is reference to customary law as being a body of customs of the natives and not much attention was given to the relevance of customary law as far as the Land Code was concerned (Richards, 1961).

The natives do not owe their customary rights to statute (Ian Chin, 2001). According to Porter (1967), the natives refused to pay premiums and survey fees in return for a lease subject to rent and conditions of occupation. They even believed that their customary rights to land were extinguished upon payment for a lease (Porter, 1967) As understood by the natives, rights to land are interpreted as ownership rights, and hence legally binding due to their understanding of customary law or the *adat* system (Richard 1961, Ngidang, 2005). However, as the customary right is defined as usufruct rights (Richards, 1961) natives only have the right to use the land but not own the land (Zainie, 1994; 1997; Bulan, 2000). Due to contradicting interpretations of customary law on land rights, efforts to integrate land rights into the Land Code are problematic (refer Table 2). The issue of sovereignty and proprietary rights over lands has become a major point of contention between the government and the natives (Ngidang, 2005: 54-55).

The history of the enforcement of the land regulations and amendments in Sarawak is summarized in Figure 2.

Figure 2: The history of the enforcement of land regulations and law in Sarawak

Year	Enforcement	Implications	Native Rights	Legislation of land
Before 1841	Native Customary Law	System of land tenure based on *adat*. Native ideas: clearing & cultivation of virgin land confers permanent rights on the original clearer.	Native customary rights to land: to cultivate the land to the produce of the jungle hunting and fishing rights to use the land for burial and ceremonial purposes rights of inheritance and transfer	None
From 1841	Native Customary Law & Brooke government	No interference with the customary land rights, allowing a degree of self-governance. No scheme of alienation or land development was introduced except to land where no rights or claims, whether documentary or otherwise existed.		English law Order L-4 (Laws of Sarawak Ordinance)
1928	English law Order L-4 (Laws of Sarawak Ordinance)	Applicable to native customs and local conditions. Regulation of customary tenure & land use touched on a social consciousness in which land has economic, social & religious significance.		Memorandum on native land tenure was published by means of the Secretrarial Circular No. 12 of 1939
1946	Application of Law Ordinance 1946	The Instrument of Cession transferred the rights of the Rajah, the Rajah in Council, and the State & Government of Sarawak in all lands to His Britannic Majesty.	Subject to existing private rights and native customary rights.	Land (Classification) Ordinance 1948
1948	Land (Classification) Ordinance 1948	System of land classification: Mixed Zone Land (land which may be held by any citizen without restriction)	Native Area Land (land with a registered document of title but to be held by natives only) Native communal Reserve (use by any	

		Native Area Land Native communal Reserve Reserved Land (reserved for public purposes) Interior Area Land Native Customary Land	native community, regulated by the customary law of the community) Interior Area Land (natives entitled to occupy for the purpose of creating customary rights but they were to be licensees of the Crown) Native Customary Land (land in which customary rights, communal or otherwise have been created)	
1949	Application of Law Ordinance 1949	Reception (afresh) of English common law & doctrines of equity together with statutes of general application.	Applied only 'so far as the circumstances of Sarawak & of its inhabitants permit & subject to such qualifications as local circumstances & native customs render necessary'	Land (Classification) (Amendment) Ordinance 1955
1955	Land (Classification) (Amendment) Ordinance 1955	Precluded the creation of customary rights over Interior Area Land from 16 April 1955 unless a permit was obtained from the District Officer.		The basis of Land Code that came in force in january 1958
1958	Sarawak Land Code 1958	Based on a Torrens registration system, only recognises registered interests in land. Claims on ownership or interest based on grant, lease or other document as evidence of title or interests.	Native Customary Land under Section 5(2) limited to specific methods: the felling of virgin jungle & the occupation of the land thereby cleared the planting of land with fruits the occupation of cultivated land the use of land for a burial ground or shrine the use of land for rights of way; and by any lawful method	

			(deleted in 2000)
1994	Amendments	To empower the minister in charge of land matters to extinguish native customary rights to land.	
1996	Amendments	The onus was placed on a native claimant to prove that he has customary rights to any land against a presumption that the land belongs to the State.	
1998	Amendments	To pave the way for extinguishment or compulsory acquisition of land, the mechanisms for assessment & payment of compensation were put in place.	
2000	Land Code (Amendment) Ordinance 2000	Harmonised the processes & procedures of Native Customary Land with other types of alienated land in respect of the resumption of land & the adjudication of payable compensation for termination of rights. Provided for the creation of a Registry of Native Rights. Deleted 'any lawful methods' under Section 5(2)(f)	Section 7A(1) streamlines " Native rights" into three categories : rights lawfully created pursuant to Section 5(1) or (2) rights & privileges over Native Communal Reserve under Section 6(1) rights within a kampung (village) reserve, Section 7

Note: Information for creating this table is adapted from a section written by Ramy Bulan as indicated in the source.
Source: Native Customary Land: The trust as a device for land development in Sarawak. Downloaded from
http://epress.anu.edu.au/apem/borneo/mobile_devices/ch03s02.html

Natives losing their *adat* land: Practical reasons

Based on information collected from households interviewed as part of this research, the Kenyah-Badeng understood in more practical terms about the ancestral land loss. The practical terms are referring to what Hooker (1999) explained to be the loss of ancestral land (*adat* land) as determined by code and courts. Land losses can be categorized based on two distinct ways of loosing land.. In other words, if native customary land is not used effectively and the land has reverts to a forest-like condition, then their rights towards that land are diminished. To date, no clear decision or statement with regards has been made by the state on the issue of the diminishing of rights on native customary right; hence, many problems related to this issue brought to court, were decided based on guidelines and decision made on earlier cases by the High Court in Sarawak. Second, if the holder of Native Rights moves out of his longhouse or goes to another district under the jurisdiction of another local leader (*penghulu* or *tuai rumah/tua uma*), he loses his rights. Basically, this is an old rule both of *adat*[8] and of Brookes However, the rule can be more complex in practice. For example, if an individual holder of rights in "communal" land removes himself from a longhouse, he may still retain his rights so long as he remains within "reasonable farming distance" (Hooker, 1999).

The claim by natives over a territory is best stated in Mundy (1848: 210), where Brooke acknowledged that the livelihood, culture and survival of natives surely centered on:

> The fruit trees about the *kampong*, and as far as the jungle round, are private property, and all other trees which are in any way useful, such as bamboo, various kinds for making bark-cloth, the bitter kony…..and many others. Land, likewise, is individual property, and descends from father to son, so likewise, is the fishing of particular rivers, and indeed most other things……(as quoted in Hong, 1987:39 by Ngidang, 2005).

In general, the native cultures in Sarawak are based on oral history, thus the absence of written records make it difficult to maintain a significant amount of information, particularly for the recognition of territories. It is common that the natives of the region use natural features such as mountains, hills, slopes, ridges, rivers, streams and creeks, stones, or clumps of bamboo as traditional boundary markers between farms and between different commu-

[8] Now restated, for example, in the Adat Iban of 1993, and Adat Kayan-Kenyah of 1994, both made under the Native Customary Laws Ordinance, Cap 51 (cited from Hooker, 1999).

nities. The extent of the Native Customary Land (NCL) of each longhouse community is defined by boundaries mutually agreed between that particular longhouse community and all the other longhouse communities surrounding it.

Map 1: Native classification on Customary Land

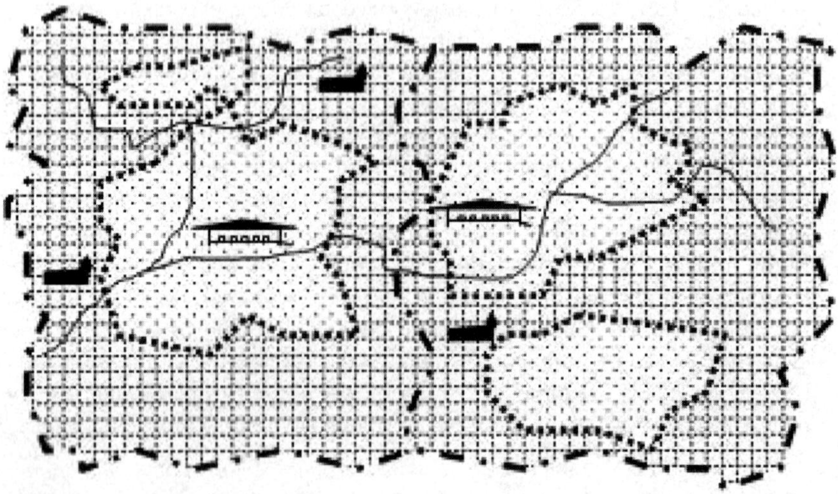

Longhouse (uma´)

Grave yard

Boarders between ´menoa´ in Iban (oma in Badeng)

"Temuda" (in Iban) or swidden cultivation area (békan in Badeng)

Communal land or swidden left to fallow for 7-8 years (juwe in Badeng)

Rivers

Note: The legend has been modified and translated.
Source: Booklet on Dayak´s Interpretation of Native Customary Rights Land (in Bahasa Malaysia) http://brimas.www1.50megs.com/ncr_konsep.doc

Dale (1997) stated that people are territorial by nature, and they relate to land in both formal and informal ways. For many generations before Brooke created the personal kingdom in Sarawak, indigenous people had defined their personal and cultural space, community boundaries, decision-making processes, and human relations in terms of their customary system passed down from their ancestors. These land boundaries are also recognised by the law and they are officially recorded in the government Land Boundary Register kept at the District Offices following a legislative decision through the Secretariat Circular No. 12 of 1939 which requires all land boundaries to be recorded (quoted from Eddie Roos[9]). However, there is also some doubt if the record is updated and is still valid as a reference. Furthermore, as Ngidang (2005) notes, the problem of verifying landmarks of these ancestral lands due to the increased density of population, lack of official documents of ownership, and the realization of the monetary value of land resources, resulted in competing stakeholders making claims and counter-claims to the same territory.

Compensation and counter-claims over *adat* land by the Kenyah-Badeng

Based on an ethnographic study by Tan Chee Beng (1995)[10], Kenyah-Badeng at Long Geng were swidden cultivators who practiced shifting cultivation. At the time when, individuals or households claimed the land by opening up new land, which had not been claimed by anyone. All lands claimed had been opened up for cultivation at least once.

The households that were interviewed claimed compensation only on swidden cultivation areas (e.g., *békan* and secondary forest as shown in Map 1). All households taken for case studies confirmed that the compensation was calculated based on how much the land was supposed to be flooded by the water from Bakun dam, that is, up to Bakun water perimeter and not based on how much land owned by households. All of the lands claimed for compensation by Kenyah Badeng at Long Geng were categorized as common land and compensation was given by the state government to be shared with the whole population of Long Geng. Lands that were claimed were grouped and compensated in a category of common land. For Long Geng, according to main informants, MYR18 million has been dispersed to compensate *békan* and *juwe* areas. The MYR18 million of compensation was divided amongst the whole community (1485 people) of Kenyah-Badeng in Long Geng.

---

[9] http://www.wald.org/docs/report1.htm

[10] The categorisation of Badeng´s lands was confirmed as written by Dr. Tan Chee Beng by my key informants at Uma Badeng, Sg. Koyan,

The ambiguous understanding of rights to the land made it very difficult to evaluate and estimate the lands and farmland. In addition, the absence of reliable landmarks, boundaries, and community land mapping confounded the calculation and estimation for compensation. In other words, what criteria were taken into account when accessing the value of the land?

The 20 households interviewed as case studies in this research confirmed that they did not know much about how to evaluate and what to evaluate for the claims except the obvious property such as their houses and the farmland that they were working on at the time. Neither were they aware of how the evaluation was conducted. According to all of the households interviewed, no one knew exactly the process of accessing the value of the land and, most interestingly, when the time came to post claims, people were actually very excited but no one seemed to know exactly what they were supposed to do. Furthermore, the borders of their land with each other were ambiguous landmarks such as rivers or slopes or trees or hills. Not only do these landmarks change over time, people often forgot their exact locations. For example, when one claimed that he or she owns a piece of land at the other side of the river, the accurate location of the borders cannot be identified especially when these lands have not been often visited. Without these borders, two situations occurred: first, they could claim just any land in nearby forest presuming that no one had put any claims on it; second, there were no questions asked about their claims. How this was possible? According to the households, the officers-in-charge surveyed and visited the lands in the area surrounding the longhouse and farmlands that were in use. However, fallow lands, which were further away from the longhouse, were surveyed based on estimations. In addition, there was very little discussion within the Kenyah-Badeng community before making land claims and no decisions arose from these discussions. As a result, overlapping land claims became the major issue and many claims were disputed.

Basically, the Kenyah-Badeng did not understand the evaluation of their claims and they did not have a clear idea about the important aspects that were included in their compensation. They also were not aware that the reason the lands were evaluated as communal land, and not by individual claims, was due to the absence of individual land title. Nor did they really know the boundaries of their land with their neighbors. In this situation, claiming lands was like a competition where each individual or household was looking for land that was assumed had not been claimed or marked by others. If the local leaders had possessed even a basic understanding of the administration of ancestral land via their *adat* system, confusions and problems could possibly have been minimized.

Dispute: The role of local leaders in the land surveyed

Compensation was only given to fruit trees claimed by households. Nevertheless, prices for fruit tree claims were not stated in the document details. This compensation slip was known as *surat kuning* amongst the Kenyah-Badeng because of the yellow paper used. According to the households interviewed, surveyors listed fruit trees claimed but there was no copy of the lists given to households. Therefore, no one knew, for example, what the cost was of a cocoa tree or a durian tree. The surveyors listed type and number of fruit trees without checking the farm or lands that later had underwent alteration by having a second ´spot-check´ as the locals called it; this reduced the claim by not really doing the job based on reliable information. The alteration was made without surveying. Amongst the households interviewed, this method was known as "remote control" as most surveyors had not been to any farm or lands claimed by the people except to surrounding area of the longhouses. The farmlands that were claimed were not nearby or even close to the longhouse.

Based on the household and key informants' interviews, in general the information gathered on dispute and the role of local leaders (*penghulu* and *tua uma*') during the process of surveying land revealed that both were not playing their roles in the decision of determining borders between their people's lands. Both were unaware of the territories; hence, they were unable to become the reference for the people and surveyor when there were problems. Therefore, without any consultation, the households claimed lands with clear demarcation between one's territories and the local leaders were unable to stand as reference for dispute. Basically, this situation showed that the Kenyah-Badengs were deciding for their household or for the households of their family members; they acted as if the community had no leader. The first 30% payments have caused great disappointment amongst the Kenyah-Badeng of Long Geng as they received not even close to the expected amount. The compensation receipt (*surat kuning)* was sent to native settlers with the amount stated without any indications of details on what had been compensated. If the amount was not what was agreed upon, the owner of the receipt was able to dispute the compensation and filled in an application form. Later, the person was supposed to wait for another confirmation about a court hearing before any revision on the compensation.

However, the greatest impact of these compensation assessments has been on the image of the *penghulu* and the *tua uma.* Their role as local leaders have been regarded as fairly weak and ineffective from the beginning but with the result of the compensation evaluation based on the second land survey, their reputation as leaders had become even more damaged. According to key informants, no one turned to them for reference after that first payment. From that point on, the Kenyah-Badeng in Long Geng organized themselves without any advice from these leaders.

Box 1 : Overlapping decision

According to a main informant, who is the son in-law of *penghulu*, after the Kenyah-Badeng in Long Geng finished submitting their claims on lands, and confirmation of land surveyed was signed by both local leaders and by the head of the Land and Survey in Kapit, there was big dispute on overlapping land claims. For example, there was an overlapping claim between two individuals from Uma Kelap. The case was brought forward to the land and survey in Kapit and the overlapping land claims were investigated. During the investigation of this overlapping claim, the local leader from Uma Kelap refused the claim and managed to avoid having to re-survey all of the claims from his longhouse. In the beginning the dispute did not involve the Kenyah-Badeng of Long Geng. However, one of the individuals who was involved in the dispute was married to a woman from Long Geng and he also had some land claims around Long Geng territory. As a result, the overlapping claim was not only surveyed where there was dispute between him and the other individual from Uma Kelap but it also extended to the land occupied by this individual in Long Geng area. With this dispute, there was some doubt on the method of surveying and claims over land. Therefore, Land and Survey in Kapit requested that all land claims in Long Geng had to be re-surveyed.

Box 2 : Compensation dispute

OL Household (OLH) claimed for their two houses (these houses were used when they had to sleep at their farms and the materials used to build these houses were good quality woods), rubber trees, and two fishponds nearby the longhouse area. According to OLH, the surveyors refused to survey and to measure the land he was claiming even though he did know exactly the size and some landmarks of the land he was claiming. The measurement was only taken on the land where the fishponds were located. Later, when he received the compensation slip, the value of all what he claimed on this farmland was only MYR11,400 and did not indicate the value of any of the items claimed. OLH was unhappy about the amount and he went to file dispute compensation at Land and Survey Office where he was asked to fill out an application form and wait for further action. He started waiting for the response in 1996 and when they moved to Sg. Asap in 1999, he received another letter and compensation slip in response to his previous query. The value of the claim had been downgraded to MYR180.00, showing a drastic difference from the first one. He was even unhappier and again he filled in the same application form as he did the first time; this time he awaited a court hearing about his claim. A few months later, another compensation slip came and the value stated was the same as the first amount, and he realized that he was not even called for a court hearing as he had expected. Knowing very well that his claim would not make any progress, he decided to keep the MYR11,400 after discussion with his wife.

Final settlement of compensation

In the final settlement of the compensation, the payment was made in two stages for both personal claims and communal land compensation – 30% before they moved to the resettlement and 70% after they have moved to the resettlement.

Box 3 : Final settlement of compensation

For example, from OLH the breakdown of the real amount received for compensation is shown below. OLH claimed approximately 30 ha of lands; fruit trees were also included in the survey. From MYR18 million of the communal land compensation, the first payment (30%) received was MYR4000 per person before they moved to Uma Badeng in Sg. Asap and the second payment (70%) received was MYR8600 per person after they h moved to Sg. Asap. OLH comprised of nine members, OL, his wife, and their seven children. Overall, each member of OL household received MYR12,600, totalling MYR113,400 received by OL household from communal land compensation.

Box 4 : Final settlement of compensation

The first 30% payment :

Name	Reference no.	Survey no.	Date	Total Value (MYR)	First payment 30% (MYR)	Type of payment
OKANG	LS/BK N/9192	168A/95	13/11/97	725,90	217,77	Crops
	LS/BK N/9878	174A/95	18/11/97	796,20	238,86	Crops
	LS/BK N/A010	179A/95	18/11/97	571,90	171,57	Crops
	LS/BK N/9751	176A/95	19/11/97	6 460,50	1 938,15	Crops
	LS/BK N/C282	177A/95	19/11/97	5 339,90	1 601,97	Crops
	LS/BK N/5449	168/95	25/08/97	3 978,05	1 193,42	Crops
SIOH	LS/BK N/9411	172A/95	13/11/97	2 158,20	647,46	Crops
	LS/BK N/9543	173A/95	14/11/97	4 067,40	1 220,22	Crops
	LS/BK N/A031	179A/97	18/11/97	211,00	63,30	Crops
	LS/BK N/9913	174A/95	18/11/97	1 261,20	378,36	Crops
	LS/BK N/C960	169A/95	19/11/97	38,40	11,52	Crops
	LS/BK N/9821	176A/95	19/11/97	1 249,60	374,88	Crops
	LS/BK N/C374	177A/95	19/11/97	126,20	37,86	Crops
	LS/BK N/C444	178A/95	19/11/97	520,10	156,03	Crops
	LS/BK N/5503	172/95	21/08/97	664,98	199,49	Crops
	LS/BK N/7080	173/95	21/08/97	215,00	64,50	Crops
	LS/BK N/5457	168/95	25/08/97	5 827,50	1 748,25	Crops
TOTAL					10 263,61	

Box 5 : Final settlement of compensation

OL personally received MYR22,000 for fruit tree compensation from his personal claims and his wife received MYR19,000 from her personal claims. Therefore, the total compensation of the OL household for their assets in Long Geng, personal claims of OL and his wife, plus the communal land compensation, was MYR154,400.

As mentioned previously, the compensation of 30% on personal and communal lands was given even before the households moved to the resettlement; thus all of the households interviewed claimed that this compensation was used to prepare for the move and trips to the resettlement. The remaining 70% of the compensation was received after they moved due to resettlement, but was used to furnish and improve the house, children's schooling at the new school, and to buy food and other needs during the first and second years following resettlement as they did not earn regular income.

With respect to the compensation installments, the other 19 households chosen as case studies as well as the other 55 households taken for household surveys shared similar experiences to OLH. Unfortunately, the amount of compensation received by the other 19 households and the 55 household surveys cannot be described in detail because they were unable to release their receipts because most of them did not keep the receipts or lost them during the transfers to Sg. Asap. Perhaps they also purposely did not want to share the information in this research. All of the households chosen for case studies and for household surveys received between MYR60,000 and MYR160,000. The way they spent their compensation was more or less similar to OLH since they moved to Sg. Asap in 1999. Most of them depleted the compensation between 1 and 2 years after resettlement, since many had no other source of income.

Land rights and ownership at Sg. Asap

To quote Rousseau (1994)[11], the resettlement area

> "is inadequate. Planners have failed to consider the current needs of the people; they have failed to plan for a population increase; they have failed to consider the needs of the people from the lower Balui, who currently face a shortage of land. The Government is also ignoring the fundamental issue of land tenure. Without long-term secure rights to land, effective development is impossible; feelings of insecurity will sap the enterprise of the population concerned".

The Kenyah-Badeng in Sg. Asap received the right to use 3 acres of land for each household. However, none have received land title for these 3 acres to secure the ownership of the land. Beyond the resettlement, lands have been leased to oil palm companies. SOLID Oil Palm Company[12] proved its lease of land to the people in Sg. Asap with the document and certificate of leasing during an official meeting in 2004. The Kenyah-Badeng, as any other group in Sg. Asap, are still unclear about the status of the three acres that they were granted use-rights to. The question is whether there is ever going to be any land title given to the 3 acres of land they received as part of their compensation. Another question is whether the 3 acres are also under the lease of SOLID Oil Palm Company. For subsistence farmers who work prominently with shifting agriculture, the 3 acres is inadequate. The majority of the households grew only peppers and fruit trees on the land they obtained. Therefore, there is an urgent need for more land for paddy and vegetables. All of the households interviewed for this research admitted that they opened up state land to plant paddy hill and vegetables. The size of the state land farmed by each household ranges from 5 to 8 acres. Unfortunately, by opening up state land, they have dragged themselves into problems with oil palm plantation companies, particularly SOLID Oil Palm which officially has the lease and document for the land. The Kenyah-Badeng was not aware that these lands have been leased to the companies since 1996. A few households gave up the land they have farmed to the company and received small compensation for their work to clear up the land while others refused to do so. This has created another problem for them and as there is no sup-

---

[11] "The Bakun HEP and Resettlement". Paper presented to a seminar on the Bakun project, December 1995 (quoted from Gabungan, 1999:49).

[12] SOLID Oil Palm Company is under SOLID Timber Company directed by Dato Ding Lian Cheong based in Sibu, Sarawak. This company has about 500,000 ha concession in Malaysia. The area where the oil palm plantation is located was a logging area.

port from any government agencies to inform the people in Sg. Asap resettlement about the real situation on the lease of the land. The oil palm companies have had to handle this problem and resolve conflict as diplomatically as possible.

Conclusion

This paper concludes that implementation of a resettlement, especially an involuntary one, is in itself a portrayal of all but good governance. The transparency and accountability in decision-making on the implementation of the Bakun hydroelectric project the resettlement program, and issues related to it such as compensation on properties have undergone major public criticism because of the persistent secrecy involved. The native settlers were left without clear directions in the whole process of the implementation of the project and the resettlement program. First, there was a chain of communication problem between the state and the natives in which the state failed to be transparent on the information on land tenure, its amendment, and policies. There are publications, such as the book on *Adat* Kayan-Kenyah or *Adat* Iban, that provide information to the public about Native Customary Land in familiar local indigenous language, but it is written in a fashion that makes it complicated and is barely understood even by policy makers or government personnel. Without an understanding of the meaning of ancestral land or native customary land or *tanah adat* and the other issues attached to it made a native landless because as demonstrated in this paper, for the payment of compensation, none of the individuals claiming compensation received payment for the land they have claimed rights. Instead, claimants were compensated for the rights to use which were on the number of fruit trees they had on the land they claimed as theirs, and even that was barely counted. Secondly,after analyzing the whole situation, the role of local leaders is local governance of resources. Their authority through *adat* system, is not and has not been a guarantee for a better stand for the claims to compensation. Their appointment as the custodian of land tenure seemed to be artificial because many parts of the Land Code have been amended. The amendments made are directly affecting every aspect of the *adat* system, but the Kenyah-Badeng do not understand how to claim their rights through the *adat* system.

References

Agrawal, A., Gibson, C. 1999. Enchantment and Disenchantment: The Role of Community in Natural Resource Conservation. World Development. 27/4: 629–649.

Appell, G. N. 1971. System of Land Tenure in Borneo: A Problem in Ecological Determinism. Borneo Research Bulletin 3: 17–20.

Bulan, R. 1999. Native Status and the Law. In: Wu, M.A., (ed.). Public Law in Contemporary Malaysia. Longman Malaysia. Petaling Jaya.

Bulan, R. 2006. Native Customary Land: The trust as a device for land development in Sarawak. In: Cooke, F. M. State, Communities and Forests in contemporary Borneo. ANU E Press. Canberra. Cited from http://epress.anu.edu.au/apem/borneo/mobile_devices/ch03s02.html.

Bulan, R. 2000. 'Indigenous Peoples and Property Rights to Land: A Conceptual Framework.' Paper presented at a workshop on 'Customary Land Rights: Recent Developments', Faculty of Law, University of Malaya, 18–19 February.

Chee Beng, T. 1995. The Kenyah Badeng of Long Geng: An ethnographic report. A report submitted to the State Planning Unit, Chief Minister Department, Sarawak.

Dale, P. 1997. Land Tenure Issues in Economic Development. Urban Studies 34/1: 1621–1633.

Department of Statistic Sarawak, 2005. Yearbook of Statistic Sarawak. Department of Statistic Malaysia (Sarawak Branch).

Freeman, J. D. 1955. Iban Agriculture: A Report on the Shifting Cultivation of Hill Rice by the Iban of Sarawak. Her Majesty's Stationery Office. London.

Hong, E. 1987. Natives of Sarawak. Penang: Institut Masyarakat.

Hooker, M. B. 1999. A Note on Native Land Tenure in Sarawak. Borneo Research Bulletin 30: 2840.

Hooker, M. B. 2002. Native Title in Malaysia Continued: Nor's Case. Australian Journal of Asian Law 4/1: 92–105.

Hemmati, M., Gardiner, R. 2002. Gender and Sustainable Development, World Summit Papers of the Heinrich Böll Foundation, No. 10. Berlin: Heinrich Böll Foundation.

Ingold, T. 2000. The Perception of the Environment: Essays in Livelihood, Dwelling and Skill. Routledge. London and New York.

Ian Chin, H. C. 2001. Judgement Made in the High Court in Sabah and Sarawak in Kuching, Suit No. 22–28–99–1, on 12 May 2001.

Jehom, W. J. 2008. Development and Displacement: Kenyah-Badeng in Bakun Resettlement Malaysia. Center for Development Research. Bonn.

Langub, J. 1998. The Ritual Aspects of Customary Law in Sarawak with Particular Reference to the Iban. Journal of Malaysian and Comparative Law. 25: 45–60.

Mundy, R. 1848. A Narrative of Events in Borneo and Celebes from the Journals of James Brooke Esquire. John Murray. London.

Ngidang, D. 2005. Deconstruction and Reconstruction of Native Customary Land Tenure in Sarawak. Southeast Asian Studies. 43/1. June 2005.

Porter, A .F. 1967. Land Administration in Sarawak: An Account of Development of Land Administration in Sarawak from the Rule of the Raja Brooke to the Present-Time (1841–1967). Government Printer. Kuching.

Pierre, J., Peters, G. B. 2000. Governance, Politics and the State. MacMillan. London.

Richards, A. J. N. 1961. Sarawak Land Law and Adat. Government Printing Office. Kuching.

Rousseau, J. 1994. "Review of Socio-economic Studies and Preliminary Recommendations for the Resettlement of the Kayan and Lahanan of the Upper Balui". A report submitted to the State Planning Unit, Jabatan Ketua Menteri, Sarawak. Extracted from http://www.irn.org

Wet, C. de 2008. Improving Outcome of Development Induced-displacement and Resettlement Projects. Cited from http://www.fmreview.org/FMRpdfs/FMR12/fmr12.2.pdf.

Zainie, Z. K. 1994. 'Native Customary Land: Policies and Legislation.' Paper presented at a seminar on 'Native Customary Land', Kuching, 29 September–3 October.

Zainie, Z. K. 1997. Native Customary Rights and the Creation of Land Bank. A special briefing on the "New Concept of Land Development," jointly organized by the Ministry of Land Development and the Society for Progress, 30 August 1997.

Sources cited from internet:

"Booklet on Dayak´s Interpretation of Native Customary Rights Land (in Bahasa Malaysia)" http://brimas.www1.50megs.com/ncr_konsep.doc

http://www.developmentgateway.com.au/jahia/Jahia/pid/192

http://www.unescap.org/pdd/prs/ProjectActivities/Ongoing/gg/governance.asp

http://www.hri.ca/fortherecord2003/documentation/commission/c-cn4-2003-90htm

http://www.nativescustoms.sarawak.gov.my/web/rit3.html

http://www.wald.org/docs/report1.htm

ZEF Development Studies

edited by Solvay Gerke and Hans-Dieter Evers (Center for Development Research (ZEF), University of Bonn)

Caleb R.L. Wall; Peter P. Mollinga (Eds.)
Fieldwork in Difficult Environments
Methodology as Boundary Work in Development Research
Fieldwork in difficult environments – Methodology as boundary work in development research contains personal accounts of PhD researchers on doing field research in politically and otherwise difficult environments. The methodological flexibility required in development research is discussed around four themes: cultural difference; methodological style and the scale level; communication and interaction; and political and ethical legitimacy. The volume argues that the choice and deployment of methodology is an ongoing, reflexive process of "boundary work".
Bd. 7, 2008, 192 S., 19,90 €, br., ISBN 978-3-8258-1282-9

Solvay Gerke; Hans-Dieter Evers; Anna-Katharina Hornidge (Eds.)
The Straits of Malacca
Knowledge and Diversity
The Center for Development Research (ZEF) is an international and interdisciplinary research institute of the University of Bonn, Germany. The Straits of Malacca are one of the world's most important shipping lanes connecting Europe, the Middle East and East und Southeast Asia. This volume throws new light on the Straits of Malacca region by highlighting its cultural and bio-diversity, knowledge-based development and economic hazards and opportunities. Cross-Straits Passenger Ferry, photo H.-D. Evers, 2007.
Bd. 8, 2008, 224 S., 29,90 €, br., ISBN 978-3-8258-1383-3

Caleb Wall
Argorods of Western Uzbekistan
Knowledge Control and Agriculture in Khorezm
Argorods of Western Uzbekistan: Agricultural knowledge is important in rural Uzbekistan, it is also contested. This book illustrates how risktakers and rule-makers negotiate knowledge in rural Uzbekistan. The author Caleb Wall is a development consultant with a PhD from the University of Bonn.
Bd. 9, 2008, 344 S., 29,90 €, br., ISBN 978-3-8258-1426-7

Nayeem Sultana
The Bangladeshi Diaspora in Malaysia
Organizational Structure, Survival Strategies and Networks
The study explores the organizational structure, modes of networking and the survival strategies of Bangladeshi migrants in Malaysia. Looking at the very diverse social reality, differentiation and power dimensions within the community this study will facilitate our understanding of the Bangladeshi Diaspora in selected multi-cultural social setting of Kuala Lumpur, Penang and Johor Bahru.
Bd. 12, 2009, 368 S., 34,90 €, br.,
ISBN 978-3-8258-1629-2

Phuc Xuan To
Forest Property in the Vietnamese Uplands
An Ethnography of Forest Relations in Three Dao Villages
The Center for Development Research (ZEF) is an international and interdisciplinary academic research institute of the Rheinische-Friedrich-Wilhelms University of Bonn, Germany, EU. ZEF's research aims at finding solutions to global development issues. A 10 years strategy plan outlines land- and water use, biodiversity, public health and renewable energies as priority transdisciplinary research areas (www.zef.de).
Bd. 6, 2007, 296 S., 29,90 €, br., ISBN 978-3-8258-0773-3

LIT Verlag Berlin – Münster – Wien – Zürich – London
Auslieferung Deutschland / Österreich / Schweiz: siehe Impressumsseite